Interpreting the Pentateuch

by

Seán McEvenue

A Michael Glazier Book
THE LITURGICAL PRESS
Collegeville, Minnesota

About the Author

Seán McEvenue teaches scripture at Concordia University in Montreal. He completed his studies at the Gregorian University and at The Pontifical Biblical Institute. He is a regular contributor to scholarly publications; and this book is the first on many years of research and reflection.

A Michael Glazier Book

published by

THE LITURGICAL PRESS

Typography by Brenda Belizzone and Phyllis Boyd LeVane.
Copyright © 1990 by Seán McEvenue. All rights reserved. No part of this book may be reproduced in any form or by any means, electronic or mechanical, including photocopying, recording, taping, or any retrieval system, without the written permission of The Liturgical Press, Collegeville, Minnesota 56321. Printed in the United States of America.

1	2	3	4	5	6	7	8	9

Library of Congress Cataloging-in-Publication Data

McEvenue, Seán E.
    Interpreting the Pentateuch / by Seán McEvenue.
        p.   cm. — (Old Testament studies ; v. 4)
    "A Michael Glazier book."
    Includes index.
    ISBN 0-8146-5654-4
    1. Bible. O.T. Pentateuch—Criticism, interpretation, etc.
I. Title. II. Series: Old Testament studies (Wilmington, Del.) ; v. 4.
    BS1225.2.M34   1990
    222'.106—dc20
                                                                                    90-62039
                                                                                    CIP

Contents

Preface

I am grateful that I have been able to write this book, as it meets the intellectual and spiritual needs which have concerned me over the past thirty years and more. One can only hope that it will prove helpful to others as well.

The nub of the question is very simple and very important: what is the relation between the meaning of biblical literature and reality? Does the Bible really matter?

The answer to this question is not to be found in reading the eminent literary critics who have moved into the biblical field (Northrop Frye, Robert Alter, Meier Sternberg), for whom literary reality in itself is the object of study and interest. Nor is it to be found in reading the most brilliant biblical scholars who are concerned with Hermeneutics (James Barr, Brevard Childs, and many others), for whom there is no real distinction between hermeneutics and theology, between meaning and truth, between biblical meaning and faith. And the answer is not even to be found in reading the most penetrating analyst of theological method, Bernard Lonergan, since he held that historical consciousness has built a wall between biblical and contemporary faith.

I am grateful to these scholars, and their many followers, whose precise and solid contributions to thought have enabled me to write this book. I would like to express special gratitude to Frederick Crowe, S.J. of Regis College in Toronto, to Dr. Ben Meyer of McMaster University in Hamilton, to Dr. Philip McShane at Mount St. Vincent University in Halifax, to Dr. Hugh Kierans of York University in Toronto, and to William Thompson, S.J. of the Loyola Pastoral Institute in Chicago, who by their practical and intellectual interventions, and their incisive conversation, have steered me and motivated me to pursue this topic to the end. Finally, I would like to thank Michael Glazier who made the decision to publish it.

Sean McEvenue

1

Biblical Criticism
and Literary Theory

A leading American literary theorist writes that "There are many tasks that confront criticism, many things we need to advance our understanding of literature, but one thing we do not need is more interpretations of literary works." He goes on to give his reason for saying this: "We have no convincing account of the role or function of literature in society or social consciousness . . . we need a fuller explanation of its historical relation to the other forms of discourse through which the world is organized and human activities are given meaning."[1]

The challenge is issued both more generally and more pointedly by a popular French philosopher: "What relation is there between language and being, and is it really to being that language is always addressed—at least language that speaks truly? What, then, is this language that says nothing, is never silent, and is called 'literature'?"[2]

The Bible is surely a literary work, even if it is not fiction, or purely literary in a modern sense. Have we no "convincing account" of its relation to our culture? Is it a never silent text which "says nothing?" The Bible is, in fact, an excellent place to start in answering the general question about literature, because the Bible is written and read as a language which always does deal with being, and in fact with BEING, with the divine Persons who are revealed in it. Moreover the Bible is read as the principle source for Theology, a form of discourse which proceeds from religious experience to accurate statements about reality, i.e., to truths which are usually termed "doctrines," or "dogmas."

This topic presents a jungle of problems, of theories, of authors. If this book were to address them all, it would break down into a maze of observations, insights, and refutations, which might not advance the argument very much. And so it will attempt, rather, to cut one straight path through the jungle. It limits its discussion to the Bible, and even to the Pentateuch within the Bible, so that the abstract concepts which are used might constantly and easily be referred to real text. The first chapter presents a paradigm of biblical criticism as practised over the past fifty years, showing the inadequacy of this scholarship in so far as it stops at the original or historical meaning; then it argues for the validity and necessity of beginning with this approach, and offers refutations of the most commonly affirmed counter-positions in contemporary literary theory. A second chapter proposes the adoption of a further dimension to interpretation, namely the search for elemental meaning. The next four chapters provide examples of the implementation of this proposal, interpreting in turn the major authors of the Pentateuch. A final chapter directly addresses the question we began with: how does interpretation of Scripture relate to theological discourse, to religion, and to reality?

Underlying most discussions of meaning are implicit theories about human cognition, theories about culture and civilization, and theories about the nature of Theology. Differences in these foundations of thought result in conflict and failure to communicate between those who think and discuss at a less philosophical or universal level. I would state at the outset that in this book I depend upon the work of the late Bernard Lonergan for that theoretical foundation. If that may seem to be a limitation, it does offer the advantage of coherence in terminology and perspective, and it does serve to maintain a relation between the discussion of fine points and the discussion of religion. At the very least it should serve to ease the tasks of understanding, and of correcting, and of refuting!

A Paradigm of Traditional Interpretation

Ex 3:1—4:17 is an important and familiar Pentateuchal

text. Part of it is reproduced in translation below, but the reader is invited to read now the complete text in the Revised Standard Version (which is the translation usually cited in this book) as the full citation of this and other texts would uselessly lengthen the book and increase its cost.

If the reader reacts to this reading as I did, he or she will have experienced a certain interest, mixed with a warmth, in reading 3:1-8. Then, there intervened a sense of confusion, almost distress or boredom, all the way to the end of the chapter. The original feeling was restored, less sharply, in ch. 4.

Such feelings are not just chance occurrences, as, for me at least, they recur always and in about the same way. I suspect that every reader will have a similar or analogous reaction. Reactions are to be trusted, and attended to, as they are important clues about the text.

Now there is a basis in the text for a change of feeling at v. 9, because this verse begins "And now," as though God were introducing a new direction of thought. In fact, the Hebrew conjunction here is most often used to introduce a conclusion from the foregoing material. Instead we get a repetition of the contents of v. 7! The reader has been experiencing a feeling of awe and gratitude toward God as He appears in vv. 1-8, but suddenly he/she must exercise the sort of manipulative patience one adopts when old people repeat themselves needlessly. The confusing demands of the text, and the experience of contradictory feelings within oneself, may lead a reader to resolve the confusion by going numb, and closing down the brain! Otherwise we find ourselves in awe before an apparently senile God. Moreover, the rest of the text in ch. 3, in varying degrees, seems repetitive and a bit illogical. Certainly the crisp narrative style of vv. 1-8 has been lost. The reader does not easily maintain an attentive attitude.

Source-Criticism

It is in this connection that source-criticism is most helpful. The traditional view of source-critics is that not only is our story told again in Ex 6:2—7:7 by a later author (conventionally called the Priestly Writer, who wrote during the Exilic period, i.e., after 587 B.C.E.), but also the present text itself is a composite of two texts, which were written by a 10th-century author called the Yahwist and an 8th-century author called the Elohist, and which were interwoven by an Editor at some point prior to the Exilic period.[3] The underlying text is attributed to the Yahwist, with roughly the following verses attributed to the Elohist: 3:1, 4b, 6, 9-15. In ch. 4, vv. 13-16 appear to be a still later addition. Moreover, in ch. 3, the intriguing v. 14 appears to be a later gloss within the combined Elohist/Yahwist. This hypothesis of diverse sources in Ex 3-4 enables us to understand confused repetitions in the text, and to remain attentive. Instead of going numb, we become more alert and read more attentively, doffing our cap, as it were, when a new author enters. It may be helpful to present the opening verses of the text analysed for sources as follows: (The Elohist is printed across the whole page; the Yahwist in the column on the right; the gloss in verse 14 in the centre.)

1) Now Moses was keeping the flock of his father-in-law, Jethro, the priest of Midian; and he led his flock to the west side of the wilderness, and came to Horeb, the mountain of God.

2)   And the angel of the Lord appeared to him in a flame of fire out of the midst of a bush; and he looked, and lo, the bush was burning, yet it was not consumed.

3)   And Moses said, "I will turn aside and see this great sight, why the bush is not burnt."

4)   When the Lord saw that he turned aside to see.

God called to him out of the bush, "Moses, Moses!" And he said, "Here I am."

5)   He said, "Do not come near; put off your shoes from your feet, for the place on which you are standing is holy ground."

6) And He said, "I am the God of your father, the God of Abraham, the God of Isaac, and the God of Jacob." And Moses hid his face, for he felt afraid about looking at God.

7)   Then the Lord said, "I have seen the
                           affliction of my people who are in Egypt,
                           and have heard their cry because of their
                           taskmasters; I know their sufferings.

8)   And I have come down to deliver them
                           out of the hand of the Egyptians, and to
                           bring them out of that land to a good
                           and broad land, a land flowing with milk
                           and honey, to the place of the Canaan-
                           ites, the Hittites, the Amorites, the
                           Perizzites, the Hivites, and the Jebusites.

9) And now, behold, the cry of the people of Israel has come
to me, and I have seen the oppression with which the Egyptians
oppress them.

10) Come, I will send you to Pharaoh that you may bring
forth my people, the sons of Israel out of Egypt."

11) But Moses said to God, "Who am I that I should go to
Pharaoh, and bring the sons of Israel out of Egypt?"

12) He said, "But I will be with you; and this shall be the sign
for you, that I have sent you: when you have brought forth the
people out of Egypt, you shall serve God upon this mountain."

13) Then Moses said to God, "If I come to the people of Israel
and say to them 'The God of your fathers has sent me to you,'
and they ask me, 'What is his name?' what shall I say to
them?"

14)   God said to Moses,
                  "I AM WHO I AM." And He
                     said, "Say this to the
                    people of Israel, "I AM
                     has sent me to you."

15) God then said to Moses, "Say this to the people of Israel,
'Yahweh, the God of your fathers, the God of Abraham, the
God of Isaac, and the God of Jacob, has sent me to you: this is
my name forever, and thus I am to be remembered throughout
all generations."

16)   Go and gather the elders of Israel to-
                           gether, and say to them, 'Yahweh, the
                           God of your fathers, the God of Abra-
                           ham, of Isaac, and of Jacob, has ap-
                           peared to me, saying, "I have observed

you and what has been done to you in Egypt;

17)   and I promise that I will bring you out of the afflictions of Egypt, to the land of the Canaanites, the Hittites, etc. etc."

First, then, the Yahwist has written a story about the call of Moses, or his commissioning as a leader of the Exodus. The structure of his story appears to be roughly as follows: a *divine confrontation* in which the position of God and the position of Moses are revealed (3:2-4a, 5, 7-8); the *commissioning* (3:16-22); an *objection* and answering *sign* (4:1-9); a second *objection* and an answering *confirmation* (4:10-12, 17).

The Elohist has told the same story. His account is shorter but it follows the identical form, except that he replaces the second objection with a question. The Elohist story proceeds as follows: a *divine confrontation* (3:1, 4b, 6); the *commissioning* (9-10); an *objection* and answering *sign* (11-12); a question and an answering *confirmation* (13, 15). The Priestly Writer in ch. 6 has followed the same form, introducing marked changes. However, the discussion of method in this chapter will be better served by restricting ourselves to chs. 3-4.

One suspects that the Elohist was pleased to retain the Yahwist story without changing its form, but felt he had to write his own version in order to introduce some corrective materials. First of all we may notice that the Elohist has taken pains to make the encounter much more personal and intimate. In the *divine confrontation*, Moses' response, "Here I am," gives the whole scene a remarkably intimate feeling. This is reinforced when, in answering the *objection*, the Elohist has God say "I will be with you." It is true that Moses then hides his face in fear, but, as we shall see, in the Elohist source the word "fear" denotes authentic religious experience, or conversion.

A second, and greater, change introduced by the Elohist is in the question and answer about God's name (vv. 13, 15). Whereas the Yahwist had humans invoking this name as early as Gen 4:26, the Elohist makes a point of having God reveal it for the first time here. One suspects that the Elohist has rewritten the story of Moses' call specifically to connect Moses with the use of the name "Yahweh," and to give that name a special force by connecting it to the Exodus tradition.

Thirdly, a later writer has introduced a gloss in 3:14. This verse confuses the reader because it cannot be understood as an answer to the question in v. 13. It is an etymological discussion of the name "Yahweh," saying something unexpected about God's attributes, namely the freedom of God.

It will prove helpful to explain this gloss. To do so, however, we must first read Ex 33-34. The Yahwist discusses God's attributes in 34:5-7: "Yahweh, Yahweh, a God merciful and gracious, slow to anger, and abounding in steadfast love and faithfulness . . . who will by no means clear the guilty, visiting the iniquity of the fathers upon the children, etc." The Yahwist presents a very predictable God, very different from the God of our gloss in Ex 3:14!

Now Ex 33 is a compilation of sources which discuss God's presence to Israel in ways which contrast with Ex 34:5-7. And particularly Ex 33:17-23 contrasts with that Yahwist view (in just the same way as did Ex 3:14). Verse 19 presents God as refusing to show his face to Moses. Instead He says: "I shall display *all my goodness* before you, and I shall *explain* the name of Yahweh in your hearing: 'I favour whomever I favour; I take pity upon whomever I take pity.'"

Two points must be made about this untranslatable text. First, the Hebrew word which is here translated "explain" normally means merely "call out." The context justifies our translation: had God wanted to "call out" His name, He would have called "Yahweh" or "El Shaddai" or some other divine name. Instead He articulates a description of his way of acting. Hence the translation "explain." Second, the translation "all my goodness" is literal, but it remains inadequate because the context indicates that what is meant is something like "my essence" or "my whole activity." What follows then is a description of the essence of God according to this author. The description is not in terms of good versus bad or mercy versus cruelty, but rather in terms of unpredictability and freedom: God favours and has mercy, but only upon his own decision to do so.

It must be noted that the connective, which is translated "whomever" in this verse, is the same Hebrew word (*'asher*)

which is translated "who" in the clause "I am *who* I am" in Ex
3:14. In both cases the turn of phrase is striking. One suspects
that the writer of 33:19 was the glossator of 3:14. In both texts
he intends to describe God as free. In adding the gloss to ch. 3,
he creates an etymology of the name "Yahweh" in order to
add a new dimension to the meaning of the text: Yahweh will
intervene at this point, not because of Israel's merit, or because
of His covenant, but purely because He has freely chosen to
do so. The gloss here does not change or correct the Yahwist/
Elohist text. Rather it answers a question which arose later in
Israel's religious thought. Thus it made the text more directly
relevant to the glossator's day. In another era, Christian theology will be concerned with the same question, and will
develop a whole doctrine of "grace."

In conclusion, we may point out that by separating and
isolating sources, we have removed the confusion and boredom
experienced in reading; and we have also been able to clarify
distinct meanings. Of course the final biblical meaning is a
complex of these, resulting from the composition of sources.

But once one has isolated individual authors (sources), one
inevitably begins to wonder where they lived, for whom they
wrote, what they were trying to prove, and so forth. At this
point one enters "historical criticism."

Historical Criticism

It may well be because of the extreme difficulty of proof,
and the uncertainty of conclusions, and the endless controversy
between scholars in this area, that many readers of the Bible
want to find a way of bypassing historical scholarship. They
may treat the Bible as literature, or speak simply of Bible
reading. But historical scholarship goes on, and it continues to
throw light on the biblical text. We have no alternative but to
draw whatever good we can from it, remaining content with
whatever degree of certainty, or uncertainty, is possible in each
instance.

If one is prepared to accept the consensus of classical source-
criticism for the moment, namely that the Yahwist wrote in
Jerusalem, from the sophisticated perspectives of Solomon's
court or shortly thereafter, and that the Elohist wrote a century

or so later in the Northern Kingdom, *historical criticism* will be seen to yield some further light in interpreting our text.

In the Yahwist's story, inevitably the image of Solomon, who was unique in Israel's history as a very powerful ruler of a great empire, shapes the image of Moses. As we read the Yahwist text in Ex 3-4, we find it different from the Elohist in that there is no question about Moses' right to rule the people of Israel.The text tells of a commissioning for conquest, and it expands notably on the issue of Moses' credibility and power in Egypt. The Yahwist, in this text, had a powerful theological assurance to offer to the court in Jerusalem, and a specific explanation of the source of Solomon's power over Egypt at the end of the 10th century B.C.E.

In the Elohist version of the story, three differences should be noted. First, Moses doubts his authority within Israel, and before Pharaoh, until God confirms it (vv. 11-12). Second, the name "Yahweh" is here revealed for the first time, and is now proclaimed to be the normative name in the liturgy forever (v. 15). (The Hebrew verb translated "to remember" does not primarily designate an internal act, but rather a public evocation or recital.) Third, care is taken to emphasize by repetition that this Yahweh is the same God who was revealed to their ancestors (vv. 6, 13, 15). These differences may reflect in turn three aspects of the writer's background in the Northern Kingdom. First, in the North the authority of kings always needed confirmation, because the succession to the throne was always uncertain. Dynasties were repeatedly overthrown in the Northern Kingdom. In v. 12, the Elohist may well have intended to indicate three signs by which one could judge about the charismatic election of the king: God was with him; he leads the people toward liberty; he celebrates sacrificial liturgy at Bethel. Second, in the North the central place of worship was the king's temple at Bethel, where other names of God appear to have been "remembered" for many years. Clearly "Baal" was generally used until the reformation of Elijah; and the Elohist himself calls God "Bethel" in Gen 31:13, a fact so shocking that most translations disguise it. The Elohist is calling for liturgical reform. Third, in the North the many tribes of Israel were in conflict with each other (whereas Judah was more unified as a single tribe). The need of assuring all the tribes that Yahweh was identical to the gods "remembered" in their various traditions may well have been quite acute.

Of course such hypotheses about the original intent or "messages" of a biblical text for its successive original hearers can be established only with varying degrees of probability, and only on the basis of complex historical argumentation taking into account all the data of the whole Yahwist or Elohist text.[4]

When we come, finally, to the original meaning of the gloss in 3:14, it is possible to devise hypotheses about historical context. However, the text is too minute (even if it is linked with Ex 33:19) to provide data sufficient for any satisfactory verification. For example one might speculate that the freedom of Yahweh to act or not to act in times of disaster must have been a theme when the Northern Kingdom was destroyed in 722 B.C.E. Neither the cult practised at Bethel, nor the covenant which existed between God and Israel, nor the interventions of prophetic mediators were able to force God to intervene when Samaria fell. If one accepts this historical hypothesis, then the text of Ex 3 receives a very pointed meaning for a specific moment in its history, i.e., the fall of Samaria. If one refuses the hypothesis, still the historical thinking has helped us to examine the meaning of the text.

It must be pointed out that even if subsequent historical research were to establish new theses with greater probability for the historical context of the Yahwist, the Elohist, or the glossator, or for all of them, this might change little in the original "messages" which we have proposed. The historical hypotheses have led us to find meanings in the text which are really there. Subsequent historical hypotheses may reveal further meanings, and may nuance meanings already perceived. For example, if someone established that the Elohist wrote, not in the 8th century in the North, but rather in the court of Hezekiah, i.e., in the 7th century in Jerusalem, it would remain true that "the point" or "message" or "kerygma" of his text focussed on the exclusive use of the name "Yahweh" in the liturgy. Concretely, it would be the liturgy in Jerusalem, and in the context of the early Deuteronomic reform, rather than at Bethel. Thus even an erroneous historical hypothesis is usually better than no historical hypothesis, for had we not asked historical questions about who was saying what to whom, and why, we would probably never have realized that the Elohist text had implications for the liturgy, or that the Yahwist text spoke to questions about Israel's international power, and Egypt, or that 3:14 gave the whole passage a note of delicate inquiry into questions of providence and predestination.[5] An historical hypothesis serves to remind us that biblical texts deal with human living.

Form-Criticism

Finally there is the contribution of form-criticism. We pointed out above that the form of the Yahwist story was preserved by the Elohist. The same form was used by the Priestly Writer in his rendition of the story in Ex 6:2—7:7. Form-critics have further pointed out that this form appears to have been a fixed literary logic found elsewhere in the Bible. It is found notably in the story of the call of Gideon (Judg 6:11ff), the call of Saul (1 Sam 9:1—10:13), the call of Jeremiah (Jer 1:4ff), the call of Zechariah and of Mary (Lk 1:8ff; 1:26ff). The form also influenced part of the call narrative of Ezekiel 2.

This discovery has the immediate effect of removing the temptation of trying to read psychological history into these narratives. We are dealing with a formula, not a personal memory. However, the formula links in a common experience Israel's charismatic leaders: Moses, the founder of Israel, the early Judges, the Prophets, the family of Jesus. If it is true that the form was first used in the story of the call of Saul, then it follows that that expression of call experience formed a specific literary type by which subsequent experiences could be progressively interpreted: one who is called by God will free the people of Israel from oppression, and God will be with him.[6]

The contribution of form-criticism to our understanding of Ex 3 is to make us aware of a sharp signal or tone in the text: the form signals that this story is about a radical mission. In interpreting Ex 3-4, form-criticism allows us to sense that this is not only an interesting legend about Moses, it is also a theologico-historical statement about the intervention of God in human history. Moses meets God face-to-face, and changes the course of events as God desires.

Conclusion

Through these methods of interpretation, we have come to understand quite a bit about the meaning of Ex 3. This study was rapid and incomplete. The most visible omission is the lack of redactional analysis or canonical criticism, which would show the meaning of Ex 3 within the larger contexts of Exodus, the Pentateuch, and the whole Bible. We have not gone into that, because to do so would entail considerable study of texts other than Ex 3 itself. This would be disproportionate to the purpose of this section, which is not to write a commentary on Ex 3, but only to give examples of the sorts of contributions which biblical scholarship has provided.

Despite the value of these contributions, however, the most important benefit expected of biblical interpretation is lacking: namely, inspiration and direction for living with God today. Most of the meanings we have discovered are not directly relevant to us today. For example, that God intervened in the life of Moses, or that God was free in liberating ancient Israel from the Pharaohs, or that "Yahweh" is the right name for liturgical use, or that Israel is more powerful than Egypt, all these teachings are historically intriguing, but spiritually irrelevant to a modern reader. All that happened three thousand years ago. And one cannot easily see a justification for applying, for example, to Canadian politics the "messages" given to Solomon or later Northern kings in ancient Israel. And as for the obligation to use the name "Yahweh" ... who could agree to that? The original meanings of the biblical text, even if they were to be securely established, do not seem to be very useful in a contemporary religious context.

Moreover, when we first read the verses at the beginning of this chapter, we felt a warm glow, identifying with Moses. This glow has gone, because we no longer identify: we have assumed a critical stance, objectifying Moses, focussing on historical facts, watching a series of writers use and reuse a story to make specific points with a variety of readers remote from ourselves. Scholarship has enlightened our understanding of the text, but taken the warmth out of that understanding. It has sharpened our knowledge, but dulled our desire for it. This observation leads us to the second section of this chapter.

The Problem of Original Meanings

It is the triumph of modern historical writing that we have been able to discern sharply between historical and current horizons of thought and meaning. We take for granted that we must do so. Moreover, historical methodology has enabled us to establish original, i.e., critical, texts, to define criteria for the credibility of historical witnesses; and to move back in imagination to the social structures, perspectives, and culture of ancient writers so as to grasp their original meanings.

We shall consider and refute three grounds for rejecting the use of this approach in reading the Bible: practical grounds, philosophical grounds, and theological grounds. These considerations will lead to the conclusion that an historical approach is both possible and indispensable.

Practical Grounds

The most practical ground of all for rejecting scholarly approaches to the Bible is the experience that the most unscholarly, fundamentalist, readings of the Bible produce the strongest effects among religious people. That "old time religion" can fill arenas and stadia, and attract very large numbers to watch television. In contrast to that, the most gifted biblical scholar will have a hard time getting even good friends to come to his/her lecture, to read his/her books. The demands of life are so imperious, and the call of God so strong, that cultural refinements in this area seem misplaced and trivial. If God revealed His word to all humanity in a book, surely He did not expect everyone to get a doctorate in order to read it!

It is easy to soften and nuance that argument, but it is impossible to deny its real force. In fact our discussion of "theological grounds" below will reformulate it, and derive important conclusions from it. However, the conclusion appropriate to the practical argument as stated here is not that we should reject scholarship. Rather it is that, since the bible is so powerful in people's lives, there is a need for scholarship to protect us from errors. Those who are serious about biblical religion surely should take the bible seriously enough to read the scholars. Scholars who are funded by Society surely must make their knowledge available in appropriate form. The hatred and violence our generation has seen under the Nazis, or in Northern Ireland, or in the Middle East, or in Bible-belt America, which have partially been based on simplistic readings of the Bible and of the Koran, have led many to re-examine and re-evaluate the fervours of the Reformation and Counter Reformation, and often to question the value of religion itself. Massive criminality carried out in the name of God, and on the strength of "revelation," has marked our memories! We have been led to violence and murder, not of course by the saints who are recognized later, but by prominent "religious" leaders.

It is true that scholarship cannot directly stem a flood of hysteria. Rather, the scholar's task is to check the first beginnings of such floods by illuminating the real bases for religious conviction, and by enabling religious groups to think accurately when they gather together, or prepare for action. Biblical scholarship contributes here by defining exact meanings of biblical texts, establishing their historical horizons, with their limits as well as their values.

For example, the ethics in the Bible were conceived at a period in our cultural development when slavery was hardly questioned, when political power was charismatic rather than democratic or controlled by law, when women were often thought of as private property, when war consisted of small skirmishes controlled by opposed gods, and when the biblical writers were aware of Israel and its neighbours, but largely ignorant of the rest of the world. Upon the basis of that culture, the Hebrew Bible taught the Jews an admirable and advanced ethic, an ethic whose basic principles have formed the backbone of the Western world. However an ignorant and simplistic reading of those texts today can motivate and justify acts which, in our society, are criminal. In this area, a scholarly critique, placing the texts in their original historical perspective, is indispensable.

If it is clear in the case of ethics, it is equally necessary in other domains of religious expression where the need may not be as patent. Every religious enthusiast tends to see his or her doctrine for salvation as so urgently needed that there is no time for cold analysis, particularly if that analysis is to be produced by a dry scholar who does not appear to be very alive in any religious sense. And there is some truth in that view. However, if the enthusiast reads meanings into the biblical text which are not there at all, then his/her own salvation demands an inquiry: what is the origin of the false meanings? what inner flaw blinded him/her as to the meaning which was really to be found in the text? Of course we are all flawed, and all heretics, and we require many years on earth to get it right about ourselves and God. The heretic in us tends to project its own untruth into the Words of God. Scholarship provides the method for a direct remedy against such projection. In fact, it is hard to name any other effective method.

Philosophical Grounds

Another ground for rejecting scholarly approaches to the bible may be found in one's theory of knowledge, or one's philosophy of culture. To put it more accurately, one scholarly method, i.e., philosophy, may tend to discredit many others. In fact, at this time a whole sea of opinion among theorists of literary criticism is available to support those who would like to reject the kind of biblical scholarship which was presented in the first section of this chapter.[7]

This book is concerned with proposing a method which may embody some aspects of these currents of thought. However, either because they have all evolved from "The New Criticism" of Leavis, or because of the wide influence of Hans-Georg Gadamer in hermeneutic discussion, or possibly because of the popularity of Jacques Derrida, it seems that most contemporary theories share one conviction which must be examined now and refuted.[8] It is the conviction that the author of a text (i.e., his mind or intention in writing) is irrelevant to literary criticism or to interpretation of texts: only the text itself, free of its historical roots, may be considered. This doctrine implies questions about the value of source criticism and historical criticism.[9] According to this doctrine, once a text is published its umbilical cord to the historical author is cut. The text itself is preserved and reproduced at will, and in a sense it becomes timeless. The text then means whatever the reader understands, regardless of any "original" sources, or intentions, or contexts. Applied to Biblical texts, this doctrine risks lending divine authority to interpretations which the original author might see as reflecting, not his/her original belief, but rather the later prejudice of some social class or the blindness of some heresy.

Many philosophical reasons may be adduced in support of this doctrine. A good number of these may be classed as forms of skepticism. It may be argued, for example, that we simply cannot ever reproduce the exact meaning which a set of words had in the mind of the writer, because the writer's history and perception are necessarily far removed from that of the reader. One may ascertain exactly what you *said*, but one can never really know what you were *thinking* as you said it. Moreover, for ancient texts we usually know nothing about the writer— often not even his/her name. And the little we claim to know is invariably disputed among scholars who never agree. What do we know about Shakespeare, let alone Homer, or the Elohist?

The refutation of skepticism is unchanged, but it needs always to be recalled: if you don't know what I am thinking when I say these words, why do you bother to argue with me? Are you trying to change my words? or my mind as well? If you do change my mind, how will you ever know? It is hard to believe that anyone who argues with me can sincerely claim not to know what I am thinking. Whenever the skeptic affirms his position he implicitly refutes it. Now it is true that we are not sure of the identity of Shakespeare, if identity is to be defined in terms of external historical referents. But studies of the evolution in Shakespeare's political beliefs, or in his use of archetypes, or in his use of literary techniques, all imply some assured knowledge of the mind of an author who is evolving in these ways, even if his street address is never ascertained. Skepticism is helpful as a caution, but indefensible as a doctrine.

To really free oneself from undue skepticism about understanding texts from remote cultures is a task which each individual must undertake for him or herself. It might help, for example, to read foreign literary critics who write about North American authors, and to discover how well they understand.

If I may adduce my own experience, I was astonished many years ago, while studying textual criticism in Europe under an elderly Swiss scholar who published an Aramaic dictionary, to find that that retiring gentleman was able to appreciate the humour and subtle nuances of Salinger's *The Catcher in the Rye* every bit as well as I. If he could understand Salinger so easily and assuredly, and understand it as it resonated in my North American young mind, why should I doubt his ability to understand the historical Ezekiel?

However, many of those who deny the relevance, or possibility, of studying texts as expressions of the mind of an historical author are not just skeptics. Granted the large number of these on the one hand, and the space this argument merits in the scope of this book on the other, the only practical approach will be to focus on one exponent of this position, and to restrict discussion fairly rigidly to the exact point at issue. Hans-Georg Gadamer appears to be a dominant figure in this group, and we shall focus on him.

From Gadamer one can draw two major reasons for arguing that the text goes beyond the author, making the author irrelevant to criticism: the first has to do with the nature of language, *Sprachlichkeit*, and the second with the nature of published texts, *Schriftlichkeit*.

In dealing first with the *nature of language*, Gadamer leans on his analysis of playing.[10] Playing is a coming and going which is consistent in itself, tirelessly repeated. It is primarily a phenomenon of nature (as in the play of light on water, or as in kittens) but humans have also appropriated it as a cultural form. Humans set it apart from purposeful activity, and assign it a special space, typically a playing field, or a cultic place. In playing, one is totally given over to the game, in such a way that one is played by the game rather than the reverse. The game has its own rules to which one agrees, and the game elevates the player, often in conjunction with others, often including spectators as essential participants (e.g., in theatre), imposing these rules in its own spirit, coming and going. Each player has his or her tasks, but these tasks are not purposeful beyond the game. The game itself is the whole purpose. A game is presentation (*Darstellung*), including a self-presentation of the participants.

Language is such a game. All of culture is such a game. And, since text is a speaking, a participation in the language game, its meaning is taken up in the play of language, independently of any intention or purpose which the author might have had. A text is a participant in the culture game, and its meaning transcends any historical moment. Both the writer and the reader are elevated in a common experience, carried by the spirit of the game which is common to both.

This image (for in its application it is an image rather than an analysis) makes the following paragraph from Gadamer fully intelligible:

> Moreover, the texts of the New Testament are themselves already interpretations of the Christian message; they do not wish to call attention to themselves, but rather to be mediators of this message. Does this not give them a freedom in speaking that allows them to be selfless witnesses? We are much indebted to modern theological study for our insight into the theological intentions of the New Testament writers, but the proclamation of the gospel speaks through all these mediations in a way that is comparable to the repetition of a legend or the continual renewal and transformation of mythical tradition by great poetry. The genuine reality of the hermeneutical process seems to me to encompass the self-understanding of the interpreter as well as what is interpreted.... The real event of understanding goes beyond what we can bring to the understanding of the other person's words through methodical effort and critical self-control. Indeed it goes far beyond what we ourselves can become aware of. Through every dialogue something different comes to be. Moreover, the Word of God, which calls us to conversion and promises us a better understanding of ourselves, cannot be understood as a word that merely confronts us and that we must simply leave as it is. It is not really we ourselves who understand: it is always a past that allows us to say, "I have understood."[11]

One cannot deny the validity of this statement, nor its seductive quality. It describes a "peak experience" in writing, or reading, or watching a play, in which one feels united with all of humankind and all of Being. Gadamer himself compares this experience to "ecstacy."[12] There is never a simple relation between writer and reader, but always a triangle with language at the apex.[13]

Northrop Frye seems to be writing of the same experience in dealing with the "Logos of Literature," and he writes of it as an experience of the "unlimited" or of "omnipotence." He writes:

> The center of the literary universe is whatever poem we happen to be reading. One step further, and the poem appears as a microcosm of all literature, an individual manifestation of the total order of words. Anagogically, then, the symbol is a monad, all symbols being united in a single infinite and eternal verbal symbol which is, as *dianoia*, the Logos, and, as *mythos*, total creative act. It is this conception which Joyce expresses, in terms of subject-matter, as "epiphany," and Hopkins, in terms of form, as "inscape."[14]

Even Jacques Derrida appears to have the same experience of the presence of "what we call God," who is a "Witness." He terms it an experience of "revelation."[15]

It is true that in the act of creative writing, and creative reading, the human psyche is stretched, as it were, until one's capacity for unlimited love and truth and beauty is drawn to the surface, and is heard, and sometimes is answered. The classical tradition deals with this in terms of invoking the Muse, and by speaking of "inspiration." Thus the text goes beyond the author and the reader, and the meaning goes beyond the text. God is present as ultimate meaning in all of thought, as He is present in all of reality.

If this were a sermon, it could end there. However, a colder look at Gadamer's text above will raise doubts about the end of the first sentence: "they (i.e., N.T. texts) do not wish to call attention to themselves, but rather to be mediators." That is precisely as true as saying that trees do not want to be trees, but rather to be expressions of God's glory. But, in the first instance, texts are texts and trees are trees. Biology must study the trees as trees first, and Theology or Literary Criticism or

Exegesis must first attend to the texts themselves. Otherwise we fail to read. T.S. Eliot once wrote a very famous, and very acid, analysis of a sort of literary critic who hasn't quite enough vitality to write a poem, but who, on the occasion of reading the poems of other authors, emits a sick little song of impressionistic reaction. This is neither poetry nor literary criticism![16] One must add that it is also not exegesis or theology.

We can agree with Gadamer that "It is in the sermon, therefore, that the understanding and interpretation of the text first receives its full reality."[17] And in this sense the meaning of the text really does go beyond the writer. However, if this "full reality" takes place in the absence of foregoing exegetical scholarship, i.e., before these texts have "called attention to themselves," we may find ourselves trying to find God within horizons set by the limited piety of the preacher. Gadamer himself has a most sophisticated hermeneutic which took a very long book to explain, and which presupposes in fact the most sophisticated scholarly reading of texts. However, he never focusses on the scholarly effort itself, or explains its usefulness. He constantly thinks rather of performing a text, as in a theatrical or musical performance, systematically overlooking the research required before this can be done. A less sophisticated reader is easily led by his reflections to argue to a timeless, history-free reading of texts. Gadamer's own reflections on breaking out of subjectivity implicitly refute such conclusions.[18]

The fact is that usually one cannot participate in the play that is being played in a text without historical research. Even in music, one is very much helped toward hearing the brilliance, rather than a heaviness, in Bach, because research can reconstruct a harpsichord to play it with its original sound. Recently, much historical research and modern technology has been used to justify the removal of dark pigmentation which had clouded Michelangelo's vision on the Sistine chapel. And one will find it easier to focus on Hopkins' imagery after one has heard his conflicting consonants smoothly read with an Oxford accent. And, if one is to understand more than the bawdy humour of Chaucer, considerable historical research is required in explaining the whole medieval framework and vocabulary and belief systems which shape his expression, which give meaning to his words. If this were not required, Chaucer would be as popular a writer now as he was in his own day. Anyone who has tried to read Jonathan Swift's *Gulliver's Travels*, or John Dryden's *Absalom and Achitophel* to a child (or to him-or herself), will have discovered that the most charming and witty texts demand a great deal of "attention to themselves" before they yield any understanding at all. No matter what the nature of playing, or the nature of speaking and of language, there is no access to the "thing" (*die Sache* or *das Gebilde*) of which a text speaks, and which the reader is to consider, unless one begins with a scholarly understanding of the words and literary forms of the text itself, and an historical awareness of the realities and thoughts to which reference is made.[19] And there is no participation in that Muse or that Word of God which a text actually conveys, unless it begins with taking the text seriously in itself.

We must conclude that we have no way of studying the text in itself seriously which can exclude the traditional scholarly approaches, involving source-criticism, historical criticism, form-criticism, and others as well. Even though the text participates in play of Language, and even if the game of Language itself transcends particular moments in history, still some important aspects of any text (the "small-l language" of the text) do *not* transcend the historical moment of their creation. Reading requires not only a shift of horizon, but also the learning of a language, a dead language, a language which died with the author, and which is revived by scholarship. Chapter 2 of this book discusses steps beyond scholarship, steps which recover parts of Gadamer's insight. But we must retain the first step: reconstruction of the original meaning.

Taking the text seriously in itself leads us into the second of the themes of Gadamer which would make the text go beyond the writer: the *nature of writing or of text*, i.e., *Schriftlichkeit*. For Gadamer, the text goes one step further along the line of timelessness and abstraction which already marks speech and thought off from the rest of nature. By writing, the author withdraws himself, his subjectivity and biography, his body as it were, from his ideas, in order to leave these free in a timeless state, to be read and interpreted by any reader quite beyond the author's control. Reading, therefore, does not consist of getting back to some past life, recovering the thought of some past thinker, but rather it is a sharing in something said in the present. The reader does not relate to the author, but rather addresses the content of a text. Thus the meaning of a text is not limited by the subjectivity, the thought world, the horizons of its author. Nor is it limited by some hypothetically reconstructed thought world of the first hearers or readers.[20]

Once again Gadamer has given us a seductive image. And once again it will prove inadequate, or even misleading, in discussing the interpretation of ancient texts like the Bible. The fact is that ideas and truths, or even words and sentences, are not left, or contained, in texts. Texts are signals which lead the reader to *reconstruct* the ideas and truths, the words and sentences, which (as the reader must *suppose*) directed the production of this text. The universal presupposition in all reading is that an author created a coherent construct, and that the reader, possessed of similar mental processes, can detect or deduce the rules of coherence which were followed, and can reconstruct the intended meaning. This activity of reconstruction on the part of readers cannot be treated as irrelevant to the nature of text: rather it defines that nature, since texts are written precisely to meet the activities of readers. The act of reading defines a text as a directive for reconstructing an intention to communicate something. By writing, the author has *not* distanced himself or herself from the text. Rather, he/she has carefully aligned clues whereby a reader, at any time, might attempt to imagine the author's intention at the time of writing. Of course, having reconstructed this intended meaning or thing, the reader is free to criticize it, or understand it better than the author, or compare it to things subsequent in history. But the first step, historical reconstruction, remains the first step.

Let us take a concrete example, so that this effort at reconstruction, which our theorists tend to overlook, might be clearly seen. This chapter began with the text of Ex 3-4, and the revelation of the name Yahweh. It became text when a number of Hebrew letters were written down in a specific order, on a specific piece of papyrus or animal skin, probably in the 5th century B.C.E. If two moderns differ as to its meaning, and discover that their diverse English translations offer diverse meanings, they will not agree that each is free to give it the timeless meaning he or she pleases, rather they will have recourse to the Hebrew text, the "original," in order to settle the dispute. This original is to be found in medieval manuscript form, in Leningrad, Jerusalem, Rome, and elsewhere. Scholars have taken all this into account, and critical editions have been prepared, in Stuttgart and Jerusalem notably, which present one manuscript and then footnote the variants found in others, so that the reader can weigh the arguments for or against a given disputed word or letter. In all of this, the text is hardly free and timeless—it is ruled by the original writing.

Now if the manuscripts contained a spelling mistake, or omitted a necessary word, even if it were the original papyrus manuscript, a scholar would correct the text in a footnote, on the supposition that the author intended to write a correct text. In this case, the original *writing* would not be the authority, but rather a supposed intention of the author. And if the author were brought back to life, he would be invited to authoritatively emend his text. Because, even if authors are supposed to be poor literary critics, still their authority over their own text is absolute.

All of this may seem trivial, but it reveals the nitty-gritty activity of reading as reconstructing the text on the basis of authorial intention. Moreover, the words and sentences of the text are written in Hebrew, and not in Modern Hebrew. Who can say what this word, or this sentence, means? Scholars have painstakingly reconstructed the language of Ancient Israel. The meanings of words and grammatical forms evolve radically over centuries. And the meanings connected with verb tenses in ancient Hebrew are quite different from any modern tenses, and quite elusive. Scholars are still attempting to reconstruct the grammatical rules which applied to verbs, particularly in poetry. The meaning of many Psalms remains very uncertain at present, because we know too little about ancient Hebrew grammar. There has been a lot of discussion about the meaning of the name Yahweh, which appears to have a specific Semitic verb form called "hiphilic." The fact that it has a hiphilic form is known, not through the manuscripts (which falsely read "Yahovah"), but through a Greek transliteration made by Origen. Scholars have used that fragment to reconstruct the original sound of that name (and the pronunciation of classical Hebrew in general), and even to draw conclusions about the meaning of the name Yahweh. However uncertain these conclusions are, it is clear that, without this work of reconstruction, many passages of the Hebrew Bible would be misunderstood. If one were to read the Bible on the basis of Modern Hebrew, for example, not only would the original sound of the text be lost forever, but many sentences of the Bible would be massively misunderstood.

Another level of reconstruction is the reconstruction of meaning. In reading Ex 3:14 in the first part of this chapter, one might have interpreted "I am who I am" in a Greek philosophical sense to mean that God is infinite Being, "being as such." In fact the Septuagint did translate it precisely in that sense. Some readers might prefer this interpretation, considering it more fertile, or profound, or useful in theological argument, or helpful in preaching. But then the original meaning (i.e., the freedom of God, the gratuity of His favour) would be lost.

Now we are not bound by the intention of the author in any sense that would forbid going beyond his/her thought, once we have discovered it, or in the sense that an ancient attempt to express God's freedom could not be improved upon. But we are bound by the original intention in this sense: if we overlook the original meaning and replace it with a Greek meaning, then we have simply not understood that text at all. The Greek meaning was developed in Greek speculation, and not on the basis of reading Exodus. The Hellenistic translators of the Septuagint used a phrase which in fact obliterated the biblical author's meaning, replacing it with a philosophical category which the original author could never have thought of. Interpreting in that sense is not an understanding of the Bible; rather it is an imposition of Greek philosophy.

Moreover, if we retain the original meaning, and add the Greek understanding of God, and add other more modern understandings as well, we will be writing a history of ideas. But should we fail to distinguish between these various meanings, lumping them all together as though they were interpretations of Ex 3:14, or as though they were biblical in origin, we would merely confuse our thinking and deceive ourselves.

The point of all this is that the meaning of a biblical text must be reconstructed. It is not in the text, but rather must be *supposed* to have existed *in the mind of the author.* Interpretation will be shown to be right or wrong, not simply by adducing marks on an ancient papyrus, but also on the basis of shrewd conjecture and complex arguments concerning the plausibility of reconstructed intentions of authors. The criterion here, as in all historical research, is the following: which hypothesis best accounts for all the data? i.e., which original meaning in the author's mind best explains the choice and ordering of letters and words and sentences which I find here, within the context of what is securely known about the era of its writing. Not only scholars, but all modern readers instinctively perform this mental gymnastic constantly. We choose that hypothesis (i.e., we conclude to that meaning) which best provides both a plausible coherence within the text and a plausible correspondence to the realities, timeless or historical, to which the text seems to refer.

In dealing with biblical texts, where there is such a complex history of theories of interpretation, it may seem arrogant to restrict the definition of interpretation to this one sense of the word. However it has been the failure to conceive and define accurately, and to distinguish carefully between diverse activities such as reading the Bible, preaching, writing polemically, formulating doctrine, writing history, and so forth that has led to an endless and often sterile discussion of hermeneutics in this century. This book hopes to deal somewhat narrowly with the interpretation of biblical texts, in the sense indicated above and refined progressively in what follows, distinguishing accurately that arduous task from the various other tasks of systematic theology and pastoral care.

One reads ancient texts with the hope of broadening and deepening and correcting one's contemporary understanding of self, the world, and God. It is not helpful to this purpose if we fail to distinguish between our own ideas and the ideas of an ancient author. Nor is it helpful to plunge into a timeless world of vision in which one is overwhelmed by the author. Such an experience may be wonderful in the aesthetic moment of viewing a play or reading a poem; but afterwards there must follow a moment of critique in which the message of the play is objectified on the one hand, and our feelings about that message separated out and examined on the other. In the case of the Bible, whose normative character in our society has given it great power, there is all the more need for distinguishing and critiquing.

Theological Grounds

The theological grounds for rejecting scholarly approaches to biblical interpretation will be the undeniable fact that the body of belief and practise which has formed Judaism and Christianity was conceived and developed on the basis of pre-scholarly interpretation of Scripture. Does it not follow that the tedious labour involved in scholarship has not been, and therefore is not, necessary for theology, and that the distance and uncertainty which scholarship establishes between modern reader and ancient text is sufficient reason for refusing to use this method? We shall first introduce a discussion of past and present in theology, illustrate theology's overlooking of this, and then argue against these theological grounds by showing that the rejection of scholarship cannot be tolerated once scholarship has become a cultural possibility.

First, then, theological discourse is inevitably composed of present concern and past data. Moreover, in its classical definition Theology is *fides quaerens intellectum*, "faith seeking intelligence," a phrase which could mean "belief in search of contemporary expression," or "conversion in search of philosophical underpinnings," or "religious experience in search of analysis," or "dogma in search of proof," and so forth. Whatever Anselm originally meant, and whatever the reader might like to hold, all will initially agree that *fides quaerens*, "faith searching," designates something relatively timeless, a subjective stance constantly to be renewed. It is a constant present, or an eternal presence. Its form may alter subtly with time, but its term is unlimited, infinite, and in that sense without time. However, the *intellectum* which it seeks will never be timeless, but will be an historical expression using the intellectual patterns of a specific culture. Once faith is expressed within a specific culture, it becomes past, tied to a moment, limited by the meaning of an author. In doing theology, it is essential to retain both aspects: present aspiration for a timeless God, and timed expression within a limited culture.

Gadamer's contribution has been to detail brilliantly the historical-cultural nature of aspiration. Our questions about God do not arise unmediated from human nature, but rather mediated by language and beliefs which shape and limit our way of thinking and asking. In this, Gadamer appears to introduce time into the aspiration. However he overlooks the point that the purpose for reading Scripture within a theological project is precisely to escape time, i.e., to escape historically induced blindness and limitation by viewing a current question in the light of another normative time.

Gadamer obscures this point in the sentence cited above: "It is not really we ourselves who understand; it is always a past that allows us to say, 'I have understood ... '" Now it is true that the theologian cannot escape his/her immediate history, or directly see a timeless God. However the theologian does make every effort to liberate that history and that aspiration from present deviations and narrow limits, at least to some extent and as an ideal to be pursued, by returning to the normative theology of the remote past and experiencing his/her present aspiration in contact with the aspiration out of which the Bible was written and tradition developed. Against Gadamer, then, we might simply affirm that it *is* really "we ourselves who do understand."

Having confused us by introducing time into "fides," Gadamer then confuses us further by trying to remove time from "intellectum." Recall the sentence we stumbled over above: "the texts are interpretations ... of the message; they do not wish to call attention to themselves." Thus the historically limited texts, read aright, are no longer limited by history because they reveal a timeless "message." When we read Gadamer, we might accept this idea uncritically, because we think vaguely of divine authorship and divine word, and so forth. And God is timeless. But notice that Gadamer is constrained to call this timeless object of aspiration a "message," precisely in order to de-historicize the texts, and yet to retain a meaningful content which could be the object of understanding, object of *intellectum* become timeless. This is indefensible, because as soon as God becomes "message" in any humanly receivable form, then that "message" is culturally defined and historically marked. Gadamer's contribution illuminates historical inquiry; but these errors in his analysis mislead us.

Gadamer's position is remarkably similar to that of the Council of Trent, though Gadamer remains Protestant and philosophical, referring to understanding rather than to simple reception of tradition. The Council refers to a timeless message which it calls "the very purity of the Gospel," "the thing promised," "this truth and discipline." And it refers also to the timed, by indicating that the message was earlier contained in prophetic Scriptures, then promulgated orally by Christ, then preached by the Apostles, and finally contained in Scriptures and in traditions which have been handed down to us.[21] In speaking of traditions the Council was thinking of a hierarchical preservation of an unchanged message, "handed on as though from hand to hand," a message which the Synod will now promulgate in its purity "after removing errors." Gadamer has gone beyond the Council in that he has become aware of the historical nature of all "handing on," i.e., tradition in the active sense; and he differs from the Council in conceiving of this tradition as occurring, not within a hierarchical community, but in an unrestricted field of cultural mediation. Still there is an important similarity in the errors of these positions. Both eliminate the present authority of the original historical meaning. For both, when faith is in search of understanding, it is in search of present understanding only. For both, what is timeless is not an unlimited aspiration or question (i.e., the faith of every religious person), but rather a mythical "message," which is handed on like a box of candies.

Secondly, theology has always simply overlooked the original meaning of Scripture. The position of the Council of Trent was a respectable position before historical consciousness became acutely present in Western culture. In fact, it is the only position one can find in traditional theology. Not that theology did not feel it had to return to the past for its data. On the contrary, both Jewish and Christian traditions have held that there was a privileged moment of revelation to which we must return. The Old Testament was largely constructed on the principle of returning to times and words of Moses and David and Solomon, and it grew by a process of editing and reinterpreting ancient texts. The New Testament was written as a reinterpretation of the Old, in the light of its fulfillment in the life and teaching of Christ. The Fathers of the Church thought that their theological work consisted roughly of interpreting the Old and New Testaments in the light of Hellenistic logic; and the medieval synthesis in its Thomistic form was a reinterpretation of Scripture and the Fathers in the light of Aristotle's philosophy. However, unlike Renaissance thinkers or Romantic writers, Judeo-Christian theology does not glorify the past, or view the past as better than the present. If anything, religious thought focusses on present love, timeless truth, and future Union with God. But what it considers to be "the Word of God," or "revelation," occurred in the past, in a unique historical sequence of events.[22]

For this reason Jewish and Christian religious groups through the centuries have expended incredible resources in assuring the possibility of returning to this past. They have preserved the original texts in Hebrew, Aramaic, and Greek, not to mention the original translations in Greek, Aramaic, Syriac, and Latin. Texts were copied by the Massoretes and by the monastic copyists; more recently they have been critically edited and published with extraordinary care for accuracy. Archeological sites have been restored, Qum Rhan texts have been purchased and preserved, institutions and funds have been made available to scholars and students, libraries have been founded, and so forth.

The astounding fact is, however, that this return to past data has been a return to the physical text, without being a return to the author's intention. Even when the return to the past was polemically motivated, namely to provide a basis for condemning current religious practice (as was the case at Qum Rhan for example, or in the 8th-century Karaite movement, or in the Protestant Reformation), theology has not in fact returned to the "original meanings" of these preserved Scriptures. It did not have the technology to do so, or even the awareness that it should do so. This we shall see in a couple of examples of authoritative uses of theologically rich texts.

The first major document of the Second Vatican Council, *Lumen Gentium*, "Dogmatic Constitution of the Church," cites a beautiful text from Jeremiah in order to describe the Church as the "people of God," interpreting it as a promise of a community which includes both Jews and Gentiles. The Council points out that "It has pleased God, however, to make men

holy and save them not merely as individuals without any
mutual bonds, but by making them into a single people ... "
and continues with the following paragraph:

> "Behold the days shall come, saith the Lord, and I will
> make a new covenant with the house of Israel, and with the
> house of Judah ... I will give my law in their bowels, and I
> will write it in their heart: and I will be their God, and they
> shall be my people.... For all shall know me, from the
> least of them even to the greatest, saith the Lord" (Jer
> 31:32-34). Christ instituted this new covenant, that is to say,
> the new testament, in His blood (cf. 1 Cor 11-25), by calling
> together a people made up of Jew and gentile, making them
> one, not according to the flesh, but in the Spirit.[23]

Now Jeremiah, were he alive today, might be pleased with
this paragraph, but he would be surprised by this use of his
text. A recent scholarly study of Jeremiah may be cited to
make the point: "From the Christian point of view the idea of
a new covenant is a very important element in early Christian
thought, but that should not entail reading Jer 31:31-34 as if it
were Jeremiah's plan for and approval of the rise of Christianity." In fact neither Judaism nor Christianity should
recognize itself in this text: "In no sense can either of these
religions be regarded as fulfilling (or being fulfillment of) this
passage ... "[24] Modern scholars have frequently seen this text
as a *locus classicus* for the breakthrough of individualistic
thinking in religion. Without going that far, it is clear that the
text is *not* about community directly, but rather about the
interiorization of religion.

One further point: the Council, in citing verse 34, has taken
care to omit some very important opening words, replacing
them with dots! The biblical text embarrassingly reads: "And
no longer shall each man teach his neighbour and each his
brother, saying 'Know the Lord,' for they shall all know me,
from the least of them to the greatest, says the Lord.... " The
Council, acting as a teaching body (a *magisterium*), very involved in teaching the brother and the neighbour, felt it had to
omit part of the text! The Council was going back to the past
data, the original words, but definitely not to the original idea.

In this case, it was close to falsifying even the original words as well.[25]

Thus a most authoritative interpretation of Scripture, in the second half of this century, is seen to refuse the limits of "original meaning" which scholarly interpretation would assign. Is this abusive of Scripture? If so, virtually the whole theological tradition has been abusive.

Again this may be seen by referring to authoritative interpretations of Ex 3, the text this chapter began with, drawn from the history of interpretations to be found in Brevard Childs' commentary on Exodus.[26]

Mt 22:31-32 presents Jesus refuting the Sadducees by citing Ex 3:6: "And as for the resurrection from the dead, have you not read what was said to you by God, 'I am the God of Abraham, and the God of Isaac, and the God of Jacob?' He is not God of the dead, but of the living." The Elohist would not have expected this use of his text. He was not proclaiming the resurrection of Abraham! He was proclaiming that Yahweh was the basis for continuity of trust, when Moses replaced the dead Abraham. Matthew's Jesus used the ancient words, but not the original idea. Rather he has applied those words to a context totally foreign to the intention of the Elohist. Childs defends Matthew here, referring to a tradition of rabbinical exegesis which the reader is to presuppose here, and pointing out that Matthew, in having Jesus comment "you do not know the power of God" (v. 29) was invoking "a *Sachkritik* or material norm, an indication that Jesus is appealing to the reality of which the text speaks and is not limiting himself to the artificial reading of the written text apart from its substance."[27] However brilliant the defence, it is clear that Childs has learned to expect little concern for the original meaning, for he adds, "while it is true that Matthew's use of the Old Testament as evidence for the resurrection goes beyond the Exodus passage, nevertheless the real issue at stake is whether he has imposed a totally foreign meaning on the ancient text."[28] Matthew's use of the text does not impose a "perverse" meaning on Ex 3:6, but it does impose a meaning which is not found there.

Classical Jewish interpreters of Ex 3 focussed on the burning bush, seeing it as an allegory for the life of Israel, which was not consumed by persecution. The Fathers of the Church, on the other hand, wrote about the angel who spoke from the bush: they identified it with the Son of God. Augustine was concerned lest this imply that Christ was only an angel, so he was at pains to point out that the angel merely represented the Son. From Augustine through the medieval period the "I am who I am" definition of God was the centre of much onto-logical doctrine: God was the one being whose essence was being-as-such. The Reformers were concerned to remove implications of a static nature from this interpretation, and to establish that God was active in governing and saving the world.

Childs himself, when he comes to "theological reflection," recalls these traditional reflections and adds one of his own on "trust in the one whose self-disclosure is a foretaste of the promised inheritance."[29]

And current Jewish interpretation is equally remote from original concerns. Cassuto, for example, in commenting on this passage explains many details of philology, literary form, and narrative coherence; he takes note that the bush is not intended to be an image of God, and explains why the Jews were fully justified in taking wealth with them from Egypt; and he spends much effort in refuting the evidence for source criticism in this text.[30]

Nowhere do these authoritative interpreters return to the meanings we indicated as the original intentions of the text of Ex 3-4. There is no mention of the imposing of the name Yahweh, or of the doctrine of divine freedom in electing Israel. It is not that the original meanings of the Yahwist and Elohist have been lost to Western thought—it is just that they have not been retained in connection with, as interpretations of, this specific text. Certainly the name Yahweh has been much dis-cussed in Jewish theology, and the freedom of God (or the doctrine of Grace) has been much discussed by Jews and Christians over the centuries.[31]

The point which must be retained here is that in Jewish and Christian theological writing, one dealt with contemporary thought on its own terms, and returned to biblical texts, not to be limited by their horizons and concerns, but for an illumina-tion which the author often could not have intended. One was almost fanatically concerned to cite the text faithfully, and to grant it specific biblical authority, and to distinguish it from glosses and commentaries, but one was not concerned to retrieve the original meaning. So astounding is this attitude, that it may be well to cite a medieval text which makes it explicit. The meticulous scholar of the 12th-century, Robert of Melun, wrote as follows:

> If a person pronounces the words only of an author, even though he applies them in a sense other than that of the author, it is agreed beyond doubt that he should be granted to be the spokesman of authority. So we are bound by our own judgement to admit that authority resides in the words rather than in the opinion of the author. And so what we have said must necessarily be true: there is no authority in glosses which differ in their wording from the authorities whence they are believed to have been excerpted.[32]

Still it is clear that textual interpretation for the past two thousand years cannot be reduced to respect for the physical words, without regard for meaning. In fact there has existed in both the Jewish and the Christian traditions a veritable jungle of rules for interpretation of meaning. Medieval exegesis, for example, was concerned to begin with a literal sense, which was as close as they could come to a combination of our literary plus historical studies, before going on to spiritual senses: allegorical, moral (tropological), and anagogic (eschato-logical). Hugh of St. Victor, for example, wrote scathingly in the 12th century about those who were careless of this literal meaning:

> The mystical sense is only gathered from what the letter says in the first place. I wonder how people have the face to boast themselves teachers of allegory, when they do not know the primary meaning of the letter.... "The letter does not interest us. We teach allegory." How do you read Scripture then, if you don't read the letter? Subtract the letter and what is left? The outward form of God's word seems to you, perhaps, like dirt, so you trample it underfoot, like dirt, and despise what the letter tells you was done

> physically and visibly. But hear! that dirt, which you tram-
> ple, opened the eyes of the blind. Read Scripture then, and
> first learn carefully what it tells you was done in the flesh.[33]

Examples could be found of every shade of understanding and of misunderstanding of texts in the history of biblical interpretation. Still the important truth is that later interpreters, who could choose to reconstruct the original meanings in various degrees, were never limited by that original meaning. As they did not distinguish theology from interpretation, and as they wanted to do theology, they were led to confuse their intellectual operations endlessly. This confusion continued until very recent times in which exegetes have been defined as such, and systematic theologians defined differently. This confusion has been the matrix within which virtually all our religious beliefs have been born. The separation of exegesis from theology has led to great intellectual production, but to very little enrichment of doctrine. It has also led to the ever greater isolation and impoverishment of exegesis.

If theology has traditionally been done without biblical scholarship, may we not conclude that it should continue to be done independently of biblical scholarship? The answer is simply no, because we just can't do it. In this history-conscious and scientific age, we are limited. And the limit is not imposed by others, but rather by our own understanding of what constitutes honest thinking. If we do not think as hard and as critically about God and Bible as we do about medicines, about investments, about the daily news, it will then follow either that we are not serious about God and Bible, or that we are building an escapist form of religious thought, placing real life in one category of consciousness and religious living in another.

Advances in awareness are irreversible. Once you know the earth is round, or that solids are composed of infinitesimal particles, or that your best friend has deceived you, it is just not possible to think seriously of those things on any other basis. Once you have an insight into bias in narrative, you simply can never again hear an "eye-witness" account with uncritical acceptance. We are all aware of the distance in millennia and in culture between our lives and the lives of biblical writers. There is no reversing that. It is only through self-indulgent sentimentality, and certainly not from the toughness of real religious commitment, that one can read biblical texts as though those words were directly written for oneself.

We can understand the words of Scripture in some approximation of their original meaning. If we love Scripture, we have no choice but to do so. This is a first step in reading Scripture, and it will be well to retain the world "interpretation" to name this first step. This is not theology, though it is a part of theology. What is needed is not to abandon scholarship, but rather to discover a new approach to Scripture in which scholarly reading can lead securely to theological enrichment. The relation between the two is the main concern of this book, and it will be directly addressed in a concluding chapter.

Towards a Definition of Objectives

We have constantly run up against apparently opposed objectives in reading Scripture: the technical search for past meaning (precise, historically remote, scholarly); and the listening for a timeless voice of God (faith, mysticism). The first objective is thrust upon us by our current culture, i.e., our general approach toward understanding and dealing with reality. If we try to read the Bible independently of that culture, we will either trivialize religious thought by reducing it to private and unsubstantial sentiment, or else inflate religious thought in a gnostic direction by making it into a "real" alternative to reality as we know it. The second objective is thrust upon us because the Bible understood itself that way, our traditions have read it that way, and the constant, most profound aspiration of human consciousness is to hear from God.

How can both these objectives be achieved at the same time? This question is parallel to questions about reconciling Science and Religion, Science and Humanism, the University and the Church, or even Truth and Love. A reconcilation must be found, because in each of these cases the one without the other goes dangerously mad.

In this section, we shall first attempt to define objectives in respect to original meaning, and then in respect to faith.

Objectives in Respect to Original Meaning

It is important to stress from the beginning that if the biblical authors were not writing fiction, they were also not writing philosophical or scientific texts. Such pure literary genres became possible only through other developments which occurred in ancient Greece and centuries later in Europe. It follows that the meanings which one can hope to recover from the Bible will not be systematic theories, or precise analyses of reality, or abstract laws of nature, or anything which can be phrased in non-literary abstract language. Thus studies which result in abstract formulations such as a résumé of the meaning of a text, or a brief definition of the "kerygma" of an author, or the reduction of a story to its *Tendenz* or "point" (especially its "whole point"), will normally be alien to original biblical meaning. Such studies are helpful only if handled with care to recognize this difference. They are modern, in that they appear precise and objective, and they demand nothing of the reader. Still such paraphrases are emphatically not the meaning of an ancient text. The Bible does not want to be a book of doctrines.[34]

Recovering the meaning of a text consists in reconstructing from every clue we have (i.e., all the data) a whole world-view and way of thinking within which selected aspects are related and emphasized in a specific way. Just as the word is given its meaning by the larger context of the sentence, and the sentence its meaning by the larger contexts of the paragraph, and chapter, and book, so all of these are given their meaning by the larger social, historical, and language contexts within which the writer wrote and understood what he or she wrote. The "whole point" of an ancient text can be expressed only by the text itself understood in this large context.

Recovering this is not easy. I don't want to refute skepticism once again, but I would like to point out two aspects of the process here. A reader of ancient texts must come to know that one's own world-view, or context for understanding and reacting, is unique, and that others are there to be discovered through reconstruction. Any one who has penetrated a non-contemporary author such as Jane Austen, or John Keats, or Dante, or Homer, and who has read enough of and about that author to be totally at ease in understanding each sentence as it occurs, as though it were written by a familiar friend, will understand the kind of patient, attentive, and imaginative work required. Such readers will also know the possibility of actually achieving this result, and the special pleasure it affords. Most important, they will know the measureless distance there is between one world-view and another. One who has not had this experience may not readily understand how scholarship operates, and may not easily sympathize with the perspective on interpretation presented in this discussion.[35]

In regard to biblical texts, however, a second aspect of the process of recovery through scholarship must be specially indicated. These texts are the product of faith, and they require conversion in the reader if he or she is to recover their meaning. Just as some detective novels are written as puzzles and require of the reader an inquiring attitude, or just as some poems are attempts to express elusive feelings and demand refined sensitivity on the part of the reader, so the faith horizon of biblical texts will elude any reader whose world-view excludes God. Such a reader can have no idea about what the text might be about, and will tend to reduce it to some ethical teaching, or political message, some dispute between factions, some comment on another text, and so forth. Even if faith is explicit in the text, such a reader will inevitably underestimate the breadth and depth of the control of meaning which faith exercises, reducing it to superstition, or search for security, and so forth. Such a reader will also have to leave unexplained, or even unnoticed, some of the clues in the text. An example of this will be provided in the following section of this chapter.

It will be helpful now to introduce some distinctions. There is an important difference between recovering the meaning of a text for oneself, and reformulating that meaning for others. Activities of recovery we shall term *interpretation*, and activities for reformulation we shall term *communication*. Interpretation then will presuppose the research required to establish the original text, and presuppose also whatever historical knowledge we have concerning the circumstances of the

writing; but in itself interpretation denotes all the further procedures required to understand the ideas, affirmations, feelings,
horizons, aspirations, and passions expressed in the text.

The word *communication* then will denote the formulation
of interpretation for others. Communication can be *of the text*
or *of the meaning.* Communication of the text is, of course,
called *translation,* and it attempts to render in another language, or in the same language in a later era, the text itself.
Translation of the text may be *literal,* in which case it will find
equivalent words and grammar and structures; or it may be
literary, in which case it will also attempt to find equivalent
idioms, rhetorical conventions, and systems of symbols and
metaphors. Communication of meaning, on the other hand, is
far reaching. One might communicate the meaning of Ex 3-4,
for example, by writing laws about cultic practice, or by writing
cultic texts, or a novel, or a set of doctrines. Or one might
communicate its meaning by actions such as joining Solomon's
army, or by forming a group to study the life of Moses.

The main motive, and final objective, in reading Scripture is
to enhance the spiritual life of ordinary people. This means
bringing biblical revelation as a real factor into their "ordinary
lives" (i.e., our daily lives as we understand them), by making
this revelation available to them. To this end, communication
is the principal means. This is a technical matter, a functional
specialty of Theology.[36] It is often studied under the title of
"pastoral theology." All the range of communications listed
above are required. Where this range is lacking, for example
where only literal translations of the Bible are read in a Bible-
believing community, we risk all varieties of unscholarly communication, from silly to dangerous, or even monstrous.

This final aim of communication presupposes, however,
that the intellectual community has first achieved prior objectives of interpretation. There must be research to establish
critical texts. There must exist a complex process of history
writing to establish contexts for the meaning of these texts:
social and political history, history of ideas, history of the
languages. Finally there must be interpretation of the texts
themselves.

Now between interpretation and communication Christianity has instituted the whole discipline of Theology. The relation between these two will be the burden of chapter 7 below.

Objectives in Respect to Faith

So much for the historical, or timed, aspects of interpretation. As we pointed out above, it cannot be adequately accomplished without conversion, or faith, on the part of the interpreter. We shall turn, therefore, to a formal consideration of this timeless aspect of inquiry, the *fides quaerens intellectum* of Anselm. This inquiring faith motivates the interpreter and communicator, just as it motivated the biblical author in the first place. It is the constant in human experience which makes it possible for us today to understand texts from long ago.

A clear example of inquiring faith may be seen in the, perhaps, familiar story of "The Patriarch's Wife," which is told three separate times in Genesis: chs. 12, 20, and 26.[37] The story seems to have been originally a travelling legend, told possibly in Philistine circles, about an adulterous situation which resulted in sterility, or impotence, in the royal court. The Elohist account in Gen 20 may be closest to the original tale, though it was written subsequent to the Yahwist.[38] For present purposes, we shall concentrate on the first Yahwist account: Gen 12:8—13:4.

This account must be considered a very free, even an abusive, translation of the text, and even of the meaning, of a Philistine story, contours of which can be found in Gen 20, which is studied below in chapter 4. The irreverent spirit of an early Israelite adaptation has been retained. The most striking change introduced by the Yahwist has been to shift the tale from a Philistine setting (from Abimelech at Gerar) to a Pharaoh's court in Egypt, and to transpose the original sterility/impotence motif into a plague. These changes make the story implausible and problematic, but they fill the old tale with a religious meaning, suggesting as a context for interpretation that religious experience which originated Israel, namely being saved by Yahweh through the plagues visited on Egypt. Thus Egypt becomes a sort of sacrament, and Gen 12 creates a myth which implies that the Jews received this sacrament in the person of Abraham, long before Moses. A tale which celebrated the survival skills of a tribe has been transformed into a religious legend expressing God's constant care for Israel.

In this translation-Scripture-writing, just what has the Yahwist done? First, like the theologians who followed him until very recent times, he has not been restricted by the discipline which we have described under the term "interpretation." Secondly, he has provided an unscholarly, but powerful communication of an ancient tale. Thirdly, he has deliberately added a dimension of mystery to the tale, a dimension which proceeds from his own faith in Yahweh, and which demands the same faith of the reader.[39] Not faith in the historical accuracy of this story! It is not historically accurate. But rather faith in a specific shape of the salvation which Israel experiences.

The Yahwist is interested in preserving traditions and memories, and he is interested in being a clever story-teller; but above all he is interested in discovering ultimate meaning in these memories, traditions, and stories. This is basic in his attitude. It is his foundational stance as a writer. It is this inquiring faith which directs his curiosity about the past, about reality, about the universe.

The Yahwist mentions the faith of Abraham in Gen 15:6, for example; but he never discusses faith, or adverts directly to his own faith. There is no mention of faith in Gen 12, even though we now see it as the heart of the chapter. The Yahwist was a theologian, writing theology for his time. He used the most advanced intellectual procedures of his day to articulate his faith in that he gave verbal expression to his faith by retelling an old and bawdy tale. Surely that precisely is what is meant by *fides quaerens intellectum*.

In discovering the faith dimension of this text, we too used the intellectual procedures of our day, i.e., inquiring into the sources of the Pentateuch, and contrasting their texts in order to discern the focus of each. The Yahwist's faith was discovered in the gaps in the Yahwist's text, the failure of adequate apparent meaning. The discovery was later reinforced by the introduction of a source hypothesis based on the shift from Gerar to Egypt.[40] Our own faith was needed to understand the Yahwist here, for without it we would have settled for an interpretation of this story as a witty tale of Jewish survival, without looking for deeper meaning. Having interpreted the Yahwist's faith, we can now attempt to communicate it by writing commentaries, by giving homilies, by writing analogous stories, and so forth.

The Bible is a book which speaks of God primarily, and its interpretation will always need to discover this horizon if it is to be adequate. The faith horizon is often only implicit in the text, but experienced as driving the author and challenging the reader. To read the Bible adequately, we must find a method of literary criticism which systematically includes this interpersonal dimension of the text. Any approach which excludes the mind of the author, or overlooks the foundational stance of the author, or which would explain the text as merely an order of words, will have excluded the heart of biblical literature.

Conclusion

This chapter has established the need of recovering the original meaning of scriptural texts. However original meanings in the form of historically defined "messages" have never been recovered until recently, or been directly normative in Western theological tradition. Moreover, such meanings, whether they be expressed as doctrines, or exhortations, or *Tendenzen*, however useful they may be, are not *the* original meaning. The latter is a personal world-view with a specific set of relations, focusses, and emphases: a view which was held by the original author, expressed in the data and especially in the gaps of the text, recoverable in part at least by the reader, and not susceptible of résumé. At this point, we leave open the question of normativity with regard to the original meaning understood in this sense.

What is needed, then, is a method of reading Scripture which retains traditional scholarly methods; which defines and distinguishes between the activities of interpreting, communicating, and theologizing; and which provides explicitly for the interpersonal aspect of reading.

2

Elemental Meaning, A
Further Dimension to Interpretation

The aim of this chapter is to propose a specific method of interpreting biblical texts, which will be applied in subsequent chapters to the major authors of the Pentateuch. Traditional methods of scholarship will be integrated into the discussion as needed, but their nature and necessity will be taken for granted, as we have already discussed them in ch. 1, and they are otherwise well known. The focus of this chapter will be precisely the neglected and almost forbidden area of interpersonal reading.

We shall first consider the unique Voice or unnamed Speaker which a reader hears, and must react to, in a text, even though it is only obscurely felt as a presence both in what is said and in what is not said (the gaps) in the text. Second, we shall discuss the authority of Scripture in terms of the unnamed Speaker: whereas the paraphrased original meanings have never been normative, we shall show that an unnamed Speaker, precisely because it is only implied, and remains subliminal as it were, is in fact normative. This is the nature of authority in all literature, but in a special way in biblical literature. Third, we shall name the primary effect of biblical texts, i.e., they challenge the reader to conversions of various kinds.[1]

The Speaker in a Text

Literary critics, hoping to make of their discipline an objective and scientific one, condemn the project of evaluating works of art, and in particular of listing authors along a comparative scale of preference.[2] However, such evaluation is unavoidable: it determines which poets and poems get published; it determines which publications will be noticed and written about by critics; it rules the syllabus in English Literature courses and the selection of poems to be included in anthologies. Eventually, through a cumulative process of opinion building, there arises a canon of literary works accepted as such in a given culture.[3] There is no reason to doubt that all these decisions, and their complex interdependence, serve us well enough in the end. However, it is surely an unpardonable omission in literary theory to give no attention to, or satisfactory account of, this surreptitious process of evaluation.

Evaluation is overlooked because it is highly personal, inter-personal and subjective. Conventions of thought about scientific study have barely begun to accommodate the inescapably subjective nature of certain aspects of knowledge. What we shall say about the inter-personal, inter-subjective, inter-faith experience of reading Scripture will, in fact, join contemporary attacks upon these conventions.[4]

Evaluation of texts occurs in the reader spontaneously, and often without our noticing. One takes to an author, or one "just doesn't like" an author. Sometimes, one just doesn't like an author because one has no idea what the author is writing about. But at other times, one can fully understand an author, recognize the author's depth and intelligence, and yet still reject him or her. Sometimes we find ourselves inexplicably drowsy, unable to keep our eyes open, when reading a given book; other times we may be agitated or feel angry in reading it. But why? The ideas explicit in the text, the subject treated, the use of language, and so forth, frequently do not seem to justify this reaction. I have experienced this in reading recognized great writers such as Samuel Beckett, for example, or Dylan Thomas. And the experience is unshakable, even after years of trying. Yet these authors appear to have entered the canon, leaving me a heretic.

Let us try a few concrete examples, drawn from texts which, I hope, will prove to be familiar. John Gray's *Elegy Written in a Country Churchyard* begins:

> The curfew tolls the knell of parting day,
> The lowing herd wind slowly o'er the lea,
> The plowman homeward plods his weary way,
> And leaves the world to darkness and to me.

It is important for the present discussion that the reader take time to become aware of his or her reaction to this poem: excitement, delight, admiration, sadness, coldness, weariness, and so forth. One should find the whole text in an anthology, and read it, if it is not already very familiar. Do you really like this text? To what in the text are you reacting? For an immediate point of comparison (i.e., for a forbidden comparative evaluation) we might consider William Wordsworth's *The Solitary Reaper*:

> Behold her, single in the field,
> Yon solitary Highland Lass!
> Reaping and singing by herself;
> Stop here, or gently pass!
> Alone she cuts and binds the grain,
> And sings a melancholy strain;
> O listen! for the Vale profound
> Is overflowing with the sound.

Does the reader prefer one to the other? Can the real reasons for preference be identified? They both seem to be about nature, both somewhat warm and sweet, both have a slightly melancholy tone, both are written with equal sensitivity to sound and language.... And yet I, for one, love the one and dislike the other. It is instinctive, and immediate.

This is very much like being introduced to two people at a cocktail party, and feeling drawn to one but not to the other. One might explain it on grounds of "intuition," but that explains nothing. Appealing to intuition means only that one has not as yet been able to identify the data to which one is reacting. There are reactions to colours, to styles of clothing, to body language, to subliminal body odours, to the sound of voice, to rhythm: myriad barely perceived sense data, which we evaluate subliminally. Later we correct misleading "first impressions," and include further data in our evaluation. There result various degrees of accepting or rejecting a person. And such decisions determine most of what matters in our lives.

What subliminal, or barely perceived, data in these poems motivate our reaction? There is one gross difference between poems, which affects variously all aspects of both poems, and which certainly evokes my personal reaction. That is the expectancy about where meaning or fulfillment will occur. Gray builds his poem through countless images of nature, but nature leads only to darkness, and the grave, and a sad solitude. We learn from the final three verses that what Gray wants ("'twas all he wished") is a friend. He expects to find this, not in nature, but only after death, in God.

Wordsworth has an entirely different expectation. He does expect to find meaning and joy in nature. In the verse cited above he wants nature to be undisturbed by thought so that he can contemplate it: "Stop here, or gently pass!" There results a wondrous song from the peasant girl, and the whole valley "is overflowing with the sound." At the end of the poem we learn that "The music in my heart I bore,/ Long after it was heard no more." Similarly at the end of *I Wandered Lonely as a Cloud* he tells us that his joy often comes in recalling the dancing daffodils, "when on my couch I lie/ In vacant or in pensive mood." He even provides us with a reason for this: his *Ode on Intimations of Immortality* explains that undisturbed nature evokes in him obscure memories of a prior life in Heaven.

These are two very diverse expectations for meaning and fulfillment, even though they are expressed in similar imagery. The expectations are not the content, or subject matter, of the poems. Content and subject matter in poetry are really conventional materials which are drawn upon again and again in diverse poems with diverse expectations. Nor are expectations the "message" of the poems, as the poems clearly have no message. Poetry, as John Steward Mills observed, is not addressed to anyone, but rather is overheard. Such expectations are not immediately perceived by the reader, as they usually are not made explicit in the poems. In fact, one could understand and enjoy the poems without ever adverting to expectations. Certainly most of a reader's or critic's attention will be drawn to other matters. And yet these expectations directly affect the author, shaping his authorial stance, and therefore forming the elemental meaning of the text, its tone of voice, its body language as it were. These expectations subtly address the reader. They may challenge the reader, if the reader's expectations for meaning and fulfillment are quite different. Instinctively the reader reacts to the author behind the poem, evaluating, preferring one to the other, accepting or rejecting in varying degrees.

Now implicit expectation, or elemental meaning, is not a whimsical, or sentimental, point of evaluation. Even if a professional literary critic feels that he or she must put aside personal preferences in writing criticism (although I doubt this is ever successfully done), still each human being as such relates to others on the basis of what the other expects of life, what the other loves and hopes for. If that cannot be shared, then relation to the other remains purely pragmatic: one deals with the other only insofar as something extraneous to the person is to be gained.

The difference in expectation may be large, as in the example above, or it may be very fine. We shall cite another example within the same category of expectations from nature. Gerald Manley Hopkins, in his poem *God's Grandeur*, certainly is like Wordsworth in expecting to find meaning in nature, and in nature undisturbed by humanity. The poem begins like this:

> The world is charged with the grandeur of God.
> It will flame out like shining from shook foil;
> It gathers to a greatness, like the ooze of oil.
> Crushed. Why do men then now not reck his rod?
> Generations have trod, have trod, have trod;
> And all is seared with trade; bleared, smeared with toil;
> And wears man's smudge and shares man's smell; the soil
> Is bare now, nor can foot feel, being shod.

Which does one prefer? There is a kind of self-conscious and mannered style in Hopkins which takes getting used to. The style itself is expressive of the fundamental expectancy expressed here. So if a reader finds the style either delightful or off-putting, he or she will find the expectancy more so. For Hopkins, nature is not lovely in itself, but only insofar as God specially changes it, "charges" it. Moreover, at present, nature reveals none of its meaning because it is obscured by human intervention. One feels a very different Speaker in this text—an agitated and unhappy and combative voice, appropriately expressing itself in a self-conscious and mannered style. Later in the poem, the voice will warm with hope in the future: "Because the Holy Ghost over the bent/ World broods with warm breast."

In these examples, we react to three poems. The poems are not trying to say something about something else; they merely present a unity of felt meaning; they perform for us like a person at a party. Within them, we hear three very different Speakers, and we react personally, evaluating and ranking the Speakers in an order of preference. At least one important basis of evaluation will be the stance of expectancy felt in the Speaker, and expressed as elemental meaning.

In these examples from lyric poetry the Speaker is explicitly the poet himself, who speaks of himself in the first persons. It is for this reason that the stance of expectancy is almost articulated in the text. In other literary genres the "I" or "me" in a text is not the author, and the stance of expectancy is much farther from the surface of the text. For example, the popular "spy-novelist" John Le Carré appears to be concerned, partially with a story, but mostly with depicting what T.S. Eliot called "the hollow men," a society peopled by totally inauthentic and loveless non-people. From *The Spy Who Came in from the Cold* to *The Little Drummer Girl*, his stories are only partially sustained by action and suspense. The Speaker has other concerns: he presents his material as harrowing studies of personal squalor, illusion, and betrayal. Smiley is a sensitive genius, but never a hero, because his own mind is constantly drawn back to something irrelevant to the stories, namely the failure of his marriage. The reader feels that Le Carré's expectancy is a hopeless search for traces of authenticity, trust, love, in the realm of "The Wasteland." Eventually he wrote *The Naive and Sentimental Lover*, the other side of the coin, an equally harrowing discovery of authentic love as chaos. Some Le Carré fans were confused, and even displeased, as the aspiration of the familiar Speaker, which had been hidden beneath the surface of the texts over many years, suddently was displayed on the surface and almost made explicit.

We must now attempt to evoke a more accurate awareness of the Speaker in literature, and to define precisely what this notion includes. There is of course the named speaker in a text, whose words are placed in quotation marks. This speaker may be fictional, and the text is attributed from time to time in such texts to familiar personages in order to give it authority, or to give it a special tonality, or simply as a literary convention. For example, the Pentateuch is attributed to Moses by extra-pentateuchal tradition, but within the text itself Moses is the named speaker of the book of Deuteronomy; similarly the book of Psalms is generally attributed to David in biblical and extra-biblical tradition, and even within the book of Psalms itself a series of editorial headings designates many Psalms as "a Psalm of David"; all but the last two chapters of the book of Proverbs are presented by the text as words of Solomon, as is the Song of Songs, and also, by imprecise allusion, the book Qohelet (Ecclesiastes). All of this is a technique of assigning a specific authority and literary genre to these books. For example the collection of love songs in the Song of Songs is heard differently because it comes from the mouth of the all wise Solomon: it becomes a parable or allegory of some sort. Outside the Bible, "The Ancient Mariner" is a tale told by a survivor, using "I" or "we" throughout. This technique fills all the narrative with the immediacy of an eye-witness on the one hand, and the spectral horror of the living dead on the other. This named speaker is merely one literary technique among many other techniques chosen by the unnamed Speaker. Our interest lies with the latter. When we talk of "the Speaker" in this discussion, we do not mean the named speaker, but rather a more general Voice which includes and overrides named speakers.

Other voices in some texts which are distinguishable from, and yet absorbed by the overall Voice of "the Speaker" are the voice of an unnamed narrator, and that of an unnamed editor. For there is in narrative an unnamed narrator, who is present to all events, and provides a continuity and interrelationship for all that is related. For example, in Genesis an unnamed narrator tells about God creating the world in ch. 1, and about burying Joseph in ch. 50. The narrator is not God, since he speaks of God in the third person; he is not Moses as Moses is not born yet, and the same narrator will tell of Moses' birth in the following book; he is not named or inquired about, and yet his continuous presence, and the unbroken consistency of his viewpoint, are essential to the unity of the book. The unnamed narrator chooses devices for conveying information to the reader, and controls the flow of information between participants within the text: sometimes the narrator directly informs the reader that something occurred at such a time, and at other times he will have one of the characters, or God, or a clue, reveal this information to another person within the text, or to the reader directly. The unnamed narrator is certainly a voice in the text, a voice chosen and shaped by the Speaker. The voice will have its own characteristics, for example relating the narrative in a smooth slow rhythm, as in George Elliot's novels, or relating it in abrupt, unconnected spurts as in the spy stories of John Le Carré. The voice is never adverted to by the text, and often not adverted to by the reader. It exists in the style of the text, and it emerges perhaps most visibly in the gaps in the text, the leaps in logic, the omissions, where the narrative trails off. The reader spontaneously constructs this narrator and reacts to it.

Sometimes the unnamed narrator does demand to be adverted to, or named, as for example in the case of the editor of the Pentateuch. The gaps in the text were so disturbing that one could not successfully fill them without consciously questioning and painfully constructing an hypothesis of editing. This editor is an unnamed narrator, insofar as the text never names or acknowledges him, even though scholars have done so.

Parallel to the unnamed narrator in non-narrative texts, and often overlaying him in narrative texts, is an unnamed editor who writes the title and subtitles, or who introduces the personage who will tell the story, or who writes the introductory verses to the prophetic books, or framework verses such as Deuteronomy 1:1-2; 4:44; 28:69; 33:1. This, too, is an unnamed voice, chosen by the Speaker, who resides in the gaps of the text as elemental meaning.

If the text is introduced and read by an official reader in a religious ceremony, that will constitute an external speaker, assuming a totally different voice, a voice from another era and another culture. But the unnamed editor is heard from within the text, a voice as ancient as the text itself. It is the major tone in the voice of the Speaker of the text.

This Voice of the text is profundly affected by the literary forms which the Speaker adopts. There is, for example, the intimate one-on-one tone of a private letter, signaled by "Dear Harriet"; or the fairy-tale convention signaled by "Once upon a time"; or the scabrous rollicking suggestiveness signaled by the lymerick meter of "There once was a lady named Rachel"; or the authority of a royal messenger signaled by "Thus said Yahweh" in prophetic texts; or the ambience of public worship signaled by the imperative plural of *alleluia*, "praise ye the Lord" in the Psalms; and so forth and so on. Recognizing the literary forms in the Bible, discovering the social contexts for meaning implied by these forms, and acquiring a fine feel for the kind of meaning to be looked for in texts marked by them, has been perhaps the major contribution of biblical criticism since Hermann Gunkel introduced the topic at the beginning of this century. These forms and the levels and kinds of knowledge they imply, and the tone they impart, are signaled but not stated in the text. They constitute an elemental meaning of the text. A reader who has become familiar with a given form will not directly advert to it in reading, but will experience it as a special character in the Speaker's voice, and react to it by constructing the Speaker's meaning with perfect accuracy.

Finally, there are all the tricks of style which are peculiar to an author, making his or her texts recognizable among others, and expressing a unique taste and stance. These tricks of style can sometimes be described as objective data in the text, such as the preference for active or passive verbs, the use or avoidance of adjectives, the signals for structuring a text and techniques for emphasis. Sometimes tricks of style are more implicit, or perceived in the gaps, as for example the pervasive use of bombast, or hyperbole, or humour, or the tendency to appeal to visual phenomena rather than auditory, and so forth. Among the tricks of style are included the techniques of the unnamed editor and narrator, and the choice of literary forms.

All of these together give the reader a distinct impression of the author. The impression may be totally wrong if the reader is either insensitive to text, or perversely sensitive. Right or wrong, the reader constructs a distinct impression of the author, an impression which is not easily conceived in verbal form, but which will make the reader tend to believe or disbelieve, to accept or reject, to like or dislike. The community of readers, by comparing notes, as it were, tends to correct the measure of insensitivity or perversity found in each individual reader.

Ultimately the Speaker in a text is the historical author, insofar as he or she chooses and harmonizes in one coherent Voice all the voices we have enumerated. The historical author's world view and value system and horizon is implied in this Voice, and is objectified and affirmed in this literary text. It is not the historical author in a biographical sense, i.e., in the sense of an assortment of biological and historical data collected by some one else. Rather it is the historical author insofar as his or her internal consciousness as a writer is united in the writing. To use a category made popular by Karl Jung, the Speaker is the *persona* of an artist engaged in creative expression, which appropriates and incorporates an historically limited complex of awareness, attitude, expectation. If we know that the Speaker in a text wrote in the year 1940 C.E., that external fact will provide helpful clues toward hearing the author aright. But we may also hear aright if we feel through the text to form an exact impression of the author's awareness, horizon, attitude, and expectation, without being able to assign a specific year, or century, to the work. Much biblical scholarship in particular has consisted of attempts to establish contexts for meaning by arguing to the personal and historical context of the author. Such reaching for the author is always helpful, even if the results are terribly uncertain.

Biblical scholarship has also included a rarely acknowledged amount of accepting and rejecting biblical authors. This phenomenon is called "proposing a canon within the canon." I have to confess that all my life I have successfully avoided teaching apocalyptic texts simply because I dislike them. I do not dislike their message or their content. I dislike the Speakers within them, all of whom share a similar attitude and expectation. This reaction would be irrelevant in the face of literature in general; but in the face of biblical literature it becomes something to be confessed.

The Normativity of Biblical Speakers

Generally a reader begins a book uncertain whether or not he or she will buy it, or read it. If one is a professional reader, one will steel oneself, hold one's nose, and read it anyway for professional purpose. However when a reader begins with a biblical book, her attitude is different. If the reader is not a believer, then the unique pretensions of the book will offend her radically. If the reader is even vaguely a believer, she will be prepared to consider herself defective in reading this book: she will be prepared to be challenged as to her human authenticity, exhorted to greater virtue, invited to radical conversion. If she does not like the Speaker, she is prepared to find that the fault lies in herself, not in the Speaker; and her dislike will trouble the reader, leading her to examine her conscience, or engage in religious discussion with friends or religious authorities. In the famous "Spiritual Exercises" of Ignatius Loyola, the exercitant is instructed to reflect after each meditation on scripture, and to focus on the parts of the meditation where one experienced particular feelings of "consolation" or "desolation." In subsequent meditations the exercitant is asked to return precisely to these parts. One's subjective reactions, positive *or* negative, were to be the focus of intense prayer, and eventually the guide to major decisions. Ignatius offered two sets of rules for discerning whether one's feeling of consolation or desolation were to be ascribed to good spirits or evil spirits.

Some modern readers of the Bible may not readily admit to taking the texts as seriously as all that. We are talking here, they will argue, not of accepting or rejecting biblical doctrines, or teachings, or messages in paraphrase, but only of questions of "taste"! But the truth is that some who say this may not be as objective as they pretend. Some overlook "taste" on a doctrinaire basis of fundamentalism, and they risk reading the Bible with ears that do not hear its inter-personal challenge. They may focus on surface details involving miracles and historical facts, closing out the Voice of the Speaker within the text. Others politely avoid reading or thinking about the Bible. Participants in Western culture who close themselves off from the biblical Speakers in these two ways may be compared to children who break off honest relations with their parents, either by external subservience or by simple rejection. A key function of personal growth is lost. In an important way one ceases to be a member of the family. Similarly, in breaking off relations with the biblical Speakers, one may no longer spiritually be a Christian or Jew, even though one proclaims the contrary.

The original sense, which may not be reduced to some paraphrase, as we have argued above, is normative and limiting in important ways. For example, all doctrines aside, if the biblical Speakers tell stories about the virgin birth of the Savior, and no stories at all about the sexual activities of the gods, the reader meets a world-view with a certain slant. If the biblical Speakers frequently present men as the channels of divine activity, and rarely present women in this role, then they do not need to formulate anti-feminist teachings to be anti-feminist! Readers have always felt this profoundly, even if they have articulated a protest about it only in recent times. (Of course answers are also to be found: e.g., the role of Sarah, and Miriam, and Deborah, and Huldah, and Mary; the feminine images of God in Second Isaiah; the cultural conditioning within which the biblical texts were written, and so forth.) Such reactions and counter-reactions are to the Speakers in the text, and they take place because the Speakers are normative.

Similarly, if the biblical Speakers present king Solomon in story after story as supremely wise, while not really giving any picture of the extent, the power, and the wealth of the empire he forged, and while passing over in relative silence the brillant feminine society which certainly developed in Jerusalem during his reign, inevitably through these gaps the reader all unawares arrives at a general view of good government which is normative, without its ever being a Kerygma, or a *Tendenz,* or "the point" of the stories. And yet, if one asks about the biblical teaching regarding kingship, biblical scholars will feel obliged to point to the Deuteronomist's explicit teaching that the kings must read and obey the law and so forth, overlooking elemental meanings such as these. And they will do this even though this explicit teaching of Deuteronomy has not been normative as law since the 6th century B.C.E. when Israel stopped having kings, and since the 1st century C.E. since Paul's epistles explicitly liberated Christianity from the law.

The Speakers have been normative in Western Society precisely because their teaching has been subliminal, i.e., felt without being adverted to, accepted without being noticed. If you feel you must come to accept the Speaker, who is expressed as elemental meaning of the text, because you believe in scriptural authority as the voice of God, then you will come to accept his or her foundational stance and basic world-view, usually without adverting to it, or being able to formulate it. When you find some biblical book distasteful, and only then, you will inquire into the subliminal teaching or attitude which offends.

Foundational Stance as Normative

In the foregoing, the reader's attention has been indirectly drawn to his or her own foundational stance by various analyses of the experience of writing, and by the variety of descriptive terms used, such as "the world-view of the Speaker," or "expectancy about meaning and fulfillment," or "horizon," or "elemental meaning." This inner force or dynamism has been consistently contrasted with articulations in the form of paraphrased meanings, propositions, and directives. The affirmation which is proper to literature is not the affirmation of some objective truth or prescription, but rather the self-affirmation of the subjective *persona* of the author, the affirmation of the foundational stance of the Speaker. This inner force must now be more accurately described, so that the reader may become directly aware of his or her own subjective activity in the act of writing, and so that some implications concerning meaning in all texts may be seen. What is the precise nature of this inner dynamism of the Speaker which challenges the reader, and which has been normative?

We shall call this force a foundational stance.[5] It is merely a stance, rather than a set of articulated propositions, or images, or axioms, or canons, because normally one has never troubled to articulate the fundamental mainsprings of one's thinking.

If one reflects on the experience of writing, one realizes that one both knows in advance and does not know what one will write. This is partially because the logic of words and their associations, and the structures of language, lead us as we write in unforeseen directions and beyond foreseen boundaries; and partially because, as our understanding of the subject matter is articulated, new aspects of the subject matter invite consideration. You begin to define one term, and end up needing to define a cluster of terms; or you intend to describe a person's face and soon find yourself writing a story.[6] At the same time, we are not passive in this development, but rather our whole psychic structure controls the outcome, making choices between possibilities, deciding questions of taste, evaluating evidence and probability, establishing conditions for the validity of proof, determining the range of inquiry and of subject matters, and so forth. All of these acts of choice constitute the author, i.e., the Speaker. There are reasons for each choice, and it is not inconceivable that in each case these reasons could be articulated. However, the choices are so numerous, and frequently so subtle, that the task is not practical. Often we choose by eliminating options without fully adverting to them, certainly without troubling to articulate the options in detail, not to mention the many reasons for and against each one of them. Now if we reflect on options we have made, we can discover a number of guiding principles which were implied in the choice. All of those principles exist as realities of the author's psychic dynamism, and they form a live force, growing and changing with time, without ever being fully objectified. It would be impossible to deduce all of them, as the human psyche is far too subtle, and the history of its growth far too complex.

Allow me to adduce a brief example. In writing these paragraphs, I added footnote 6 above. At that moment there flickered through my mind the possibility of collecting a number of texts from Jacques Derrida in order to establish my point. I rejected the idea in an instant, and without reflection. Why did I decide in this direction? And what was implied in this choice? As far as I can recall, the following dialectic took place in a flash: I felt (without fully expressing it) that to cite texts would involve adding at least a page to this chapter. Moreover, I disagree with so much of his thought that I would have to refute, even as I used, his paragraphs. The result would have been a form of proof disproportionate in length to the importance of the point. On the other hand, the brillance of his prose would enhance my text, and his name would add authority to my position. Still external authority is not nearly as convincing, particularly when surrounded by complex argument, as drawing attention to the internal experience of the reader. So the answer was no.

Implied here was a stance toward writing: I am not simply examining evidence, but also selecting it with a view to persuasion. Moreover there is at work an aesthetic canon of some sort including a taste for brilliance in prose and a concern with proportionate length.

When I actually made my decision, I was only subliminally aware of the foundational material I have just sketched. It has been easy to formulate this material, but I am aware that behind it there lies a further foundational stance, extensive and complex, which would require limitless time and patience to articulate. It includes patterns for writing paragraphs, norms of accuracy in recalling and reporting subjective experience, a grasp of the relation of this paragraph to my whole book, and to other diverse lines of inquiry which I pursue in different contexts, and so forth. At a deeper level there are foundational principles, such as recognition of truth as a value, the affirmation of continuity between personal experience and universal truth and revelation, and so forth.[7]

The foundational stance of an author as such is not his or her whole psyche. It is those aspects of the psyche which shape the writing. It is foundational in the sense that it underlies other psychic activity, directing choices without being a choice at the moment of directing, determining objectives without being one itself, enforcing criteria without necessarily being prepared to define them. It is a living value system, and an operative theory of knowledge, which could be partially articulated but which usually will not even be reflected upon.

Most specifically in the case of writers, the foundational

stance is a stance of expectancy about meaning and human fulfillment. An author knows a great number of things, possesses a language, and disposes of a traditional set of metaphors and symbols and useful images. These are his tools, not his foundational stance. The foundational stance motivates him to write in the first place, and directs him in writing as to what sort of creation it should be, and ultimately which tools he should select to achieve it. The process of writing will clarify the expectancy, and yet the expectancy will steer the writing from first to last. The author will be satisfied when his text displays his tools correctly on the one hand (good use of language, accurate knowledge, effective imagery), and when it fulfills his expectancy about meaning and fulfillment on the other.[8] The text must not only be true, in the material sense of closely following the data or objects discussed, but it must also reflect a stance with regard to reality which the author respects, and recognizes as his own. For example texts about a war monument must not only do justice to the material reality of the monument, but they must also do this in a form or manner appropriate to the foundational stance of an art critic in one case, or of an historian in another, or of an engineer, or of a lyric poet, or, to move to other forms of expression, the stance of a photographer, or a painter, and so forth.

The foundational stance of a Speaker, though almost never expressed directly in the text, is immediately felt by the reader. It is felt through the gaps, through the edges of the text, through what is missing in the text, through the reader's sense that he or she would have approached this subject matter differently. The reader's own stance of expectancy about meaning, however subliminal it may be, reacts very powerfully to that of the Speaker. One may be delighted by the content of a text, and yet loathe the Speaker. For example, one might read one's praise in obsequious prose![9] Or else one may virtually overlook the content and be delighted by the speaker, as in reading texts written by children, or the history of Herodotus, or possibly some biblical texts.

Finally, in the "compact consciousness" of pre-philosophical writers, and particularly in the unique case of biblical authors, the foundational stance will have the sort of expectancy about meaning and fulfillment which includes God.[10] In other words, when dealing with biblical texts and Speakers we can usually translate "meaning" as "revelation," and translate "fulfillment" as "salvation." For, presumably, all biblical Speakers will have a foundational stance which not only includes, but also is centered in, an expectancy about revelation and salvation. At least the editors who put a given text in the biblical canon both understood it that way, and gave it that character by placing it in the context of the canon.

Now each religious Speaker will have a characteristic foundational stance to which each reader will react in a personal way. A given stance will be characterized principally by favouring a specific realm of human activity and meaning in its expectancy about revelation and salvation. For example, an author's choice of topic and manner of treatment may be directed by an expectancy that revelation and salvation occur in the victory of charismatic heroes,[11] or within the confusion and corruption of political manipulation,[12] or in the mystic experience of simple and innocent people,[13] or after a soldier's death in a Holy War,[14] or in an aesthetic and magnificent celebration of the liturgy.[15] Such specific expectancies may seem to entail equally specific obligations, such as participating in national pride (e.g., joining the army), or self-sacrificing involvement in the political process, or simplicity of life style, or suicidal heroism in battle, or magnanimity in spending money on liturgy.

Now a given specific expectancy may be felt by different readers to imply diverse obligations, and religious divergence may result. For example the wonderful order of creation portrayed, and judged "good" by God, in Genesis 1-2:4a might lead one person to become a contemplative, a nature poet like Wordsworth; but it might lead another to be angry about the besmirching of nature through human intervention, as was Hopkins. And from there one might feel obliged to join an activist ecological movement, or alternatively to retire from civilization into some eschatological sect waiting in prayer for the last day. The point is that the specific foundational stance is felt to make demands upon the real life of the reader. And the reader has to react either by complying, or rejecting, or else by accepting a status of guilt.

This is the power of Scripture. It is in this way that biblical Speakers have been normative in Western civilization.

Conclusion

In discussing the objectives of interpretation in the first chapter, we saw that the original and normative meanings of Scripture are literary in character: they do not affirm abstract doctrines or universal laws. In this second chapter we have seen that they do affirm something subjective: the foundational stances of individual authors. We have called this elemental meaning. These stances are not explicit in the text. Rather they remain hidden or subliminal, and for that reason they have their maximum effect and are powerfully normative for readers and communities who read the Bible as a divinely inspired book.

Traditional scriptural scholarship has rendered tremendous service in its textual research, critical history, archeological excavation, and exact historical exegesis. The results of this enterprise are easily available in published commentaries, and these will continue to improve. However, traditional scholarship, moved by concern for objectivity too narrowly defined, has systematically avoided the elemental meanings of texts. This chapter, taking up the call for "inter-personal" reading of Scripture at the end of chapter 1, has attempted to provide an account of the experience of writing and reading which can justify academically, as legitimate literary criticism, the search for elemental meaning, and the delineation of foundational stances of Speakers as objectified in the clues (both data and gaps) of the text.

If our contention is correct, it is possible for scholarly interpretation to remain academically rigorous, while touching directly on that experience of Scripture which has shaped our religious beliefs and, in fact, the whole of Western culture.

Concretely, how does one identify the foundational expectancy of the Speaker of a literary biblical text? There may be many answers to this question, and we may expect constant refinement on any which is proposed. As a first attempt, I would propose three questions which one should ask of a biblical text:

> 1) In what realm of meaning, or human activity (for example war, liturgy, family life, politics, sports, aesthetic activity, and so forth) does the Speaker expect revelation or salvation to occur?
> 2) In what precise way is salvation or revelation expected to be experienced by the Speaker/reader?
> 3) What demands upon the reader, what conversions and what practices, are implied and demanded by this foundational expectancy?

The next four chapters will attempt to exemplify this form of literary criticism, by asking these questions of the major authors of the Pentateuch. Then a final chapter will attempt to show specifically how the results of this approach form a useful, and methodologically precise, basis for theology.

3

The Yahwist

The normative teaching of the Pentateuch is not a subject which can be exhausted in a few pages. As we have seen, the original meaning is the whole text, whose foundational stances are only implicitly expressed as elemental meaning, and obscurely sensed by the reader. These may gradually be brought to full awareness; but certainly they must not be rapidly paraphrased in a series of abstract propositions.[1]

The Pentateuch is not normally read as a continuous text, from beginning to end. And the major sources which form the Pentateuch (Yahwist, Elohist, Priestly, Deuteronomic) are almost never read as separate complete units. On the other hand, it is far easier to feel a foundational stance on the basis of a long text than on the basis of a few lines. Moreover the normativity of a foundational stance must be more significant if its author is in fact present in large segments of the Pentateuch. For this reason, the next four chapters will make use of the major Pentateuchal sources as far as this is possible.

Source criticism of the Pentateuch appears to be totally in disarray at this point, as the Wellhausen synthesis is no longer tenable on some key issues.[2] Some scholars solve the problem by adopting a purely narrative focus, establishing text unities on narrative criteria, and prescinding entirely from history. Fruitful results can be obtained in this way. However, the historical questions inevitably recur, and will eventually have to be answered.[3] And, in any case, our method requires dealing with historical authors. An edited interweaving of authors will have a composite foundational stance, of course, which will be normative. Should scholarship eventually show that the texts we treat here were in fact authored by several people, that will not undermine our approach, as the specific foundational stances will have been discovered and described irrespective of the number of writers who shared them. But obviously it will be easier for us to start with single authors as much as possible. Taking each source in turn, texts will be selected following strategies which gives us the greatest possible security about continuous authorship, and the best advantages in terms of familiarity and fruitfulness for our study.

The text traditionally viewed as Yahwist is far too long to be examined in its entirety. We shall begin with Gen 2:4b— 3:24, which is the first, and most familiar of all J Texts, and continue with a series of texts selected on the grounds that they are most generally attributed to J, that they manifest the same foundational stance, and that they will subsequently prove helpful as contrast points in our subsequent study of the E and P texts. These criteria for selection are legitimate, as our purpose is not to provide a complete study of a "Yahwist" source, but rather first to exemplify the approach proposed in the previous chapter, and second to discern any single foundational stance which marks a significant number of texts from Genesis to Numbers. Finally, to aid imaginations, we shall go along with the traditional view that the Yahwist wrote during the period of the great Solomonic empire, or the immediate post-Solomonic era when wealth and culture still flourished in Jerusalem, and when several other biblical texts saw the light of day: for example the Ark Narrative, the Rise-of-David Story, the Succession Narrative, early collections of Proverbs and of Psalms. This will be no more than a working hypothesis, and no conclusion will lean on it as a basis for proof.

No attempt will be made to provide a complete commentary. Rather we shall try to focus our observations upon elemental meanings which commentaries overlook.

Gen 2:4b—3:24

It is important to read the text as though for the first time, in order to feel the foundational stance of the author, rather than the analytic clarity of the commentators, including the present commentator. It is important to treat the comments which follow, not as answers to questions, but only as a first attempt which might lead the reader to formulate ever better approximations of the author's stance.

As a first impression, the author, in treating so heavy a subject as the ultimate origins of current experience, seems to have a light touch, leaving a great distance between himself and the reader, and between God and the reader. In the next chapter, we shall see that this is very much in contrast with the Elohist's approach. Certainly it has a different feel from Gen 1:1-2:4a.

Distance between the author and the reader is maintained by a witty style. The reader is never invited to identify, or sympathize, with anyone in the story. The reader feels the cleverness of the author, but does not feel any weighty message from the author. The story is about sin and punishment, but no narrative slant or rhetorical device is used to make the reader feel fear, or guilt, or sorrow. The treatment of sin or evil is not marked by theological or philosophical depth; rather its most memorable passages, the treatment of temptation in 3:1-6, and of guilt in 3:7-13, are characterized by a dramatic subtlety which one associates more easily with comedy than with tragedy.

As a result, commentaries which focus on mythological origins, or on doctrines about original sin, or analytical precisions about intended meaning, seem to be getting somewhere that the Yahwist may have never intended.

The story ends with the world as we know it, i.e., physical pains and economic problems, but also with two surprising focusses: first, the serpent on its belly with its head exposed to the foot of the woman's progeny, and second, man and woman seen as similar to the Lord God in all but mortality (i.e., knowing good and evil, but made of dust and separated from the tree of life).[4] It is difficult to explain the prominence of the serpent in this account of origins,[5] so we shall turn to the image of God, of man, and of woman, in this story.

For the author, Yahweh appears to be, not the creator of the universe, but rather little more than a magic giant; Yahweh is not the core of Being, but merely a force to be reckoned with. There is the charming anthropomorphism in which God enjoys walking in the cool breeze of evening, wondering where His little pinocchios are to be found, just as He will later enjoy sniffing the roast after the flood in ch. 8. But this is more than narrative technique: anthropomorphism appears to be all pervasive. Yahweh does not create the water of 2:6. The author provides it because Yahweh needs it in order to form dust into the shape of a man. Subsequently, in order to form woman He must first perform an operation to get a rib, and then like a careful surgeon he will close up the incision (v. 21). Then He acts like a good tailor in making coats for Adam and Eve, and actually fitting them on in 3:21, just as He will later close down the hatch after Noah is safely in the ark (7:16).

But there is much more limitation placed on God than this. In 2:5 it is astonishing to find man and Yahweh parallel: we are told there is no farming, first, because the Lord God has not arranged the winter rains, *and, second, because* man was not there to till the ground. When the Lord God makes trees, plants, and animals, He is not seen as doing this for His own glory, or because these creatures are good in themselves; rather they are referred directly to man, being beautiful to the sight, and good to eat, and possible mates for man (2:9, 18-20). On the other hand, man is not made in order to be useful to the gods as in the old mythologies,[6] but specifically to take care of the farming (2:15; 3:23). Thus man and nature have their own sphere of meaning without specific reference to God.

Moreover, for this author Yahweh is far from being in control of everything, or even knowing everything. The East appears to be a mysterious extremity beyond Yahweh's reach in 2:8, 14; 3:24; and 4:16. But, even where He acts directly, Yahweh has to learn gradually from nature, as we do, through experience and reflection. He makes man and then discovers that it is not right: something is missing. Yahweh is not sure what to do. At first He makes animals, but then man discovers for Yahweh, one by one, that they are not fit companions for him. Eventually Yahweh hits on the idea of making a woman. Similarly in the flood story Yahweh will discover that the heart of man is evil (6:5), but He has to learn from experience how He should react: at first He sends a flood, but then later (8:21-22) He realizes that was a mistake, and He promises stability in nature.

Moreover, Yahweh is concerned about his supremacy, and so He warns the man away from the tree of the knowledge of good and evil, threatening him with death. We later learn that this tree would make man like God (3:5, 22), and that the threat of death was not serious. When God said "you will die the death" (2:17), He was threatening something which He could not, or would not, carry out.[7]

The human couple were not to be frightened off, and they did try the tree of knowledge. Yahweh doesn't even know they have done this. Like an absent landlord He has to figure things out: He has to deduce what happened from the fact that Adam and Eve manifest shame (3:11).

Finally, in order to take no more chances, He sets up the Cherubim with a flaming sword to protect His supremacy, i.e., to keep humankind from the tree of life.

This shocking image of God is very far removed from that of the Priestly Writer, or the Elohist, as we shall see. It is not a doctrine, but it is not to be lightly dismissed as "primitive," or as belonging to narrative art. Rather it is a foundational stance expressed as elemental meaning in the text, to which the reader, willy-nilly, reacts. Reading the Yahwist, we are plunged into a universe which is not safe, ordered, divinely controlled for our spiritual well-being. Rather it is one in which people have primary responsibility for planning and establishing prosperity. God is kindly, but distant and careful to defend His own interests! In some respects a rival! God is not revealed as a glow of love at the heart of each little creature, but rather as a power which crashes around on another planet, a magic giant which one might contact from time to time for specific purposes.

Apart from the Yahwist's image of God, his image of the role of woman in this story merits some attention. For, apart from Yahweh, the only real actor here is the woman. The human action begins with the serpent's speaking to her in 3:1, and ends with her confession of guilt in 3:13. The etiological material centers on Adam/man, but the initiative in human action is on the part of the woman. Similarly, in the Yahwist legend about Esau and Jacob in Gen 27, Rebekah will take the initiative in assuring Jacob's succession in preference to Esau's; and in the Yahwist's Gen 16 Sarah, as we shall see, is the only real actor in the expulsion of Ishmael. Men give in to pressures, but women decide what the pressures shall be. The uniqueness of this narrative twist, and its gratuitous presence in these three Yahwist stories, leads one to suspect this is a mark of the Yahwist, not merely a trace of some of his sources.

This again is not a doctrine about women, but it is an elemental meaning to which the reader reacts. It does imply theologico-anthropological questions for theology, and it may have the effect of making a reader like or dislike, accept or reject, the Yahwist.

The Cain Story

In Gen 2 to 3, the Yahwist has not presented a doctrine of original sin, though he does depict the universality of sin in Gen 2-11. The Deuteronomistic historian will depict the omnipresence of sin in Israel. But all of this is literary, and there was no tendency toward a formulation of general law, or doctrine, until Paul wrote Rom 5 in the first century C.E., and eventually the Council of Carthage in 417-418 C.E. The Yahwist has expressed, not a doctrine, but rather a way of integrating the experience of senseless suffering and death within a total world-view, or myth. In the Yahwist's image, since God is so well-intentioned, and so astonishingly unmasterful, one cannot blame God for suffering and death. The Yahwist looks to the realm of psychosis, and precisely of human responsibility for breaking the barriers between the human and the divine, to explain suffering and death.

In ch. 4, the Yahwist begins to focus on evil more directly. The reflection will continue through ch. 11, in showing how evil spreads from the individual through culture, and becomes worldwide. Gen 4:1-16 is a puzzling and fascinating statement of the Yahwist's attitude toward anger and murder.

The story has three parts: the setting (vv. 1-2), the action in 3 successive incidents (vv. 3-15), and the closure (v. 16). The story is about Cain, not about Cain and Abel, as is clear from the almost exclusive focus on Cain in each of the three parts. In other words, the story is about the criminal, not about the victim of crime; it is about sin, not about suffering.

The action is told in three successive incidents, each ending with a major speech: Cain's anger (vv. 3-7), the resulting murder (vv. 8-12), Yahweh's bafflement (vv. 13-15). In the first incident, Yahweh learns about human anger, just as in Gen 2 He learned about man's need of a companion. He does not know what to do about it! (Later, in the Flood Story as we shall see, He will begin by trying to wipe out human corruption by killing everybody, but then He will learn that that is no solution.) Here, Yahweh leaves it up to the man: he warns Cain that sin is not something that happens, but rather it is an active agent whom Cain must directly fight: "sin is crouching at the door; its desire is for you, but you must master it" (v. 7b). In the second incident, Cain does not fight sin, but commits the murder. Yahweh is horrified and strikes out angrily in His turn, cursing the earth and banishing Cain. In the third incident, depicting Yahweh as baffled, we first learn that Yahweh's reaction has been foolish, as it is too heavy to bear (v. 13), and as it will result, not in suppressing sin, but rather in occasioning further murders (v. 14). Then, in v. 15, Yahweh makes a second attempt to prevent the spread of violence: He invents the mysterious sign of Cain, and a system of sevenfold vengeance (v. 15). The reader is expected to feel Yahweh's helplessness against this evil, as one cannot imagine that the original readers of this text would believe for an instant Yahweh had succeeded, and that murder had been suppressed by whatever techniques of vendetta were in place.

The closure of this story (v. 16) leaves a whole race of humankind characterized as "wanderers," threatened by all the rest of mankind. These are the murderers, and they will be depicted as founding city cultures marked with violence (vv. 17-24). The story is compelling, and archetypal. The act of murdering one's sister or brother entails a rejection of the sister- and brotherhood of people, and an acceptance of alienation, i.e., "wandering," as the truth about one's life.

Once again, the Yahwist is not teaching a doctrine. However the elemental meaning of this story is that human anger is a powerful demon that Yahweh has not been able to correct or manage. The primary responsibility for containing anger lies with humankind! This idea can be found in much of world literature, in varying degrees of deliberate thematization, from Homer's *Iliad* to Oscar Wilde's *The Ballad of Reading Gaol* with its refrain, "You always kill the one you love." A recent novel by John Knowles, published in 1960, *A Separate Peace,* studies it microscopically.

The image of God's helplessness in the face of human anger implies several anthropological and theological doctrines. Or, better, it demands of theology that such doctrines be elaborated and critiqued. Moreover, it implies much about what is appropriate in our attitude to anger in ourselves, in our loved ones, in our community, in world politics. It is a shocking image: one which challenges the reader to take position vis-à-vis the Yahwist Speaker.

The Flood Story

It is not possible, or even useful, to spend time on each Yahwist text. In 6:1-4, Yahweh watches, in a quandary once again, as women are involved in a demonic attempt to break down the barriers between the human and the divine. He intervenes by reinforcing the limitation on the length of human life. There then follows the Yahwist's basic treatment of sin, i.e., the Flood Story.

The Yahwist text for this story may be read roughly as follows: 6:5-8; 7:1-5, 7, 10, 12, 16b, 17b, 22-23; 8:2b-3a, 6-12, 13b, 20-22.

The story begins in Gen 6:5 with Yahweh learning something about humans that He didn't know: people are radically sinful. He reacts with grief, and He proceeds in ch. 7 to take care to preserve a part of His work, while wiping out the rest. One thinks of Cézanne destroying most of his canvases because they were not up to scratch in his opinion. The Yahwist does not depict the violence of this, or the suffering which it must have entailed. Again, His focus is on sin, not suffering, and specifically on God's bafflement in the face of sin. Sin is a thing that happened, like disease, something Yahweh had not foreseen in His first attempt at making humanity, something He would like to cure.

There then follows a brief period of destruction of which the Yahwist depicts nothing. Immediately we are delighted by the depiction of Noah opening a window in the ark and ingeniously sending out birds to scout for him (8:6-12, 13b). This is a unique moment in the Yahwist text where the reader is invited to identify with one of the characters in the story. Verse 11 reads: "And the dove came back to him in the evening, and lo, in her mouth a freshly plucked olive leaf." The reader is there, not hearing about it, but watching it and sharing the excitement!

There then occurs a remarkable development (8:20-22). Noah's liturgical act changes Yahweh's attitude. From now on, Yahweh accepts the defect in His masterpiece as inevitable. From now on, instead of wiping out the diseased creatures, Yahweh will retreat, and give people space to develop as they will.[8] Yahweh takes His distance, again the absent landlord, assuming responsibility only for the stability of the ecology.

In ch. 11 we will see Yahweh once again literally coming down to take a look (v. 5), and intervening to reduce human pride by confusing communications.

In what realm, then, does this speaker expect to find revelation and salvation? For the Yahwist, God intervenes at the key junctures of human history. He establishes the general conditions of human life. An individual would not expect to deal directly with God in his, or her, own life. Rather God is revealed sufficiently in the God-given order of nature and society; and divine salvation is as effective as He could make it in the order of nature and of civilization which surrounds us. The individual must flourish by taking practical initiatives in reacting to these God-given ecological and cultural realities. There is a further implication that the individual must see to it that God remains positively disposed, by providing for a liturgy of animal sacrifices.

This foundational stance is very remote from that of the mystical traditions, for example, which discover God within, and which therefore practise a discipline to arrive at specific states of consciousness. It is equally remote from the expectancy of those who find evidence of divine intervention in aspects of their private lives, or in the experience of a divine call to a specific form of life, or in miracles.

A reader has to have some reaction to this stance, either of accepting or rejecting, even though it is not a doctrine formulated as a proposition to be declared true or false. Still it invites specific reactions on the part of the reader. Dialectic is in order. If I am unhappy reading the Yahwist, is it because he seem to overlook the experience of direct union with God, the whole mystical tradition? Or is it because I am afraid of taking human responsibility for my life? The great mystics such as Ignatius Loyola or Theresa of Avila shared the Yahwist approach, in that they joined mysticism with energetic self-reliance in their efforts to reform the "real" world.

Exodus 34:1-28

It will be helpful at this point to skip to the "Yahwist Decalogue" in Ex 34, in order to consolidate our picture of this foundational stance, before examining other Yahwist pericopes. The text has been reframed, and has undergone some deuteronomic editing, but the original Yahwist text, in its feel and intent, appears to have been only superficially modified.[9] In particular the idea of a collection of precisely "ten commandments" (v. 28), and also the actual word "covenant" and something of its form, may have a post-Yahwist origin. In reading for foundational stance, we will focus on verses which show no evidence of editing.

In the Yahwist text, this law-giving occurs after the exodus, the theophany on Mount Sinai, and the idolatry before a golden calf.[10] Chapter 34 relates the inscribing of the laws on stone tablets, the making of covenant, and the content of the laws. In vv. 1-9 Yahweh is imagined on a mountain top, and Moses has to go there to meet Him. Moreover Moses has to carve stone tablets, and carry them up the mountain unaccompanied. Once again Yahweh literally comes down from somewhere. He is in the cloud at the top of the mountain, where He strides around shouting. He describes Himself as patient and forgiving. He then talks of direct intervention in human affairs: He will be relentless in punishing iniquity (which, from the context must be understood as covenanting with other gods), and promising to prove his power with dreadful deeds. Moses, for his part, begs Yahweh to enter into this special relationship with Israel.

It must be pointed out that this law will be imposed on the people because of Yahweh's power, not because of their consent as in Joshua 24. Moreover, it is Moses, not the people, who makes this covenant. This contrasts with the tradition in Ex 19:7-8, where Moses goes to the people in the role of mediator, not monarch.

And what is the tenor of the Yahwist law collection in Ex 34? It appears to be concerned only with the establishment of Jewish identity by socially structuring an exclusive relationship with Yahweh. Yahweh, who formed humankind and imposed some anthropological and ecological laws in Gen 2-11, now forms a unique culture and imposes it on the Jews with a display of explosive power. Thus they must destroy the Canaanite religious practices, and avoid intermarriage, lest they be involved in covenant with other gods (vv. 11-16); they must make no metal idols (v. 17); they must observe the feast of unleavened bread in their families, and the sabbath rest on their farms, and also all males must appear in the temple for the three major religious feasts of the year (vv. 18-24). Finally there are specific rules for the liturgy which are intended largely to separate Jewish from Canaanite practise (vv. 25-26).

These Yahwist laws may seem to make rather tame demands, when contrasted with the drama of the setting in which they are imposed. It is a brief collection which could conceivably be incised in stone tablets. However, it is shrewdly conceived as an instrument for the unification of Israel over against the Canaanites and others. It cuts deeply into family life, and it exercises supreme power in the formation of culture, and the shaping of feeling and politics.

There is an intransigent nationalism in this stance. Yahweh may be a distant giant who leaves the individual responsible to manage his or her own prosperity, but He places the individual in a special community, separated from others by its relationship to Him. The individual will not deal directly with Yahweh, because Moses had dealt definitively for all Jews. One can easily imagine how this story would feel in the age of the great emperor Solomon! And how this feeling would grow with the growing splendor of the temple, the growing power of Jerusalem, and eventually the centralization of all cults in Jerusalem.

If all of this is correct, one would expect an anti-establishment reader of Irish descent, brought up in a democratic tradition, to read the Yahwist with acute displeasure. And yet I do not seem to feel any negative reaction while reading the Yahwist text. Why not?

The Yahwist foundational stance of expectancy names only the remote figure of Moses in a fabulous past. He never mentions his contemporary, Solomon, however much its readers may have applied it all to that unique emperor. His foundational expectancy implies some application to political reality, but still it imposes no specific political theory. The figure of Moses implies no doctrine of monarchy, since Moses is clearly a unique figure of the past. All of this is merely the historical-literary material through which, as elemental meaning, the Yahwist expresses his aspiration for revelation. Now, a contemporary reader can easily identify ancient ancestors whose decisions before God have set the culture and limits of his or her own life. There is the ancestor who decided to move from Europe to North America. There is the series of decision-makers who brought about the industrial age, and now the technical era. At a family level, there are the series of psychological reactions whereby one ancestor, perhaps, chose between rebellion and alcoholism, or another between hope and despair, another opted for creativity or for security, and so forth. Such decisions have resulted in a family atmosphere which provided the specific problems, the range of unconsciously appropriated attitudes, the specific pressures, within which each individual has shaped his or her life. All of that is irreversible cultural imposition, imposed subliminally, passionately, upon infantile awareness, but shaped before God in the past. One might resent the authority of emperors and kings, and yet accept the imperious power of the past expressed as elemental meaning.

What demands does this text make on the contemporary reader? Each one will feel it differently. One could feel obliged to be more observant in regard to his or her own historical religious tradition, to fight assimilation by fostering social connections within the traditional group, and by practising the cult of that tradition. Another, who has become acutely conscious of the total family of humans, might expect to find God responsible for all cultures, imposing all religious traditions. Such a reader of the Yahwist might feel obliged to break away from exclusive traditional religion, and to participate in the creation of a more universal community and culture. All will feel a demand to take seriously one's civilization and culture as vehicles of union with God, and to link politics with religion. The Yahwist stance demands some cultural expression of collective relatedness to God.

The Yahwist view of religion has come into disrepute where religion has been linked with nationalism, or racism. Modern communications have made us conscious of a human collectivity which transcends races and nations. In this regard, secular culture has often seemed more spiritual than the religions! The origins of Christianity broke away from racism two thousand years ago (Galatians 3:28), even if many subsequent expressions of Christianity have been less transcendent! The Yahwist Speaker demands a searching and refined dialectic on the part of a modern reader.

Gen 12:8—13:4

This story follows upon the Yahwist's account of the call of Abraham (12:1-3), in which the Speaker's concern with political theology is made explicit: Yahweh is intervening once again in the world, placing Abraham's family there as a touchstone of blessing for all nations. In 12:1-3, God was depicted once again as caring actively for humankind, and setting up a regime in which He will make prosperous those nations which favour Israel, and cursing those which persecute Israel. This much commented "Kerygma" needs no further discussion here.[11] It finds its first application in our story.

Commentators differ about the exact limits of this pericope. I would argue to the limits indicated above, first by pointing out that what begins in 12:1-3 ends very convincingly in v. 7. Second, after our pericope, a new story clearly commences in 13:5. Third, our unit is heavily framed within the following inclusion: "Bethel ... Ai ... altar ... invoked Yahweh by name ... Negeb ... famine ... Egypt" (12:8-10), and then "Egypt ... Negeb ... wealth ... Bethel ... Ai ... altar ... invoked Yahweh by name" (13:1-4).

There are, of course, parallels to this story in Gen 20, and again in 26. At present we shall attempt to discern the Speaker's Voice in this text alone, reserving for a study of Gen 20 in the following chapter of this book the insights made possible by comparing sources.

We might first note that God is made absent, or distant, in this story by the Speaker's narrative technique. Certainly it was God who sent the plague, and who somehow told Pharaoh the true status of Sarah. But the Speaker has managed to make this intervention all but invisible in the telling.

Secondly, the heavy framework around the story has the effect of making it very much a special excursus within the flow of an Abraham cycle. It is a sort of curtain-opener, a cameo depicting symbolically the Egyptian experience of Israel. We see Abraham offering sacrifice at home, in Bethel, at the beginning and at the end; and in between the story's action consists of the exodus theme in résumé. It is told in two parts: vv. 10-16 depict the immigration to Egypt, and Israel's initial prospering there; and vv. 17-20 depict the exodus proper.

Thirdly, even though initiative is not given to the woman, Sarai, still feminine beauty is a central factor in the first part of the action as perhaps nowhere else in biblical literature. Sarai's beauty is specifically mentioned in vv. 11 and 14, and praised in v. 15. Abram will be saved because of Sarai (v. 13), and subsequently Pharaoh makes Abram wealthy because of her (v. 16). Finally the second part of the action is introduced with the remark that Yahweh sent a plague "because, of Sarai, Abram's wife" (v. 17). Sarai is the focus and motor of the whole story.

Missing here is the narrative art of which the Yahwist is a master. The interplay between Abram, Sarai, and Pharaoh invites the writing of clever dialogue, but the Yahwist is not interested. His focus appears to be so fixed on thematic ideas, that he has no curiosity left for the human drama. He is telling a story about blessing, about Israel, about Egypt.

The Hebrew root meaning of "blessing" has to do with fertility, and secondarily with prosperity. At this point in the story, the blessing of Abram requires that Sarai have a child. Pharaoh inadvertently prevents Abram from bringing this about. However, Pharaoh does bless Abram in a lesser way by making him rich. There follows a curse on Egypt, and Pharaoh discovers the cause. When he returns Sarai, we must suppose that Egypt also prospered again. It is surprising that the Speaker does not mention this. One feels that the Speaker is not only not interested in telling a human story, but he is not even interested in the logic of his plot. (Historically, Egypt was not prosperous during the Yahwist's lifetime.) Once again we recognize in the gaps of a text the elemental intent of the author: he is not really writing a story; rather he is using an old tale (originally told about a Philistine incident, as we shall see in the next chapter) to duplicate, for Abram, Israel's experience with Egypt: an initial happy alliance, which entailed a radical humiliation of Israel, followed by an escape and return to Canaan.

There is some tension between the blessing and cursing formula of 12:1-3 and its first application here. Yahweh is depicted as cursing Egypt with a plague because of Pharaoh's interference with Abram's wife. And Yahweh's intervention does prove to be a blessing on Israel. However there is depicted no blessing on Egypt, either at the beginning when Egypt first enriched Abram, or in the end when Egypt let Israel go. Abram is said to be very wealthy at that point (13:2), and the reader might suppose that the wealth was due to Egypt, as wealth at the expense of Egypt is regularly connected to the exodus theme throughout the Bible. But the Speaker says nothing about this either. As a result Egypt is obscurely felt to be corrupt and cursed vis-à-vis Israel!

A reader today has to make considerable effort to understand this story in its original sense. In particular the word "Egypt" will not easily evoke today the complex symbol which was denoted for the original readers. Moreover, a reader today may have to struggle against an instinct to focus on the human drama which is, after all, the material of the story. Where can the reader stand in order to feel this Speaker's foundational expectancy? One wonders whether preachers have often chosen this text as a basis for a sermon.

The story presupposes an assurance of election, and of divine protection. Abram's blithe risking of Sarai is a narrative impossibility without it. Thus the story tells both of a religious home with Yahweh at Bethel, and of going out to the greatest enemy without fear. The immediate reasons for dealing with Pharaoh are simple: famine, and the beauty of Sarai. In this God is distant, and irrelevant. However this Speaker confidently expects revelation and divine intervention where the enemy is cursed, and where the chosen ones are blessed. In Solomon's day, Israel was in fact extremely wealthy, at the expense of a weakened Pharaoh. The story would have seemed particularly natural to its original readers.

What demands upon the reader are felt in the presence of the Speaker's foundational stance in this pericope? Once again, the individual feels he or she must take responsibility for his or her own life (finding food at a time of famine), since God is distant. Secondly, the earlier command to "go from your country, and your kindred, and your father's house to the land which I will show you" (12:1), i.e., the demand that one face the unknown and the dangerous, is given radical definition here. One might say that Abram leaves Yahweh and sojourns with evil, and is blessed for doing so. The elemental meaning of the text challenges the reader to the greatest courage in managing human life and family prosperity.

Not every reader will like this foundational stance. There will be room for dialectic: is the Yahwist to be rejected, or is there something in myself which must be straightened out?...

Gen 15:1-2, 4-12, 17-21

This chapter, apart from some editorial additions, appears to have been written by the Yahwist.[12] In this text the absent landlord makes a covenant with Abram following a liturgical technique which is described in Jer 34:18: He promises that Abram will become a huge nation and possess Canaan; and He invokes a curse upon himself should He fail to keep His promise.

This is a shocking text. The Speaker took care to make it a dream experience. And it is not Yahweh who walks between the animal parts, but a symbol of Yahweh. Moreover, writing in the Solomonic period, the author knew that Abraham had in fact become a nation, and that the Canaanite tribes had been driven out, and that the empire could be described as stretching from the river of Egypt to the Euphrates. Still he depicts Yahweh as binding Himself by self-curse to keep a promise, as though He needed such constraints . . . as though He were either not all-powerful or not altogether trustworthy! Nowhere in the Bible is God so humbled until the New Testament, where, for example, in Philippians 2:6-8 we read of God emptying Himself, taking the form of a slave, and humbling Himself to accept death.

Of course the counterpart to this covenant which binds God is the covenant in Ex 34 which binds humanity. But the effect of this text is to make the reader feel the very personal nature of that intervention in which God took hold of the world and its culture. Yahweh may be absent and distant, and yet He is passionate, direct, and personally involved. From now on we must expect that the landlord will not be absent in the same manner as before. Rather He will be bound to intervene instantly whenever the blessing of Abram's family is jeopardized.

The doctrine of the text deals specifically with the future, and only with the future of Abrams's family. However the Yahwist wrote this when that future was now past and present. The Yahwist's doctrine, therefore, was concerned, as in Gen 2-3, with the past, as explanatory of a present situation, i.e., the society he knew. This doctrine may have implied something about the future, but its explicit teaching consisted of explaining the present. The doctrine is limited to Israel, at the time of Solomon. The Speaker's foundational expectancy about God, on the other hand, is felt to regard the future rather than the present. A reader today will respond to that expectancy, whether or not he or she be Jewish, or whether or not there intervene some transitional doctrine which would make a present-day church or group continuous with the family of Abram. It is this unspecified stance of hopeful expectancy which has been normative through the centuries.

In this text, the Speaker's stance challenges the faith of the reader: do you believe that God cares radically about your future? The text begins with Yahweh appearing and stating "I am your patron; you will benefit very richly."[13] And in the key transition of v. 6 we are told: "And he (Abram) trusted

Yahweh, and He (Yahweh) accepted the trust as authentic."[14] There follows a powerful scene in which a "bird of prey" (the Hebrew word primarily designates "a scream"), doubtless a hawk of some kind, attacks the dead animals; but Abram "stands by them." We have largely lost all sense of what once was a familiar image, namely the hawk as a symbol of wild nature. Since husbandry has replaced hunting, we have largely forgotten the ancient techniques for taming a hawk by staring it in the eye hour after hour, often through the night, until it gives in, trusting enough to fall asleep.[15] The image here of Abram standing over the carcasses, facing the swooping hawk until nightfall when Yahweh puts Abram to sleep, does not yield an unequivocal meaning, but it remains powerfully suggestive. It is an image of a man daring to ask God to commit Himself, while he all alone faces the wild force of nature. And it is an image of God agreeing to come to man in that stance.

If one rejects the Yahwist at this point, the rest of his text is reduced to fiction. Accepting the Yahwist here means sharing in his very positive view of a world in which God ultimately assures us that it will all mean something good in the end. To use Robert Browning's phrase, "God's in his heaven—All's right with the world!" In the Christian tradition, a reader who does believe this does so because he or she has received a divine gift, or grace, of faith.[16] A reader who does not possess this gift, and particularly one whose beliefs exclude the possibility of the Yahwist's possessing such a gift, will not easily feel the stance of this Speaker, and will not easily interpret the Voice in its original sense. A reader who parts company with the Yahwist here may feel some measure of failure as a human being.

Gen 16:1-2, 4-14

In this first Hagar story it is clear that vv. 3 and 15-16 belong rather to the Priestly than to the Yahwist source. It is generally thought that vv. 9-10 are also editorially added to make possible the insertion of a second Hagar story in Gen 21. The Speaker's stance of expectancy remains the same with, or without, those verses, although it is more dramatically present to the reader if vv. 9-10 are omitted. It may further be noted that the story is clearly an old tale retold by the Yahwist, since the etymologies of vv. 11 and 13 were important factors in the telling, and they have become illogical in the retelling, as they depend on the name "El" rather than "Yahweh."

This is a surprising tale. It is all about the relationship between women, and its action is totally dependent on their feelings and decisions. Abram is almost irrelevant in the story, and the son is not born when the story ends. The conflict between the women, which forms the action, is not resolved in the story. Instead it becomes the origin of conflict between their offspring. As in the case of the other Yahwist stories we have seen, the message intended by this story consists of explaining a present situation through the past: namely the puzzling recurrence of animosity toward Jews on the part of a kindred tribe, the Ishmaelites. Within the Yahwist's general thesis that those who curse Israel will be cursed, the special case of the Ishmaelites had to be treated. The answer is that the Ishmaelites are blessed as progeny of Abraham, but they are rebellious because of their origin.

Does the Speaker here exercise any subliminal effect on a reader today? Where may God be expected to intervene? First it is clear that in this story psychological factors explain action in this life: the emotions of the women, and even the twisted attitude inherited by the son. And God is absent from all the emotions and decisions which form the action of this story. Even in the editorial v. 9 the angel does nothing to solve the conflict. In fact the conflict *must not* be solved, if Ishmael is to turn out like a wild ass. The angel merely orders her to go back and to submit. God is interested only in the fact of progeny; and He is a "God of seeing" in that He takes into account the banishing of Hagar as an explanation of the wildness of Ishmael. God is operative only on the political level, not on the personal.

This aspect of the Yahwist Speaker has been present in all the stories. In Gen 15, for example, Abram's complaint is not about personal matters, such as that he can't make a living, or that he is depressed, or that his household is always complaining. And similarly God's promises to Abram in Gen 15 are restricted to political blessings. But the Hagar story forces

the reader more directly to come to terms with this aspect of
the Yahwist stance, because the tension between the women
which creates the action and the suspense is never resolved.

This may be felt as a clarification of the apparent absence of
this passionately present landlord. On the one hand, one must
take full responsibility for arranging one's personal life, since
the absent God will not intervene. On the other, one must
trust God as the one who has set the general order of society;
and obey God as one who is passionately dedicated to preserving it.

Gen 27:1-45

The Yahwist appears to be more interested in the figure of
Rebekah than in that of Isaac, i.e., women as determining
human history rather than men. Certainly his long tale in Gen
24 about how Rebekah was chosen under Yahweh's direction,
with all its subtle narrative art, barely mentions Isaac. Here, in
Gen 27, Isaac alone possesses a God-given power of blessing,
but the whole action of the story depends on Rebekah's (not
God's) preference for Jacob.

This is a good story, told for its interest. For an ancient
Israelite, the story would have far more point, because its
explicit message, in continuity with the Yahwist's focus upon
the blessing and cursing of Israel, is that Esau's envy of Jacob
explains the enmity between Edom and Judah.

As in Gen 12:8ff. the Yahwist is not at all concerned about
the personal morality of the participants in this story. The
treachery of Rebekah, and of Jacob, including Jacob's involving Yahweh in the deception (v. 20), are not relevant to
this Speaker. His concern is only at the political level. For the
rest, he takes a purely secular pleasure in telling tales of human
perfidy, and in constructing suggestive dialogue. God is absent
from his artfulness, but very present in his horizon. In fact his
spending time on the irrelevant human subtleties of his stories
serves to jolt the reader into recognizing the irrelevance of
such subtleties. Once again, elemental meaning is read in the
gaps in the text.

The modern reader sides emotionally with Esau, who is
tricked out of everything by his mother. But the story demands

that one discipline such emotions strictly. What matters to this Speaker is not how humans treat each other, but only what God does in the midst of it. In this case God blesses Jacob, and gives the promise to him, leaving Esau to go his own way without consolation.

The Speaker too must have learned this, and felt that it was a stern lesson. We shall see in the next chapter how the Elohist felt obliged to offer an alternative reading of these same events. A reader today, with all the residues of individualism from the Renaissance, and of individual psychological awareness since Freud, must find it difficult to accept the apparent inhumanity of this stance. The text demands that one make an effort to recognize the all-powerful and peremptory presence of God in the social order. The text demands that the reader focus, not on himself or herself, but on the world at large, and on larger issues: where is the divine blessing and the divine curse operative in the world today?

The Spy Story, Num 13-14

The texts already discussed yield a coherent profile of a stance of expectancy. As the Yahwist text is too long to be considered in its entirety, and as there is little difficulty in hearing the Voice of this able writer, the question arises as to whether there is need of further pursuing this first application of a method. Moreover, the most dependable criterion for separating the Yahwist from the Elohist, i.e., the use of the name Yahweh for God, disappears in Ex 3 and 6, when the Elohist and Priestly writers also officially begin to use the name. As a result, it becomes more difficult to discuss the Yahwist as an assuredly separate source. However, a reading of one combined text from a later part of the Pentateuch, which is at least so Yahwist dominated that it can be treated for present purposes as Yahwist, may provide a useful confirmation of the insights gathered thus far. It will also prepare the way for reading the Priestly writer in chapter 5.

The "Yahwist" spy-story may be read in roughly the following verses: Num 12:16; 13:17b-20, 22-24, 27-31; 14:2-4, 11a, 23b-24, 25b, 39-45; 20:1b.[17]

This presents a coherent tale in which some gaps remain

where the editor has replaced Yahwist with Priestly material. We recognize the artful storyteller, who first presents an unfolding of events in which Yahweh is absent, and then moves on to a divine intervention. The first half of the story, roughly ch. 13, deals with the spies and their experience: first there is the speech of Moses, written as for boy scouts in a war game, telling the explorers just what they are to look out for. Then there is the vignette about the wonderful grape clusters which take two men to carry. There follows the report about seeing a race of giants there.[18] Finally there is Caleb, realistic and confident, wanting to invade the land. All of this is good story, very similar to the travel tales of Herodotus, without any advertence to religion or God. The second half of the pericope, beginning in ch. 14, is quite different: it takes place between the people (not the spies) on the one hand, and Yahweh, Moses, and the ark on the other. In ch. 14 we move from a secular tale to a religious legend. The people rebel against Moses, and want to return to Egypt. Yahweh takes this as contempt of Himself, i.e., of his salvific intervention, and decides to punish this generation by condemning them to die in the wilderness around the Reed Sea. There follows a mis-guided attempt to take the land of promise against the will of Yahweh who had promised it, and a rout. The second half of the pericope seems almost unrelated to the first! The absent landlord of the first half becomes suddenly a passionately present ruler in the second.

In the Yahwist's day, the spy tale clearly was intended to explain something about the Calebites and their power in Hebron. The Calebites must have been conscious of some title to ownership in Judah which was different from, and superior to, the rights of other families in Judah. However, the Speaker is not primarily concerned with this explanation. He retells the spy tale only to set up the sin of the people and Yahweh's intervention. His artfulness is evident in the spy tale, but his excitement is evident in the speed and importance of events beginning in ch. 14. Both Yahweh's decision to bring the people out of Egypt and into the promised land, and also Yahweh's instruments, namely Moses and the ark, are in the realm of political institutions. That is where God is revealed (this time through sin, i.e., contempt), and that is where God's salvation is granted or denied.

In the Yahwist's day, the elemental meaning of this story would certainly motivate the commandment in Ex 34:23 that all males should appear before God in the temple three times a year. The king and the ark were there, and these were symbols of Yahweh's establishing order in the empire and the centrality of Jerusalem. Three times in the year all males should acknowledge and celebrate this kingdom of God on earth. And they should not doubt about Yahweh's power, by imagining that the surrounding nations were sons of giants, or that the king's army could not always conquer the enemy. They should lead their private and family lives in the villages, from one end of the empire to the other, as they pleased, and as the initiative of women created daily vitality; but they should never forget that Yahweh gave ultimate security and meaning in Jerusalem.

That foundational stance of expectancy is easily imagined in that concrete historical setting. What subliminal impact can such a stance have on a reader today? To answer the question, one has to allow one's feeling about the story to come to the surface. Are you bored by the story? Boredom is a sure sign of rejection. Boredom means that, despite the undoubted skill of the storyteller, your stance of expectancy is not prepared to be stimulated by the stance of the Speaker. Why not? It may be that one cannot easily identify any parallel situation in one's life: a salvific place to which God is leading one's community, and for which one is obliged courageously to attack some enemy. In that case, such a stance of expectancy is irrelevant to oneself, or even offensive.

A dialectic might be called for: is the fault in me? Am I failing to hear God's voice—putting my head in the sand? For example, surely Yahweh has demonstrated the terror of atomic annihilation, and thereby commanded us all to spy out and move toward a nuclear-free world. Where is Moses and the ark in my world? Who are the enemies that unduly frighten me? Statistics indicate that many people today find life meaningless, or terrifying. This Speaker's stance may be demanding precisely for such people that some such realm of expectancy be defined in the contemporary scene. This, of course, is the work of religious leaders, and preachers.

Conclusion

There is, then a unified Speaker and Voice expressed for us as elemental meaning in the Yahwist text, whose implied demands on the reader are supported by the Yahwist's literary skill on the one hand, and by the reader's religious openness on the other.

What demands does this Speaker make upon the reader? First of all, we must live our lives, providing for our prosperity and combatting evil, as though God were not part of the immediate picture. We alone are responsible.

Second, God is passionately involved in preserving the larger social and political order, and the order of nature. We must then accept and trust these things, and actively cultivate communal awareness of social unity and common values.

Third, women play the activist role in the drama of human life, but men must speak to God, relying on the benevolence of creation and of the cultural determinant which God established long ago.

Finally, we must offer sacrifice as it will please God and encourage Him to support the order of nature and of society; but we should do so, above all, in order that we ourselves might draw strength and direction from awareness of our community, and of divine concern for social order.

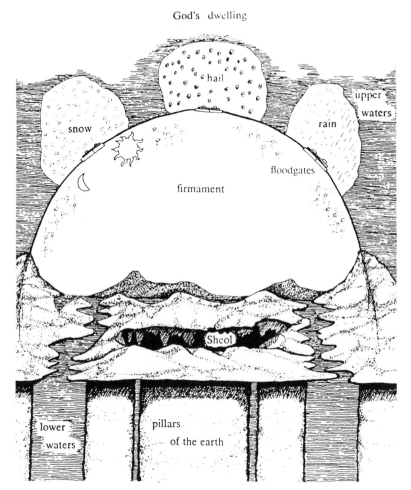

Reconstruction of early Hebrew cosmology

4

The Elohist Text

If source criticism in general is unloved these days, certainly the Elohist text is an orphan even among the children of classical critics. However, Alan Jenks, in a doctoral dissertation at Harvard directed by G. Ernest Wright, has reviewed source criticism dealing with the Elohist, has proposed new criteria for source decisions, and has concluded to Elohist authorship of a very extensive portion of the Pentateuch.[1] This work in turn was reviewed in a series of papers presented to the annual meeting of the Catholic Biblical Association from 1978 to 1983, by John A. Grindel. These papers have never been published. Grindel's project was to establish a text which could be confidently identified as Elohist on the basis of secure criteria, (criteria more critical than those of Jenks), and to determine its nature. In Appendix A there is reproduced the synoptic table of his results, comparing the findings of Noth, Jenks, and Grindel. It will be noted that after Ex 3 Grindel finds it possible to identify only Ex 13:17-19 as certainly Elohist, because from then on the key criterion (i.e., the name of God) is no longer relevant.

The present study is not a source critical study. Rather it presupposes sources and recognizes their importance. It is not primarily an historical study, attempting to define the kerygma of a text as it was adjusted to a specific moment in history. If it were such a study, it would be important to assemble all the data, and examine every clue, and therefore it would want to identify every verse written by the Elohist. Our study is interested in the elemental meanings which have reached readers in every age of our history. It needs to be sensitive to the Voice of the text, rather than the "intended messages," and as a result it needs to avoid, as far as possible, the confusion of other authors, and the disturbance of editors. For this reason it needs an assured minimal elohist text, and Grindel provides this. The proposed core Elohist text is relatively short. This chapter proposes to work through it all, beginning with some close anaysis of Gen 20-22 in order to discover and define the foundational stance of the Elohist, and then moving more rapidly through the remaining texts in order to recognize it in them, and refine its definition.

In Appendix B, we will briefly examine some other *probably* Elohist texts, whose elemental meaning appears to be in keeping with the same foundational stance.

Gen 22:1-13, 19: The Testing of Abraham

The famous story of the sacrifice of Isaac will be a good place to begin. It forms a climax to the trilogy of elohist stories (Gen 20-22) by which this author makes his or her entry in the biblical text.[2] Moreover it reveals the purpose and discovers the emphases of the first two stories in the trilogy, and it will be seen to express most fully the unique sensibilities of the Elohist.

Verse 1a provides a title for this story: "The God tested Abraham."[3]

As a contrast point it may be helpful to note that subsequent tradition will focus, not on Abraham, but rather on Isaac. Jewish tradition will see in Isaac a model of submission to the will of God. Christian tradition will see Isaac as a type of Christ crucified.[4] This shift of focus involved a radical shift in foundational expectancy as well: the expectancy for meaning is moved away from the realm of fatherly love to that of undeserved suffering.

Verses 1b-2 present God's intervention. It begins with a literary action-stopping device which we shall call *Scene-setting*: "And He said to him, 'Abraham.' And he replied, 'Here I am'. And He said...." The Elohist uses this device so often that it may be considered characteristic of his style.[5] The elemental meaning of this device is that the interpersonal nature of the ensuing conversation is of primary importance. The reader is awakened to a sense of aesthetic distance, a stance of contemplation, a self-conscious awareness: one is listening in to two people whose interrelationship is being formally expressed to each other. A Scene-setting, by making explicit the confrontation between the speakers, also challenges the reader, and induces in the reader a form of participation which is conscious and responsive.

The God then gives what has to be one of the most devastating commands in all literature, namely that Abraham must take his lovely son and slaughter him. For the Elohist what matters here are the feelings of Abraham (and the feelings of the participant readers) as can be seen in his care to focus by repetition: "Just take your son, your only one whom you love, I mean Isaac."

Verse 3 moves then abruptly to the next morning, when Abraham sets out. There is no comment on God's horrific command. There is no answer from Abraham, and no space in the text for the reader to imagine Abraham's feelings or confusion or rebellion or reasoning. In fact nowhere in the story is the reader to see Abraham talking to anyone who might understand his experience. The participant reader is not allowed by the text to objectify these feelings, but rather is condemned to share them in silence with Abraham. In effect the reader, all alone, must face this shocking command and work out his or her own response to it!

The rest of the story, as commentators have often pointed out, is laden with techniques for eliciting feeling, including the details about carrying the wood, the terrible irony of Isaac's question about the victim, and the twice-evoked scene of father and son walking alone together (vv. 6 and 8). Moreover the initial literary technique of Scene-setting is used twice more: Isaac and Abraham in v. 7, and then the angel with Abraham in v. 11. This is a story whose elemental meaning is that divine intervention occurs in the realm of family feelings, and also in the realm of the participant reader's feelings.

Again it will be helpful to note how the tradition shifted away from this focus: the editor who added vv. 15-18 takes the reader to a different place entirely, reflecting, not on feeling, but on the merits of Abraham, and on the confidence a later generation may have because of them.

In v. 13, the provision of an alternate victim seems almost trivial. The real solution after all had to do with God's revoking his command to sacrifice Isaac. The Speaker's concern lies with Abraham's fear of God. However, the Speaker had a secondary concern as well, namely to show that God took care of Abraham in a very real way. In v. 14, however, a subsequent editor has once again shifted foundational expectancy in a major way. This verse, with its double use of the name "Yahweh," cannot be Elohistic. It centres on the doctrine that God will "provide" (the Hebrew root means "see"), picking up the verbal root in the otherwise unexplained name of the mountain, Moriah, and echoing God's promise to "provide" in v. 8. By adding v. 14, the editor has underlined the secondary theme of v. 13 and made it a dominant theme in the pericope. The foundational expectancy for salvation has moved from the internal realm of Abraham's feelings about his son and about God to an external realm of God's taking material care of Abraham.

These diverse changes in the Speaker's foundational expectancy constitute the present biblical Speakers in Genesis 22, in the Talmud, and in the New Testament. Our concern at present, however, is to not lose sight of the Elohist Speaker.

What then is the foundational expectancy expressed as elemental meaning in the Elohist text? The realm of divine intervention is clearly expected to be family feelings, the love of father and son. The feelings are those of Abraham. However the Speaker uses literary techniques to demand that the reader participate personally in them. More specifically the feelings here are those of conflict between God's revealed will and Abraham's paternal love. God has intervened to create this conflict, and at the end He intervenes to resolve it. God has provided an occasion to test Abraham's (and the reader's) fear of God. When that fear is seen to be alive, then God intervenes to reveal Himself and to save Isaac. One might risk reducing this original meaning to formula as follows: God is revealed as saviour in one's fear of Him (authenticity); fear (authenticity) is activated where the heart is torn in family relationships.

I use the word "authenticity" here in a contemporary psy-

chological meaning to designate the virtue which once was
called "religion," or "ultimate concern," or the "faith" of the
Reformers, or the "fear" of the Old Testament. Today, the
word "fear" communicates an unacceptable meaning. It has
been psychologized to denote a purely subjective state which is
painful and undesirable. If "fear" in contemporary English
could be used to reflect both a subjective state and the object
which causes it, then the word would be more useful. For
example, if one stands before the ocean or the Alps one
experiences something which we prefer to call "awe," though
even that word is becoming archaic. Similarly, if we stand
before an infinite being, whose love is so pure that it is
intolerant of all else, and so communicative that it responds to
our most subtle and hidden feelings, we must experience an
overwhelming and thrilling fear. However, rather than fight
language, we shall use the word "authenticity," with all its
pompous inadequacy, to translate the Elohist's "fear."

It must be noted that Abraham's authenticity is called into
life when his heart is torn. His heart is not torn by suffering
injustice, or because he is persecuted, but rather because he
loves his son. The Elohist Speaker does not expect revelation
or salvation in the realm of the victim, as in the "Aqedah"
tradition, but rather in the realm of internal conflict between
relative and ultimate values.

Genesis 20:1-18: The Patriarch's Wife

This text has, of course, been very much studied and commented in the light of Yahwist parallels in Genesis 12:9—13:1
and again in Genesis 26:1-13. It is the most puzzling of the
Elohist texts, and it will require the longest treatment. However
it will also provide solid confirmation of our findings regarding
Genesis 22 above, and important refinement in our definition
of Elohist foundational expectancy.[6]

The first verse provides a vague Transition, and the second
presents the nub of the Complication. As it stands, verse 2
makes no narrative sense. "And Abraham said of Sarah, his
wife, 'She is my sister.' And Abimelech, the king of Gerar, sent
and abducted Sarah." The reader is not told why Abraham
would think of making a misleading statement about Sarah,

nor to whom the statement is addressed. The Elohist appears to be breaking into biblical writing with an intolerably inept beginning! And it is hardly justifiable on the grounds of a supposed familiarity with the story in oral tradition. It remains a graceless and insensitive entry into narrative. One is led to surmise that this is not after all an entry into narrative. Rather, the Elohist Speaker presupposes the *reading* of Genesis 12:9ff. This story, then, has the character of a parallel account, written as a commentary on the Yahwist version. Originally, at an oral stage, the story had been told about Abimelech at Gerar and, only possibly with a Jewish connection, i.e., about Isaac. The Yahwist retained this oral tradition (Genesis 26), and also wrote a parallel, applying the tale to Abraham and Egypt (Genesis 12). And now the Elohist has created a further parallel version, this time about Abraham at Gerar. He wanted to correct something in the tradition! He wanted to retain the Yahwist text, but compensate for some of its implications.[7] And since the Elohist was writing a corrective commentary rather than a straight story, his literary genre admits of considerable narrative foreshortening.

This surmise will receive an initial confirmation by glancing ahead to Genesis 21, where once again immediate dependence on J is required for narrative sense. Genesis 21:9-10 implies that Isaac's right to succession is seriously threatened by the son of a slave woman. Now, unless a reader is understood to have just read Genesis 16:3 (J), where Hagar is publicly recognized as Abraham's wife, the threat is narrative nonsense. Again, Genesis 21:25 introduces Abraham's complaint about a well with intolerable abruptness, explaining only later in v. 30 that Abraham had dug the well. Moreover the event narrated here took place in Beer Sheva, as we eventually learn in vv. 31 and 32, a location for which the Elohist text leaves us completely unprepared (20:1). But if one recognizes that all this is written as a corrective parallel to the Yahwist in 26:17ff which tells of Isaac's several attempts at well-digging with its final fruition at Beer Sheva (vv. 23, 32-33), then what would be narrative ineptitude is adequately explained as a literary form of commentary.[8]

In what follows, therefore, Elohist texts, and especially those which have Yahwist parallels, will be considered on the hypothesis that the original meaning includes a correction to the Yahwist. If this hypothesis is correct, one will not have understood the Elohist's concerns fully until one has identified what precisely in the Yahwist is being corrected.

Verses 3-17 contain the Action of this story, and v. 18 is a Closure. The Action is narrated in two parallel developments which may be seen as follows:

God and Abimelech	*Abimelech and Abraham*
1) The Protest (v. 3)	1) The Protest (vv. 9-10)
2) The Exculpation (vv. 4-5)	2) The Exculpation (vv. 11-13)
3) God's actions (vv. 6-7)	3) Abimelech's actions (vv. 14-16)
4) THE RESULTS (v. 8)	4) THE RESULTS (v. 17)

In telling this story the Elohist has not at all followed the chronological order of actual events, or any other easily explained narrative order. For example, we learn in v. 6, rather than at the end of v. 2, that Abimelech did not touch Sarah; and we learn only in vv. 17-18, rather than immediately after v. 6, that there was a question of impotence, or some disease, which intervened to prevent the adultery. Moreover, although the Elohist does tell us why Abraham said Sarah was his sister, still he does so only in v. 11, where it is timely for Abimelech but very untimely for the reader. Finally, there is a defect in narrative sense, not only in the order but also in logic: God threatens Abimelech as if in great anger (vv. 3 and 7b), and yet the reader learns that God had prevented all sin, or even physical contact, from the very beginning! God's anger is narrative nonsense. What then is the Elohist trying so hard to comment or correct in this way? What are the Elohist's concerns?

First of all, the emphasis here, as in Genesis 22, is deftly placed on inter-personal confrontation and feeling. Verse 2, as inept as it may be from a narrative point of view, has a very powerful rhetorical effect on the reader. By this sentence, the reader is shocked into active participation in the story, almost as effectively as by the opening verses of Genesis 22. Moreover, as indicated in the schema above, the action is presented in two parallel panels, each carefully written, not for narrative logic, but rather to create and highlight emotion-charged confrontations.

In the first panel, the Elohist has left his Yahwist sources behind in having God intervene in the story directly, at the same narrative level as the human actors. This was true in Genesis 22 as well, and we shall note it again in Genesis 21. It is an important peculiarity of the Elohist's style, and it expresses an important aspect of his foundational expectancy for meaning. God's anger is only an appearance, but his direct confrontation of feelings is the Elohist's mark in this telling of the story. Abimelech's answer (vv. 4-5) is a mixture of fear and of protest. As the protest is one which the author has taken care to justify at the beginning of the verse, the reader easily identifies with Abimelech, and also feels personally in direct conflict with God's appearance of anger. Verse 6 finally offers the narrative information that Abimelech has not touched Sarah, but its focus is a highly personal reassurance for Abimelech and for the reader. Twice we have the double-emphatic *gam'anoki*: "Not only did *I Myself* know that in all innocence you did this, but *also* it was *I* who prevented you from offending me." In v. 7 God's concern and power are reasserted. Verse 8 brings the first panel to its conclusion and climax: the men were filled with great fear. Of course this fear before God is the beginning of authenticity in Elohist spirituality, and in v. 11 we will learn that it was the lack of it among the Philistines which originally lead Abraham to state that Sarah was his sister. In this panel, then, we have revelation to the Philistine king, climaxing in conversion of the Philistines to religious authenticity!

In the second panel (vv. 9-17) we have a confrontation between Abimelech and Abraham. It opens with two separate indignant speeches by Abimelech (vv. 9-10). The reader is led to identify with Abraham. The Elohist's Abraham, unlike the wiley but amoral Abraham of the Yahwist, is a sensitive, ethical, and saintly man (cf. for example Genesis 21:11-12; 20:12, 17). We have just read that in God's eyes he is a prophet-intercessor (v. 7). Identifying with Abraham, the reader shares the abuse, and should feel confusion and humiliation at Abimelech's charges. Then Abraham answers the charges: in v. 11 he explains why he misled Abimelech; in v. 12 he shows that he was not in fact lying; in v. 13a he indicates that it was God who set the whole thing in motion; in v. 13b he recalls the moment of his obedience to God where his heart was torn. He said to Sarah, "This will be your marital fidelity which you will maintain toward me everywhere we go etc." A new and wrenching sort of wifely *hesed*, or sworn fidelity! Shocking, just as Abraham's obedience in sacrificing Isaac is shocking. And in both cases God has both created the problem and also provided so that the terrible consequences do not follow upon obedience. There follows then reconciliation, and restoration (vv. 14-17). The story has been badly told in one sense, but the feelings of the actors in it, and of the reader, have been thoroughly exercised!

A second concern of the Elohist in this chapter, as in chapter 22, is to show God as testing the heart of Abraham, while making sure in very concrete ways that no real harm comes to him or his family because of religious obedience. This concern is shown by the Speaker's invention of a divine revelation to Abimelech, and by his invention of the notion that God has acted specifically to prevent any contact between Abimelech and Sarah. The closure in v. 18, again by its very ineptness, reveals this concern. It is such narrative nonsense to place the detail about closing wombs at this point in the story, that most source critics try to assign the verse away as though the Pentateuchal editors were allowed to be fools while the Elohist is not allowed.[9] But, for the Elohist, this verse is a climax and a closure to the story. Just as in the case of the ram in 22:13, there is something trivial about the detail of the womb; and just like the ram it symbolizes a central point: God is in charge from the beginning. God not only initiates the action (by sending Abraham to wander abroad in this text, as by ordering the exile of Hagar in 21:12, and by ordering the sacrifice of Isaac in ch. 22), but He has the whole event under His beneficent control. Verse 18 concludes the story, just as v. 2 begins it, with a narratively inept detail which yet expresses the main concerns of the Elohist: clash of feelings in v. 2, and God's providing in v. 18.

In what sense are these concerns a corrective comment on the Yahwist parallels? In Genesis 12 the virtue and feelings of Abraham appear to be quite unimportant. Abraham tells an apparent lie, releases his wife to sexual abuse, acts throughout in a cowardly and opportunistic manner. The point of Gen 12 seems to be primarily to apply the Isaac story of Gen 26 (also Yahwist) to Abraham as well, and to give it the added typological dimension of salvation from Egypt. The point of Gen 26 seems to be to discuss the relations between Israel and the Philistines: Jewish women should not be given in marriage to the Philistines, and enmity between the Jews and the Philistines should be avoided by signing treaties about wells. The Yahwist remains in the realm of politics. The Elohist's foundations however, as expressed as elemental meaning in Gen 20, lead him to shift religion from the political to the personal realm. It is the virtues of individuals (i.e., no lies, fear of God, obedience) which is the stuff of religious life, rather than the Jerusalem-centred empire and international politics. The Elohist presents God, not as permitting foreigners to sin and then punishing them as in Gen 12, but as dealing directly with them, preventing sin, saving souls! The Elohist feels that God, not only has plans for the the nation of Israel, but also brings about the moral perfection of the individual, and reveals Himself directly in testing the Israelite and converting the foreigner.

What then does Gen 20 add to our definition of Elohist foundational expectancy as derived from Gen 22 above? In Gen 20 God not only tests Abraham as in 22, but He also intervenes to prevent sin and demand rectitude of Abimelech. God is active as a conscience, and not only for Israelites but for Philistines as well, and implicitly perhaps for all peoples. Thus God intervenes *wherever* the heart his torn, demanding authenticity which includes both ethics (in this case purity and justice) and obedience to god, fear of God, authenticity.

The Elohist, commenting on the Yahwist, preserves the Yahwist text, and writes a parallel which presupposes the Yahwist account. Thus he retains Yahwist nationalist political expectancy, but he consciously introduces another level of revelation, salvation, religious reflection, namely the level of individual authenticity.

Note, once again, that Abraham is not personally a victim here. He suffers only because he loves.

This foundational expectancy makes clear demands on the reader. For example one will feel challenged to risk the pains of friendship, love, marriage, children, divorce, death of loved ones, and so forth, for God intervenes where the heart is torn! One is challenged to trust God in the midst of all inter-personal stress, rather than escape stress by dismissive anger at one's parents, or escapist anger at educational establishments, or the government. One is challenged to find hope in the midst of personal or family tragedy, believing that God has provided from the beginning to prevent any real harm.

Genesis 21:8-21: A Story about Hagar

The intervening verses, i.e., Genesis 21:1-6, may contain some Elohist phrases, but certainly a new Elohist story begins in v. 8. It is a parallel to the Yahwist story in Genesis 16:1-2, 4-8, 11-14. Once again we must read it on the hypothesis that it is a corrective, or compensatory, commentary on the Yahwist, since it expects the reader to accept Abraham's shocking relation to Hagar without any explanation, apart from the Yahwist's text in Gen 16.

The Yahwist tale is about the problems of two women, since Abraham appears only as an insignificant, and almost contemptible, figure. Sarah has a problem in that she is child-less despite the promise; and Hagar has a problem in that she is unable to handle her promotion with grace. If there is a Peripeteia in the story, and a Resolution, these do not turn upon the problems they start with. Family life and emotions do not interest the Yahwist. Rather an angel intervenes, not to solve anything, but merely to explain that Yahweh knows all about the recurrent conflict between Jews and Ishmaelites, brother tribes. It is governed by His providence. The story of the women provides a legendary image for a thorny political situation which seemed to the Yahwist's contemporaries to cast doubt on Israel's favoured status. It is an image which allows the Yahwist to understand how the Ishmaelites might "curse" Israel and yet not be "cursed" in return by Yahweh. The "Resolution" of the tale does not resolve the problems of Sarah and Hagar, but rather the problems of the Jerusalem king and his Yahwist theologian.

The Elohist, on the other hand, creates a very different view of that legendary event. Here, once again, the Elohist makes

the reader a participant in the emotions of the persons involved, and here once again God enters the story at the level of
the human participants. And finally here once again non-Jews
receive direct attention and salvation from God.

Verse 8 provides a Transition and setting, i.e, Isaac's weaning
at about the age of 3 years is the occasion for a feast.

Verses 9-10 contain an Introduction which originally almost
certainly omitted the name Isaac completely:[10] "And Sarah
looked at the son of Hagar the Egyptian, which she had born
to Abraham, who was *playing*. And she said to Abraham,
'Drive out that slave and her son. No son of that slave should
inherit along with my son." The pun on "playing" (i.e., the
Hebrew root for the name Isaac) seems trivial, and in fact
inappropriate, since Sarah feels so strongly. From a literary
point of view, its only purpose is to command the reader's
attention: this is a subtle tale, so listen attentively! As a narrative technique, it is not as arresting as the openings in Gen
20 and 22, but it serves the same purpose, i.e., inviting the
reader to participate personally in the scene and its feelings.

That Hagar is an Egyptian is noted at the beginning of the
action, and that she finds an Egyptian wife for Ishmael is
noted at the end, forming an inclusion. The foreign connection
is heavily emphasized by this inclusion. Moreover, it will also
be viewed favourably, since God will make this seed into a
"great nation" in vv. 13 and 18.

The Action begins fully in the following scene between God
and Abraham, vv. 11-13. The Elohist has given an inadequate
account of Sarah's feeling in his Introduction, leaning on the
reader's familiarity with the Yahwist text, but he is concerned
to explain Abraham's feelings. Abraham feels badly about
exposing his young son (11b). Moreover, as the Elohist has
God explain, he feels badly about both the boy and the slave-
woman (12a). But it is God who makes the decision, and sets
the story in motion: Abraham is to do what Sarah wants,
because God will see to it that Abraham's family will not
suffer: Abraham will have two families (12b, 13).

God is the decisive personage who starts the previous story,
and the following story as well. In fact, all three stories in the
trilogy Gen 20-22 display an identical basic series of events:
1) divine intervention to create an horrific situation,

2) Abraham's obedience, 3) dangerous consequences, 4) divine intervention to bring good out of evil. This can be seen in the following schema:

Patriarch's Wife	*Hagar Story*	*Testing Abraham*
God tells Abraham to wander; Sarah accompanies him as his sister (v. 13)	God tells Abraham to obey Sarah and send Hagar and child away (v. 12)	God tells Abraham to sacrifice his son (v. 2)
Abraham obeys (vv. 1-2a)	Abraham obeys (v. 14)	Abraham obeys (v. 3)
Abimelech abducts Sarah; a disease in Abimelech's court (vv. 2b, 18)	Hagar's (i.e., Abraham's) child is dying of thirst (v. 16)	Abraham prepares to slaughter his son (vv. 9-10)
God prevents the adultery; tells Abimelech to return Sarah; restores health to the court (vv. 6, 7, 17)	God's angel shows Hagar a well; takes care of growing child (vv. 19-20)	God's angel saves Isaac and provides an alternative form of sacrifice (vv. 11-13)

The following scenes, vv. 14-19, have been much commented upon for their emotional focus and art. Whether God hears from heaven or on earth is totally irrelevant here—the point is that God is made to participate in the feelings between Abraham and Hagar, Abraham and his son, Hagar and her infant, the despairing infant itself. And God acts decisively to work a kind of miracle in showing a well to save the child and its mother.

Verse 20 contains an important conclusion to the story, namely that God would "be with" the boy as he grew up in the desert, and learned how to use a bow. Similarly, God will "be with" Jacob/Israel (28:20; 31:59; 46:4a), Joseph and his sons (48:21), and Moses (Ex 3:12). God is taking care of Abraham's domestic family life with all his providential care.

There follows in v. 21 a Closure, forming an Inclusion with the Introduction, as indicated above.

This story duplicates, and reinforces, what we have found to be the foundational expectancy of the Elohist in the previous two stories, even though there is no explicit focus here on the obedience, or sanctity, or fear of Abraham. The story retains too much of the original Yahwist concern for politics and the Ishmaelites for that. Still the Elohist has changed the Yahwist story by having the Complication in the plot fully resolved within the story: the infant is removed from Abraham's immediate family, saved from death in the desert, and cared for in the future. Through this change, the Elohist has God intervene where the heart is torn, and for non-Israelites as well as Israelites. The Elohist has moved the tale from being a reflection on political theology to being a participation by the reader in Abraham's and Hagar's experience of the immediate presence of God who reveals and saves at the domestic level.

Gen 21:22-32, 34: Grief and Friendship with the Philistines

The source critical analysis of these verses has a long history. The use of "Yahweh" in v. 33, and its concern for the Yahwisation of a local name for God, makes the verse look like a gloss in the J tradition. The jumbled nature of the narrative itself is best explained if one understands that originally vv. 22-24, 27, 31b, 34 took place in Gerar and formed a conclusion to the Elohist story in Gen 20. The rest of the verses (vv. 25-32) appear to be a tale about an oath at Beer Sheva, written as an Elohist parallel to a Yahwist story in Gen 26:17-33, and dependent for its narrative intelligibility, as indicated above, on that Yahwist source. The composite which we now read in the biblical text forms an appendix to the Elohist story in Gen 21. Granted its position in the Elohist trilogy (Gen 20-22), we shall do well to look at it briefly.

The Yahwist story is about the name Beer Sheva, as the major unit is marked out by an inclusion on that name (26:23, 33). It comes after three other brief preparatory stories about wells, with their etymologies, which develop from conflict, to hatred, to tolerance (vv. 17-22). The Yahwist, as usual, is concerned with international politics, and the point of the Beer Sheva story seems to be that making a sworn covenant of non-aggression with the Philistines assured blessings for Israel, blessings symbolized by the water of Beer Sheva.

The Elohist parallel is not at all about blessing, and in his story the water is only an occasion for the quarrel. The Yahwist etymology for Beer Sheva (i.e., *shaba'*, oath) is retained in v. 31, but another tradition about the etymology has been added, namely the number seven.

What corrective to the Yahwist motivates writing this parallel? The story is still about international politics, but the focus has been moved from prosperity to the feelings between Abimelech and Abraham. Abimelech's protestation of innocence in v. 26 is created by the Elohist. Moreover, where the Yahwist began his story by a lengthy development concerning the conflicts between Philistines and Israelites (26:17-22), and then contrasted this with the promise of blessing for Israel (26:23-25), the Elohist begins with Abimelech's plea that Abraham deal honestly with him, and then moves on to Abraham's complaint and Abimelech's answer, and the arrangements for sacrifice (21:22-31a). Only in 31b do we get to the basis of the conflict. In the Elohist story, the Israelites are subtly placed in the wrong: at the start Abimelech asks not to be wronged but to be treated as well as he has treated Abraham; and then Abimelech is wrongly (though not falsely) accused, and he protests his innocence. The reader's sympathy, granted the larger context of the Abraham stories, may remain with Abraham, but it is strongly solicited for Abimelech as well. God is not explicitly mentioned in the story, but the oath involves God in the very personal, mutual, loyalty between Abraham and Abimelech. The Elohist has written a story about interracial friendship, as a compensatory addition to the Yahwist's international politics.

The Elohist, or editor, seems to have placed the composite tale here, after the story about Philistines in ch. 20 and Ishmaelites in ch. 21, as a kind of synthesis of his concerns about interracial harmony within religious differences. Both chs. 20 and 21 deal with interracial marriage, and in both God backs its interdiction. In ch. 22 God will back the interdiction of infant sacrifice. But the Elohist plea throughout is to respect the religious authenticity of the non-Israelite. The present story, 21:22ff, has God backing a personal loyalty between every Israelite and every Philistine! It implies that disputes may be justified, but that the other party may be innocent, and merits a trusting approach.

The Elohist (editor) has also taken care to move Abraham to Beer Sheva, which becomes Abraham's home in this tradition (Gen 20:1; 21:14, 31, 32, 33; 22:19).

Does this add to our understanding of Elohist foundational stance? It extends our definition of the sphere of feelings where God will be revealed. For the Elohist the heart may be torn, not only in regard to family (love of wife, of child, of concubine), but also in regard to property, and to interracial sharing. We are still in the realm of domestic feelings, even though Abraham is not just any Israelite, nor Abimelech just any Philistine. The story has been deftly reduced from its original national or tribal horizon, to one which deals only with the relations between two men.

Gen 28:10-12, 17-22: A Temple at Bethel

Once again we can work with a Yahwist parallel, i.e., 28:13-16. The Yahwist story is basically a repetition, for Jacob's benefit, of the national and political promises made to Abraham and Isaac, and a promise of interim protection on his trip to Haran. Jacob discovers that Yahweh is present, not only in Beer Sheva, but also beyond the borders of Judah in Bethel (v. 16): welcome news for international travelers and traders in Solomons court, for whom the Yahwist wrote.

The Elohist, possibly because he lived in the Northern Kingdom, is not satisfied with treating Bethel as a place of theophany in exile. For him, Bethel is the central shrine, and its legitimation occurs here in the life of Jacob.

The Elohist story begins with a transition (v. 10), and has two incidents, the dream and the oath. The dream section (vv. 11-12, 17) climaxes in Jacob's "fear" (v. 17a). It is chiefly concerned with the actual sacred place, and the word magom or "place" occurs 4 times in these three verses. In the previous Elohist stories, God intervenes and reveals himself where the heart of Abraham is torn, but here there is a constant reve-

lation, almost institutionalized in a "ladder." The stone is a
divine dwelling; the place is a gateway to Heaven; Jacob
experiences "fear" (i.e., religious conversion to authenticity) in
that place.

In a second part of the story, we are told how Jacob reacted
to this experience, i.e., by anointing his stone as a "*maṣṣebah*, "
and taking an oath (vv. 18-22). The oath, like the Sinai
covenant, is conditional: *if* God takes care of me, I will build a
temple here, and tithe.

The Elohist has modified the Yahwist story in three important respects: first, he has legitimized a northern shrine,
and thereby the northern Kingdom; second, his story is not
just about Yahweh's promise, but also very much about
Jacob's authenticity, his feeling fear at Bethel; third, he has
Jacob not only learn something about God, but also personally
interact with God by putting a condition on his service, i.e.,
enter a form of conditional covenant with God.

Our understanding of the foundational expectancy of the
Elohist is slightly modified by this story. God is still revealed in
the heart of the individual, but it appears that the experience
of fear may occur, not just in domestic suffering, but also by
merely visiting the major sanctuary.[11] And this occasions the
first note of explicit Elohist demands upon the reader, i.e.,
care for the shrine, and tithing. Where Yahwist demand has
centred on national unity, and racial purity, the Elohist has
here introduced a demand centred on setting aside a portion
of family income to support the temple at Bethel.[12]

Readers may react to the Speaker's demands in different
ways, depending on religious affiliation. All will feel that the
Speaker expects religion to be externally expressed, and to
cost money, or the equivalent.

Gen 35:1-8: Bethel, a God of Flight

It will be convenient to skip ahead here to this pericope,
because of its direct connection with the foregoing, and because
it slightly corrects one aspect of the impression created by the
foregoing.

If v. 8 is viewed as an etiological note appended after the
story proper, the unit is very strongly marked by an Inclusion:
"Bethel," "there," "altar," "the God who appeared to you as

you fled from your brother Esau" (vv. 1 and 7). The Inclusion constitutes an attempt by the Elohist to define the nature of God: He is one who is revealed at Bethel, when you are in flight from your brother! This definition is reinforced by Jacob's description: "the God who answered me in my day of distress" (v. 3b). Thus we learn that God appeared to Jacob, not just because he visited the gate of heaven and slept on the sacred stone, but also because his heart was torn. Bethel is the gate of heaven because it recalls the experience of family conflict. Unfortunately, if ever there existed a separate Elohist account of how the alienation occurred between Esau and Jacob, it is not possible to discern it with any confidence in the extant biblical text.[13] It remains helpful for our purposes to note that the distress of alienation from one's brother, which the Yahwist, for his part, treats at the mythical level in purely negative terms as sin or curse (Gen 4, Cain and Abel, and Gen 11, The Tower of Babel), and, at the psychological level, in dealing with Jacob and Esau, as mere grist for the narrative mill (Gen 27:43; 32:2—33:4, 12-17), is turned now by the Elohist into an occasion for divine revelation.[14] Similarly we have seen that Hagar's conflict and flight from her mistress occasioned revelation. This was found in both J (Gen 16) and E (Gen 21). But, whereas in J the alienation became a legend for understanding political strife, E made God enter into, and reveal Himself through, the feelings of alienation. Immediately below, we shall see a parallel difference of treatment in the case of alienation between Jacob and Laban, with the Elohist taking it as something to deal with directly, and the Yahwist taking it as a given without importance.

Moreover, the Elohist makes this definition of God all the more significant in that he connects it with the rejection of all foreign gods, and the burial of clothing and earrings reminiscent of them (35:2, 4). For the Elohist, this God was revealed under the name "Bethel" (Gen 31:13), presumably a Canaanite divinity. Eventually the proper name, "Yahweh," will be revealed (Ex 3). The present text proposes to distinguish the acceptable God, as opposed to all foreign Gods, on the basis of two characteristics: the internal characteristic that He is revealed where the heart is torn by conflict and flight, and the external characteristic that his cult is at Bethel.

If the hypothesis is correct that the Elohist writes, not an independent book, but rather a commentary on the Yahwist text, then this exclusivism will not reject the nature of God as revealed in the Yahwist text, i.e., God as political master. Rather it will complement and encompass it.

The elemental meaning of this text is that the God who is revealed here is to be encountered exclusively where the heart is torn, notably on the occasion of a visit to the shrine.

Gen 31:4-16: Jacob Wins his Wives

There is no real parallel to this text in the Yahwist. In the previous chapter the Yahwist has told of the mutual trickery between Laban and Jacob, which he sees apparently as somewhat humourous, and without importance. The Elohist sees it otherwise, and writes this corrective account. Once again the Elohist text presupposes that the reader has just read some account of the events which he here interprets and explains, i.e., the Yahwist account.

In the Elohist version, there is no cleverness. Laban has directly cheated his son-in-law, and God has directly intervened to redress the injustice. Moreover, the story is told, not as it occurred between Jacob and Laban, but as it formed a basis for determining the relationship between Jacob and his wives. The climax of the story (vv. 14-16) consists of two elements: first the wives recognize that God had intervened from the beginning unknown to everyone, and secondly they decide to leave their father and go away with Jacob.

One should recognize the Elohist signature in the Scene-setting technique in vv. 11-12, which assures reader participation in the confrontation. The whole story is constructed, as we have come to expect, in a milieu of inter-personal feeling, where the heart is torn, and where God intervenes directly from the beginning. The reader is invited to participate in this experience.

This story by the Elohist contradicts the Yahwist version in the details about flock management. One might ask whether the Elohist is adding to the Yahwist here, to comment, compensate, and correct, or is he writing an alternative story which rejects the tradition? That question presupposes a process which is more simple than the evidence indicates. The Yahwist text in ch. 29 has contradictions and obscurities in abundance. Moreover, we have seen in Gen 21 that "the Elohist" denotes a writing and a subsequent rearranging or editing. This story is presented as Jacob's interpretation of events, and as such it does not reject the previous chapter and could not serve as an alternative to it.

Gen 31:17-24, 25-42: Jacob Vindicated Before Laban

In this story of the flight from Laban, there is an unresolved problem about sources. Grindel assigns the whole story to the Elohist. Wellhausen, Gunkel, Eissfeldt and Vawter consider the preponderance of the narrative to be Elohist, but assign some parts to the Yahwist. For example Vawter gives the following verses to the Yahwist: 17, 19a, 21-23, 25b, 27, 30-31, 38-40. Verse 18 he assigns to P. The following comments will follow Grindel, but will take special care with data found in questioned verses. In the 31:4-16 we have seen the Elohist contradict the Yahwist tradition, while leaving that text intact. Here we have an Elohist story, but cannot be sure about surviving traces of the Yahwist tradition.

This story again deals with the alienation between Laban and Jacob, and it appears to be thematized around the root *gnb* "to steal." Was Jacob a thief? This is a problem which the Elohist took seriously indeed, unlike the Yahwist. And he had to take on a whole tradition, including the traces of crookedness associated with the Hebrew root of the name Jacob. Here the word occurs seven times, (three of them in questioned verses). It has two meanings: first, the usual meaning of "steal" when its object is the teraphim (vv. 19, 30), or the passive "be robbed" (twice in v. 39); second, the unique meaning of "deceive" (vv. 20, 26, 27).[15] It is clear that the Elohist places some weight on this semantic play, since he makes the two meanings parallel to each other in close proximity in the Introduction to his story (vv. 19-20). Rachel has *stolen* the teraphim, but Jacob has only *deceived* Laban. This explains both that Jacob was *not* a thief, and also how it came about that "thievery" was associated with his name in the tradition.

The story is told in a manner typical of the Elohist in that it is cast in the general mode of a personal confrontation between Jacob and Laban. Another typical characteristic is that here, as in Gen 20, God appears and speaks to a non-Israelite, i.e., Laban, to prevent him from committing a crime (vv. 24, 29).

The story begins with a Preamble in v. 17, in which Jacob is seen lifting his children and his wives up onto camels, a scene reminiscent of Abraham's placing Ishmael on Hagar's back in 21:14. There follows an Introduction (vv. 19-20), and then five Actions: the flight (vv. 21-25), the challenge (vv. 26-30), Jacob's answer (vv. 31-32), the search (vv. 33-35), Jacob's vindication (vv. 36-42).

The final section is the longest, and the point of the whole story: Jacob was falsely accused (vv. 36-37), mistreated by Laban (38-40), cheated by Laban (v. 41), finally vindicated by God (v. 42).

In this story we find reinforced what we expect from the Elohist. First the innocence of Jacob is established: he is not a thief. It has been clear throughout the Elohist text that in his view ethics count: Jacob will worship Bethel, *if* Bethel takes care of him on the trip (28:20); similarly, God sides with Abraham (in Gen 20), and with Jacob here, *because* they are not liars, adulterers, or thieves. Underlying this approach, there must be the experience of reciprocal covenant.

Second, God intervenes where the heart is torn in family strife. Where the trust between father-in-law and son-in-law has been abused, a confrontation occurs, and it is revealed once again that God has taken care of the innocent party.

There is a further definition of God here. The God named Bethel (31:13) is the God of Abraham, and the family God of Isaac, Jacob's father (31:42a).[16]

Gen 33:5-11: The Reconciliation Between Jacob and Esau

In ch. 32 the Yahwist has told how Jacob made cunning preparations for meeting Esau upon his return from Paddan Aram. They meet emotionally and briefly (33:4), and then Jacob cleverly manages to separate immediately, avoiding all personal involvement with Esau (33:12-17)!

Here, once again, we have an Elohist vignette, whose intelligibility is dependent upon the reader's having read a preceding narrative about how Jacob comes to meet Esau in this way. In the biblical text, this narrative is now supplied by the Yahwist. Are we to suppose that there once was a parallel Elohist narrative, which has been suppressed by the editor? One doubts this, since the editor has chosen to retain so many parallel texts, even when they contradict eath other! Why would he have suppressed the Elohist parallel here? And in view of the evidence adduced above that at least in Gen 20 and 21 the Elohist did expect the reader to have just read the Yahwist text, it is hard to escape the conclusion that the Elohist, here once again, is writing a corrective addition to a Yahwist text, which he retains.

The Elohist story is inserted after v. 4 precisely to tell of a reconciliation between Jacob and Esau. For the Elohist, once again, domestic inter-personal relations are most meaningful. It is there that revelation occurs. And we have this expressed in Jacob's astonishing words: "Please don't say no, if you love me, but take the offering I make. For this purpose I approached you as one approaches God: that you might accept me" (v. 10). In Biblical Hebrew the word used here for "offering," *minhah*, is usually used for a sacrifice of grain offered to God; and the word "accept," *rasah,* is usually reserved for God's accepting a sacrifice. And there follows an explanation that the gift itself is a divine blessing. Thus the reconciliation between brothers is clothed explicitly here by the Elohist in a divine sphere.

The elemental meaning here is very diverse from the Yahwist source. Where the Elohist finds God in the reconciliation of estranged brothers, the Yahwist describes slick international diplomacy.

With regard to foundational expectancy, we may learn one additional point in the Elohist demands on the reader. We pointed out that the Elohist compensated for the Yahwist's approach to tension, i.e., recourse to cleverness and evasion. For the Elohist Speaker, one must approach one's estranged brother as though he were divine, and make a reconciliation based on the abundance of one's own wealth. One must *not* avoid confrontation, or manipulate inter-personal space. This demand of the Elohist has a rather modern ring, and may well make many of us readers feel challenged indeed.

Gen 46:1-5a: God Sends Israel to Egypt

In the Joseph story proper (Gen 37; 39-47; 50). Grindel agrees with G.W. Coats that it is difficult to recognize source criteria. Coats assigns only this short text to E.[17] Grindel does the same, but adds parts of ch. 48 and 50:15-26.

The unit is marked by an inclusion, as the transition (v. 1a) tells of travelling to Beer Sheva, and the closure (v. 5a) tells of leaving Beer Sheva. In Elohist geography, Abraham's centre was Beer Sheva, and Isaac's too. Jacob was born there, but eventually, along with "all who were with him," he settled in Bethel (35:1-2).

The story is about a major vision, in which "Israel and all that belonged to him" are instructed to go down to Egypt. The vision begins with the characteristic Elohist technique of Scene-setting: "And he said, 'Jacob, Jacob.' And he said, 'Here am I.' And He said 'I am the God, the God of your father.'" The reader participates in the awe, feeling the confrontation.

This is a typically Elohist story in that God intervenes decisively, at the level of the other players in the drama. The Yahwist source had Jacob making the decision to go on his own, and without any hesitation (45:28).

As a beginning, it is not the beginning of the Joseph story, but rather the beginning of the whole Exodus drama. Jacob goes to Beer Sheva, with his whole family, because Beer Sheva is the family seat, and it is fitting that "the God of his father" should deal with the whole family there. God tells Jacob to set in motion a tearing of the heart, just as he told Abraham to endanger Sarah, to banish Hagar and Ishmael, to sacrifice Isaac. God will be with them, to keep them from harm and to bring them back.

Gen 48:1-2, 8-14, 17-22: The Grandchildren, Ephraim and Manasse

This story about Ephraim and Menasse must have been of particular interest to the Elohist as a northern writer. Typical of the Elohist also is the fact that the whole story is cast as an encounter between Jacob and Joseph, an encounter which is carefully prepared (v. 2), and very emotional in character (vv. 8-12). There follows a detailed, and almost fussy, scene in which grandfatherly confusion turns into patriarchal knowledge of the future, and power over the land. The structure of the Northern Kingdom is determined where the heart is torn, if not in conflict, still in a moment of powerful domestic feelings about Jacob's grandchildren and Jacob's dying.

This merely confirms what we have seen of Elohist expectancy. One wonders whether we must take special precautions against the temptation of reading what we progressively know of the Elohist into new texts as we come to them. In this case, I would plead that any other reading of this text renders it unacceptably silly.

Gen 50:15-26: Final Reconciliation

This unit deals with the relations between Joseph and his brothers. There are two encounters: vv. 15-21, and vv. 22-24.

The first encounter is extremely emotional. It is cautiously prepared by the trembling brothers (vv. 16-17); it is filled with signs and expressions of confused emotions; its climax consists of tender reconciliation. Joseph tells his brothers that they are not to relate to him as though he were divine (v. 19). A surprising remark, but we have seen repeatedly that torn domestic feelings are precisely the divine milieu for the Elohist. In the Elohist revision, this final scene in Genesis is not a purple patch, embarrasingly sentimental. Rather it is a fitting conclusion. And the Elohist's clearest thematic statement fittingly occurs here: "where you intended evil for me, God intended it to be good" (v. 20).

This scene is in very sharp contrast with the Yahwist's handling of the relations between Joseph and his brothers throughout chs. 42-46. The feelings are there, but Joseph dissembles them, or uses them to manipulate his brothers and his father, to bring them to Egypt. Certainly they are not valuable in themselves or divine in any sense. And God's involvement is not mentioned. At best it is understood to be very distant, restricted perhaps to the weather, i.e., the famine.

The second encounter (vv. 22-24) consists of Joseph's death scene. It begins with a transitional summary (v. 22). It continues by placing Joseph in the presence of his offspring to the third generation, and then having him die. Joseph makes his brother swear to bring his bones back to the promised land. This too is a very domestic tale. The whole family of Israel is present for the dying Joseph, and Joseph's bones are to return with them when God intervenes once again.

For the Elohist, the divine milieu is family, present to each other, feeling all variety of family feelings.

Ex 1:15-21: Family Heroines

This text is not listed by Grindel in his synopsis, but since he does make it clearly Elohist in the course of his paper, we shall treat it here. The text is a vignette which presupposes the surrounding Yahwist narrative, and corrects it.

The story of the midwives is a story about the "fear" of God. Because the midwives feared God the people of Israel prospered (vv. 20-21). It is remarkable that the authenticity which saves Israel is not found here in one of the patriarchs, or in Moses, but rather in two midwives whose names are carefully preserved in the text. One could not imagine a more potent symbol than midwives for family feeling.

This story also serves the editorial purpose of getting Moses into the Nile river, as required by ch. 2. The Yahwist must have managed that in some other way, but his version has not been preserved. That the Elohist inserted this tale at this point, between the patriarchs and Moses, brings into sharp focus one aspect of the correction he felt necessary. His foundational expectancy will have Israel saved, not through great leaders, but through the interior authenticity of ordinary people, living within domestic horizons. (This is very much in harmony with Ex 19:7-8, which was contrasted with Ex 34 in the previous chapter of this book, verses which classical source critics often assigned to the Elohist.)

Ex 3:1, 4b, 6, 9-13, 15: The Name of God

Once again a typical Elohist story, structured as confrontation between Moses and God, enclosing a confrontation between Moses and the people, and marked by the Scene-setting techniques of the Elohist: "And He said, 'Moses, Moses.' And he said, 'Here am I.' And He said, 'I am the God of your father.'" The reader too participates in the awe. And the Elohist makes it explicit: "Moses hid his face, because he feared to look upon God" (v. 6b).

Why did the Elohist feel constrained to write a close parallel to the Yahwist in this instance? What was he correcting?

The Yahwist version takes care to establish a distance between God and Moses, telling Moses not to come near in v. 5.

It may well have been this *distance* which the Elohist felt needed compensation. First, the Elohist's account retains the awe of this vision using his own category of "fear" (v. 6b), but he creates a far more intimate meeting between God and Moses (vv. 4b, 6). Secondly, he solves Moses' objection that he is a nobody (v. 11) by saying that He would be with him and promising contact "on this hill" (v. 13), rather than by giving him magic tricks as the Yahwist does in 4:1-9. Thirdly he insists three times that Yahweh is the god of your fathers (vv. 6a, 13a, 15a). All of these nuances bring God closer, and make him less terrifying.

Other Elohistic meaning in this pericope, centering on Bethel and the power structure in the Northern Kingdom, were discussed above in ch. 1. Once again, this Speaker suggests a cultic demand as a condition of political well-being.

Ex 13:17-19

This final "assured" Elohist text reveals little. It begins with a pun on the root *nhm* in v. 17 ("lead them" = "repent"), to catch the reader's attention as in Gen 20:1b, and 21:9. It portrays God as acutely aware of the feelings of the Jews, and as dealing very directly with the possible outcome of those feelings. Finally, it picks up the thread of the oath to bury Joseph's bones in Gen 50:25.

Conclusion

It is dangerous to summarize. The whole point of this presentation is to lead the reader to experience the original meaning, i.e., the whole text itself, and its Speaker with its personal challenge. To paraphrase now, may seem to suggest that this meaning can be reduced to propositions. What follows is in no sense a summary of the Elohist's meaning. It is a summary of points observed by the present author. These points point toward a complex elemental meaning of the Elohist text.

1) The main points of Elohist foundational expectancy in this core text were given sharper definition when seen as corrective to the Yahwist parallels.

2) God is revealed in the realm of feeling and inter-personal confrontation. Salvation occurs where the heart is torn by conflict of personal values (family love versus "fear" of God), by misunderstanding between friends (Abimelech), by alienation between family members (Hagar, Jacob and Esau and Laban), by death (Jacob, Joseph, the infants with the midwives).

3) God is revealed in the feelings, not only of the great leaders of ancient Israel, but also in everyone's feelings, including foreigners, and particularly in the feelings of the reader.

4) God is encountered in a religious experience of reciprocal covenant, in which Jacob is loyal if God cares for him, and God cares if Jacob is ethical.[18]

5) God acts directly by telling people what to do concretely, or by working miracles. Some miracles are revealed as such only later (disease in Abimelech's court, Laban's sheep and goats).

6) Even though strife and conflict are the place of God's action, there is nothing of the victim spirituality in the Elohist. Suffering arises because one's loves are in conflict, not primarily because of external enemies.

7) God is revealed also in holy places: Bethel and Beer Sheva.

All of this implied teaching of the Elohist text affects readers all the more powerfully for not being thematized in the text. It is not at all a set of doctrines, but it does demand that theologians formulate and face up to several theological questions concerning, for example, the operation of divine providence within time, the role of personal relations in the experience of God, the relation between feeling and truth, the concept of holy places, and so forth.

With regard to direct demands on the reader, the Elohist's reciprocal covenant approach implies all the ethical traditions concerning justice. We also identified two more specific points of demand: paying tithes and caring for the temple, on the one hand, and confronting one's brother directly, on the other.

There are other texts which Grindel and others characterize as "probably" Elohist. This study has introduced a new criterion for source recognition, i.e., continuity in elemental meaning. The above study of Grindel's Elohist appears to confirm his conclusions. In some degree the same criterion confirms the "probably" Elohist texts! All of this is irrelevant to the present study. But, since it is such a disputed issue in current scholarly publication, Appendix B below presents these probable texts in the light of elemental meaning.[19]

5

The Priestly Narrative Writer

Of the four major sources in the Pentateuch, the text of the Priestly Writer is most easily discerned, and least disputed. Also the historical placing of this author in sixth century exile appears to be the object of wide consensus since Wellhausen. For the sake of simplicity, we shall consider only the basic narrative material, whose siglum has usually been Pg, leaving aside the supplemental materials which were added to the narrative, principally from Exodus 25 through to the end of Numbers.[1] The text of Pg may be read in part by considering successive pericopes indicated in this chapter, or else may be read continuously by following the chapters and verses indicated in Appendix C of this volume. The text proposed there is drawn from the minimal Pg presented by Karl Elliger in 1952, modified slightly by some of the source study of Brevard Childs for his Exodus commentary in 1974, and, finally, extended in agreement with Norbert Lohfink in his synthesis of research on the Priestly Writer in 1983.[2]

Moreover the foundational stance of expectancy of this author is most easily discerned, and forcefully present. Karl Elliger argued, on the grounds of simple length of treatment and wealth of detail, that the Priestly Writer focussed his interest on the instruction about liturgy from Ex 24 to Lev 9.[3] This focus may help to explain the relative unpopularity of the Priestly Writer among some earlier Protestant commentators, and at the same time show a particular need of this foundational stance in our own day.[4]

If one reads Pg straight through, it proves to be a coherent and refreshing text, without lacuna. It has been written in immediate dependence on a Yahwist/Elohist source, but it is fully intelligible within itself. Unlike the Elohist text, therefore, it must be understood as written originally, not as a commentary on the earlier sources, but rather as an alternative to them.

We shall begin our study of Pg by pointing out the obvious in that instruction about liturgy. Then we shall review the other major pericopes in Pg, showing how they corroborate and sharpen the stance of expectancy implicit in that text.

The Instruction About Liturgy

The Pg text may be read as follows: Ex 24:15b-18a; 25; 26; 27:1-19; 28:1-41; 29:1-37, 42b-46; 31:18; 35:1a, 4b-10, 20-29, (30-33); 36:2, (8-38 after 37:24); 37:(1-24); 38:(1-7, 9-20); 39:(1-31), 32, 43; 40:17, 33b, 34, (35); Lev 8:(1-10a, 12-36); 9:1-24.[5]

It is helpful at the outset to recall the comparable temple vision of Ezekiel 40-48. Ezekiel also wrote in exile, and at almost the same period as the Priestly Writer. His vision occurred on October 10, 573 B.C.E.[6] It provides a meticulously detailed account of a mandala-form restored temple and cult, and of the extension of the temple as a totally idealized geography of Israel.[7] This vision, like the Priestly Writer's instruction, is motivated primarily by faith in the eventual return of Yahweh to the midst of Israel, expressed through the image of the restoration of glory (Lev 9:23-24; Ez 43:1-12; 44:4-5). In Ezekiel it corresponds to an earlier vision of the departure of Glory (chs. 8-11), and it is the culmination of a gradual return to hope. The return to hope began for Ezekiel on Jan. 19, 586 B.C.E., when a refugee announced in Babylon that the city of Jerusalem had been annihilated (Ez 33:21-22). Prior to this time, Ezekiel had had no positive message for Israel (Ez 3:25-27; 14:1-11; 20:1-31). Only when Ezekiel has accepted the idea that it is all over, and that the possibility of restoration for political Israel has been eradicated, does he begin to believe in a return of glory. He recovers his ability to prophesy. The restoration is to be apocalyptic in nature, in that it is the construction of something new (though understood in traditional images), after the complete destruction of the old. Ezechiel's temple and country are theological, or spiritual, constructs. Their hope is for a depoliticized Judaism. They propose to get something exactly right in the area of imagination, in the realm of aesthetics, far removed from a real, physical temple, which would be so passionately demanded by Haggai 50 years later. When a real temple was actually built, however one reconstructs the dates and setting of that event, it was a moment of great pride and joy. But for some it was also a moment of deep disappointment (Ezra 3:12). Very likely among these latter were Jewish circles influenced by Ezechiel, who could never accept that building. Even the magnificent temple built by Herod the Great missed the point for some Jewish circles such as the Essenes, and for groups which eventually were defined as Christians, and who expected Jesus to build an eschatological temple (Mark 14:58 and parallels; Acts 7).[8] Thus Ezechiel began a tradition of other-worldly hope, based on a vision of an ideal temple, formative of a community united on religious grounds, whose demands lay in the aesthetic rather than political realm. It is this vision of temple which, in our era, provides one obstacle to the building of a physical Jewish temple in Jerusalem.

The Priestly Writer must be read against the background of this tradition. He does not present a vision or dream. But he does present a fantasy in which the remote figure of Moses is instructed about building a portable, reduced model of the destroyed Solomonic temple. His temple is not realistic, but its aesthetic commands the skill, not of the imagination alone, but also of the artisan. It speaks, not only to faith regarding the next life, but also directly to future donations of wealth and skill in this life.

The pericope is structured in two parts: God commands Moses on the mountain (Ex 24 to 29), and Moses has the people carry out the command (Ex 35 to Lev 9). Despite the myriad detail, there is a very simple line of thought, which is given at the beginning and end of the first part, when God explains that his purpose is that he might dwell among the people of Israel (25:8 and 29:43-46). The idea of dwelling is carried by a powerful image, which forms an inclusion around the pericope, and recurs as a unifying theme throughout. The image is the glory of God as a devouring fire. In the introductory scene, the glory/fire appears in the sight of the people, but up on the mountain top (24:16-17). Later, God says that Israel will be sanctified by His glory once the temple and the priesthood has been consecrated (29:43). After the tabernacle and all its surroundings have been completed, the glory again appears but now inside the tabernacle (40:34). Moses tells the people that the glory will appear to them once sacrifices have been offered (Lev 9:6). Finally, in the concluding scene, the glory does appear as a devouring fire before the tent of meeting, and the people fall on their faces (Lev 9:22-24). There is a condition for this coming about: Moses must do it all precisely according to the pattern revealed here on the mountain (25:9, and repeated in 25:40; 26:30; and 27:8).

The instruction itself is more for literary imagination than for an artisan's drawing board. For example the instruction regarding a lampstand (25:31-40), particularly when unaided by overhelpful translations from the Hebrew, is practically unintelligible. In fact it can be understood only as intended to be read aloud, and accompanied by gestures pointing to the actual menorah, or a replica of it. Secondly, the instruction regarding the tabernacle itself (26:1-8), while intelligible, is written in sounds so carefully pleasing to the ear and with so gentle a rhythm, that it seems to be intended for children.[9] Finally, the altar is to be built out of wood, so that it will be easy to carry. However that would rule out burning fires on it, although that is what is clearly intended (27:1-8). This, then, is a fanciful proposal. However, it is cast as a proposal to Moses, and was understood as referring to some actual tent which wandered with Israel of old, and with proportions reduced from the now remembered Solomonic temple. It evokes vanished realities, and provides a real directive for a future which could be obscurely imagined and hoped for.

It is helpful to note that this instruction replaces the ten commandments, the Book of the Covenant, and Ex 34, of Pg's Yahwist/Elohist source.[10] All the body of ethical and social law hitherto associated with the covenant is here suppressed. Of course the prophets had been foretelling for three centuries that Israel was doomed because it had consistently violated the covenant. And we will see in Gen 9 and 17 how the Priestly Writer creates a completely new idea around the word "covenant" in order to circumvent that whole unhappy discussion. Here he simply replaces all the laws, all thought of sin, with an instruction about liturgy.

Thus, the foundational stance of expectancy in this writer is very clear: God will reveal Himself and save Israel where a correct liturgy is celebrated.

What are the demands implied by this stance? The first demand is generosity, or even munificence, in providing luxurious materials for the liturgy (25:1-7; 35:20-29). Secondly, all aspects of the liturgy must be carried out precisely according to what was revealed to Moses on the mountain. There is an aspect of central authority in the mention of Moses here; but the mountain has to symbolize mystic depth in general, rather than an historic moment 800 years prior to the time of writing. The Priestly Writer surely did not want his readers to believe that what he himself had drawn out of memory and imagination had been historically revealed to Moses. The demand, then, is that, beyond artistic skill, the liturgy must be directed from a state of authentic prayer, or mystical experience, or vision. Thirdly, the best of contemporary technology and artistic skill must be employed. In Pg this is hinted at sporadically, but made explicit only concerning the ephod (28:6, 8, 28; 29:5). The Ps additions extend this idea throughout.

In the modern state, most of the laws concerning social justice and family life have been taken over, and explicitly secularized by governments. Religions remain directly responsible for worship. And yet, while the media spend millions, and employ the best intelligences of our era, in improving the quality of sound and vision, and in exploring all techniques of persuasion and communication, religions have fallen very far behind, to say the least. Whereas the Medieval cathedrals, or the Renaissance organs playing Bach, were at the vanguard of their contemporary technology in offering worship, and richly met the demands of this Speaker, one must ask whether our current buildings, ceremonies, and music are even mediocre. Those responsible for worship in our society may feel very uncomfortable while reading these Priestly texts.

The Proto-history

The Priestly Writer's reinterpretation of the proto-history may be read as follows: 1:1-31; 2:1-4a; 5:1-28, 30-32; 6:9-22; 7:6, 11, 13-16a, 17a, 18-21, 24; 8:1, 2a, 3b-5, 13a, 14-19; 9:1-17, 28-29; 10:1-4a, 5*-7, 20, 22-23, 31-32; 11:10-27, 31-32.

Pg begins with a happy God, who repeatedly finds His creation good, and even very good. The Yahwist story had also begun at the moment of creation (2:4b-5), but the first story was about the forming of man, the drama surrounding his mating, and the experience of sin in paradise. The Priestly Writer replaces this with a story about cosmic creation itself (1:1a and 2:4a). Humankind is presented as a culmination of creative effort, as can be seen from the special divine deliberation and from the length of this section (1:26-30), but still totally within a progressive cosmic order. Men and women are equal partners in procreation and in ruling other creatures, but the Priestly Writer prescinds entirely from all the drama between them, and simply eliminates the Yahwist fascination with sin, just as we saw him eliminate the laws in the Sinai pericope. Where the Yahwist searches for a mate for man and has Yahweh create woman, the Priestly Writer presents man and woman united and facing God as His image. Thus Pg, while turning the focus away from human drama, does so in a way which enhances the stature of humankind.

Finally, the climax of the creation story is God's rest (2:1-3). This is the universe in which we live: God is resting (Hebrew *shabat*) because all subsequent history will unfold the six-day creation, in its own count of days and months and years, within God's seventh day. Implied is the idea that we may join God in cosmic time and cosmic rest by observing our sabbath days.

In ch. 5 the basic story of humanity begins, and it is told as a rhythmic genealogy which can be described only as merry in form. It stretches to the end of the proto-history, though interrupted by the flood story. Once again Pg prescinds from human drama. All of his stories will be told without attending to the subjective dispositions of the human actors, but only to the purposes of God. The priestly narrative style, throughout, eliminates suspense as the form of story, replacing it with chiastic or palistrophic structure.[11] The genealogy form here is an extreme case.

There are gradations. For example, in retelling the Hagar story, Pg reduces that intense drama to something close to a genealogy, while retaining the element of conflict (Gen 16:1, 3, 15-16).

Pg simply drops the story of the tower of Babel, and in fact retains only three stories about sin: the flood story (Gen 6-9) which depicts cosmic corruption and its eradication; the so-called spy story (Num 13-14) which depicts denigration of the sacred and the death of denigrators; and the sin of Moses (Num 27) which depicts failure of hope on the part of civil leadership and its exclusion from the promised land.[12] All of these, and other, Priestly Narratives are not so much a review of past events as they are static models of world relation to God.[13]

The Priestly flood story is a good example of this tendency. It is not about a flood in which rivers overflow and the land is covered for some days and weeks, as in the Yahwist source. Rather it is about *mabbul,* the cosmic waters, which are released from chaos as creation is undone, and which engulf the earth for an entire year, rising over the very mountain tops.[14] Nor is it a story about a specific sin, or the sinfulness of the human heart, but rather about a general violence which is a corruption afflicting humans, animals, and the earth itself (6:11-13). In the Yahwist tale, the flood ends with Moses releasing birds from the ark window, and with God learning to accept the sinfulness of the human heart (8:21). In Pg, we must understand that "corruption" has been eradicated in nature, and the flood ends with a solemn enumeration of sonorous dates: 8:3b-5, 13a, 14. This dating system began with the formal seven days of creation, begins to control historic events in Gen 7:6 (when the flood is placed in the 600th year of Noah), and will continue to systematize the entire Priestly Narrative. It has the effect of setting up in one's mind a time of salvation, and it has been continued through history in Jewish communities right until now, as an alternative calendar within which God's realm and worship are defined.

In ch. 9 the post-flood era begins, and it is marked by a covenant. It must be noted that the covenant is not with humankind alone. Just as violence and corruption had marked the whole of creation in ch. 6, so the covenant here is with every living creature upon the earth, and with the earth itself. The Priestly form of covenant is not a contract which humans can undertake, but a state of the universe within which we can adore. This covenant is unilateral and unconditional. God binds Himself to provide order throughout nature and forever. The rainbow, a naturally joyous and beautiful phenomenon, is the sign of God's undertaking, a sign which God designates, not to remind us, but rather to remind Himself (9:14-15)!

What does the elemental meaning of these texts add to our understanding of the foundational stance of this Speaker? First, the whole realm of human interaction and sinfulness is removed from consideration. Second, God is revealed, not in social institutions and experiences, but in the order of nature. The Reader feels himself or herself directly in the force of God's presence and activity. No demands are made beyond an invitation to gratitude, joy, admiration, adoration. This clearly is fertile ground for the Priestly instruction concerning liturgy.

Genesis 17

The length, solemnity, meticulous palistrophic form, and untiring repetitions which characterize this chapter indicate the importance attached to it.[11] Circumcision, like the Passover in Ex 12, was a practise in Israel from time immemorial. However, in the exile it assumed greater religious significance, because it identified the Jews as separate from their captors. This instruction concerning circumcision, and the instruction regarding the Passover, are as close as Pg comes to writing laws. They both deal with matters liturgical. The body of Priestly law, later added as Supplements to Pg, will expand this aspect of the Priestly Writer's view.

The chapter contains two parts, each culminating in the circumcision. The first part ends with the directives to circumcise (vv. 10-14), and the second with the account of how those directives were carried out (vv. 23-27). Like the rainbow in ch. 9, circumcision is a sign to remind God of his covenant. The style of writing, with its minute precision in advancing from point to point, recalls the style of ch. 9. The covenant in both cases is characterized as eternal, and it is a divine undertaking which the human does not have to choose. We must feel grateful, and directly recipient of divine protection and favour when we perceive these signs of God's oath. There is the obligation to circumcise on the eighth day, but this is not an imposition of obligation so much as a recognition of the religious value of what was already practised by all. Moreover it officially extends the definition of Jewishness, the sphere of special divine providence, to include all those who are duly circumcised. Judaism becomes, not a racial or political society, but a liturgically determined religious society.

Once again, then, we see that the expectancy of the Priestly Speaker lies in the realm of correct liturgy.

The Plagues of Egypt

The Priestly account of the plagues may be read in the following text: Ex 7:1-13, 19-20a, 21b-22; 8:1-3, 11b-15; 9:8-12, 35b; 11:9-10.

In reading this pericope, it is important to follow Brevard Childs in attributing 11:9-10 to Pg, and in translating 7:3 correctly, as follows: "But I will harden Pharaoh's heart that I may increase my signs and wonders in the land of Egypt."[15] There results a pericope which has eliminated the Yahwist/ Elohist meditation on sin, with its mysterious hardening (literally "becoming heavy" *cabed*) of Pharaoh's heart, even after the signs are given. For Pg, God directly hardens (*kasheh*) Pharaoh's heart in order that His signs and wonders might be increased, i.e., his glory appear. The Priestly Writer does not depict the human drama, or the sinfulness of the human heart. He is focussed totally on what God does in saving the world.

In the first plague, for example, the source account has Pharaoh first refuse the request of Moses (7:13), and the plague/sign sent because of the refusal, with the hope of converting him (7:14-18). But the Priestly Writer has God command the plague pro-actively, without reference to Pharaoh (7:19-20a, 21b). Subsequently, he relates that the court magicians did the same trick so that Pharaoh's heart remained hardened "as Yahweh had said" (7:22).

In the second plague, Moses first tells Pharaoh (8:1-3, 11).

However Pg has eliminated all the attempts to convert Pharaoh which were related in the source account (8:8-10). Rather he goes directly on to relate the fact that Pharaoh would not listen (11b), that the plague took place and the magicians could not duplicate it (12-14), but that Pharaoh's heart was hardened and he would not listen "as the Lord had said" (15).

The third, and final, Priestly plague, in ch. 9, has precisely the same form.

The meaning given by the Priestly Writer to the crossing of the Reed Sea in ch. 14 will be identical, as can be seen in 14:4: "And I will harden Pharaoh's heart, and he will pursue them (i.e., Israel) and I will get glory over Pharaoh and all his host; and the Egyptians shall know that I am the Lord." The same point is repeated almost verbatim in 14:17-18.

For the Priestly Writer, unlike the Yahwist, Egypt has become an unreal power, and the Pharaoh with his magicians have become paper figures like the court in *Alice In Wonderland*. At the same time, Moses merely does what he is told to do, and is prominently accompanied by Aaron the priest in all his actions until Aaron's death in Num 20:28. The Speaker here does not expect God to be involved in any form of dialogue with Egypt or Moses. God is pro-active creator here, determining this manifestation of His glory, in all its details, and from beginning to end, without depending on human reactions. More precisely, God Himself provides the required human reaction, in hardening Pharaoh's heart.

What demands does such a stance make upon the reader? For a traditional answer we may turn to Ignatius Loyola's famous *Spiritual Exercises*. They begin with a "Principle and Foundation" whose first sentence reads: "Man was created to praise reverence and serve God our Lord, and by this means to save his soul."[16] Such an attitude responds to the demand of this Speaker. Moreover the totality of divine control elementally expressed throughout the Pg text suggests that no other created thing, or human institution, should have any meaning except insofar as they serve to express God's glory. The same Ignatian text develops precisely this idea, and concludes: "Our one desire and choice should be what is more conducive to the end for which we are created."

The So-Called "Spy Story"

In chapter 3 of this book, we studied the combined Yahwist/ Elohist "Spy Story" found roughly in Num 13-14. The Priestly Writer radically reinterpreted this story in support of his own vision of religious reality. His account of this story may be read as follows: Num 10:11-12; 13:1-3a, 17a*, 21, 25, 26a, 32; 14:1a, 2, 5-7, 10, 26-29*, 35-38. In reading these verses, one consistently mistranslated word must be corrected. The verb *twr* is translated "to spy," because in the interweaving of Pg with the Yahwist/Elohist source it came to parallel the word *raggel* which does mean "to spy." However the Hebrew word *twr* has no military connotation, and it means "to seek out something desirable," as merchants seek out excellent jewels. Where it occurs here it must be translated "to appraise": Num 13:2, 17, 21, 25, 32a, 32b; 14:6, 7, 36, 38.[17]

The story begins with an expedition, which brings back an "evil report" (literally a "calumny") about the holy land (13:32). The combined Yahwist/Elohist source had told of a military scouting expedition, which had cautiously gone North as far as Hebron, and hightailed it home with reports of giants there. Pg has turned this into a ritual survey lasting exactly 40 days, and traversing the whole land of Canaan right to the Northern-most border with Lebanon. The sacred land is presented as almost as a sacred person, since it is "calumniated" and de-picted as an evil god who devours his servants (13:32). As a result of this report, the people are not just discouraged, they are radically deceived, and they invoke a curse upon themselves (14:2). And the glory of Yahweh appears at the crucial moment (14:10). There follows the immediate annihilation of those who have blasphemed (14:26-29a, 35-37).

In this presentation, the Priestly Writer has taken a legend about an abortive military foray into Canaan and recreated it as a paradigm of punishment for blasphemy. The land is understood as sacred. To speak ill of it is punishable by death (14:37). All the people who lose faith and hope because of the blasphemy share in that sin, and perish as well. In all the Priestly Narrative, this is the only story in which human dis-positions are directly narrated, and in which sin typical of ordinary humans is narrated. It is specifically sin related directly to the sacred. It is, in fact, the precise opposite of what the Priestly Writer demands of the reader: adoration of God through correct liturgy. The land of Canaan is the place of correct liturgy, and it is to be respected almost as a sacred person.

Conclusion

The Priestly Writer has written a document of hope for the exiles.[18] With their political power gone, their community broken, their state of curse or blessing before God unclear, even the power of Yahweh vis-à-vis other gods in doubt, and the future dark, this Speaker, and this Voice, reinterpreted the Yahwist/Elohist history to present an institution of Israel which was conceivable, and which would restore Yahweh's presence and glory in their midst. It was Israel as a sacral community under the Aaronite priesthood. At the same time it was a very stern proclamation of Zionism, the need to revere, and ultimately to return to, the sacred land of Canaan.

The stance of expectancy of the Priestly Speaker, as expressed elementally in the text of Pg, is that God will not be revealed in social and political, or even family, institutions. He is revealed in the order of nature, not of society. He is discovered and adored as creator. His glory will appear to us when we spend the money and effort required to provide an aesthetic and correct liturgy.

6

Deuteronomy

This chapter is about a book rather than an author, because, on the one hand, the layers of authorship within this book are too disputed and entangled to yield a trustworthy author-defined unit of any length, and because, on the other hand, the successive authors at work in this text appear to have maintained a substantial identity both of style and of basic stance. We shall select chapters which illustrate this stance, with a view to examining that text of Deuteronomy which served Josiah's reform in 621 B.C.E., and which, subsequently, in extended form, undertook to provide theological understandings of disaster for the exiles after 587 B.C.E. In treating chs. 28 and 32, we shall see how the experience of exile caused the expectancy of the Dt Speaker to focus in a different manner.[1]

In reading Deuteronomy, one has the feeling that this is an entirely unique kind of text. Its Speaker appears not to be subliminal, but rather standing right there looking at you, giving himself the voice of Moses, who in turn claims divine authority. However, the fact is that the Speaker has taken the trouble to insert archival-type labels in Dt 1:1; 4:44; 28:69; and 33:1, interposing himself between the reader and Moses, creating an objectifying distance, causing us to overhear, rather than hear, this exhortation. Still the exhortation forms a dominant and overwhelming impression, and we feel commanded by a man, in the name of God, to get moving, to do something.

Most of the book is written in the 2nd person, addressed

directly to the reader(s). The "you" refers immediately to the hearers in Moab, but the reader is drawn to identify with those hearers. Early in the book, just as the body of the exhortation begins, the reader is direcly invited to do so: "Not with our forefathers did the Lord make this covenant, but with us, who are all of us here alive this day" (5:3). The "us" here denotes the first generations of Israelites born in the desert, but in literary effect all subsequent readers inevitably identify with them. And this literary effect is reinforced, and substantiated, as the text draws to a close in 29:14-15: "Nor is it with you only that I make this sworn covenant, but with him who is not here with us today...."

The book is a massive direct exhortation to you, the reader, to serve Yahweh exclusively and to observe specific laws. It must be contrasted with other biblical approaches. For example, prophetic literature is quite different from this. It constantly cites words of God, and contains some texts in which the speaker addresses the reader directly; but most of the prophetic texts think of Israel in the third person. Moreover, in reading most of the prophetic books one is constantly alerted to the fact that the real Speaker is an editor, because of the discontinuities between relatively short units, and the frequent shifts between prose and poetry.[2] Secondly, the Wisdom books have a different flavour. They are often addressed to the reader, "my son." However, the essence of this writing is that it is constructed cleverly with puzzles, as an invitation to think. The reader does not really feel commanded to do something. Rather one feels invited to figure out for oneself what would be the wise thing to do. Thirdly, the historical books have an entirely different flavour: if the reader is addressed at all, it is most indirectly. And, finally, the Psalms have an approach which is directly the reverse of Deuteronomy: the reader is invited to be the Speaker, and is invited to assume the attitudes of the Speaker, while the hearer (reader) is God.

Finally, it must be pointed out that in Deuteronomy the "you" switches randomly from singular to plural in exhortatory passages. This does not appear in modern English translations, but it is striking in the original Hebrew. The switching cannot be taken lightly as mere traces of originally different sources.[3]

It is intentional. The reader is made to feel that he or she is an individual, but also part of a community. One is exhorted to act both privately and corporately. And this complex awareness is supported by the verbs which carry most of the exhortation: to remember a past event (where remembering is a spoken, not only an internal act); to love and to fear Yahweh; to extirpate the Amorites, the Canaanites, etc.; and to keep the laws.[4] All of these activities must engage the individuals as individuals, but they also engage the community as a community.

Reader reactions to this Deuteronomic voice of God through Moses will be varied. And it is important to begin by noting and handling one's reaction. Certainly one is not expected to be calm about God's voice in this text. One might recall King Josiah tearing off his clothes when he heard it (2 Kings 22:11). God's involvement with human affairs is thought to be radical and violent in this text, as is made shockingly clear in the blessings and curses of ch. 28. The same feeling is to be found in many texts. For example, one might recall the detailed instruction in Dt 21:1-9 about the care to be taken to ward off divine curse on a city when a corpse is discovered. Or consider the need to forbid the reader to burn his son or daughter as an offering, or to practice necromancy (Dt 18:10-11). Moreover the message of this voice is radical. It demands passionately throughout the book that the reader adore Yahweh exclusively. It argues that Yahweh has not chosen you, the reader, above all other nations on grounds such as the magnitude of the nation of Israel, since Israel is small (Dt 7:7); or that you are blessed with prosperity because you are powerful (Dt 8:17); or that you possess the land because of your innocence or virtues, since you have only sins on your side (Dt 9:1-24). And since Yahweh alone has loved you and has made you great despite yourself, then you must ruthlessly root out all traces of love or connection with any other god. Specifically, you must annihilate the Canaanite population. (For example, cf. Dt 7:2 or 20:15-18.)

Now this radical speaker is God only indirectly. The author has interposed a male authority figure from the remote past. The speaker is Moses, not God. One might like the feeling which this evokes, identifying this voice with an agreeable archetype, a father figure, or a religious authority. One can imagine that the first readers of Deuteronomy easily heard the words as though from Josiah, speaking from "the chair of Moses." Conversely, one might tend to resent or reject this voice, identifying it with a paternalistic figure such as the figure of the negative male oppressor set loose in English letters by the novels of Virginia Woolf, or with some feared despot in one's personal past. One might simply tune this book out, or escape it by turning to purely historical thought about it, or by developing a deluded theory about Old Testament law and fear versus New Testament Jesus and love.

In feeling our way into the book of Deuteronomy, then, we must begin by paying close attention to this voice of Moses. One must note that the author, the unnamed Speaker, was the first to be concerned about it. First, he has placed Moses there only to make things easier. Three times he repeats that you, the people, could not bear to hear God directly, because God is a terrifying fire: 5:5, 24-27; 18:16. It was your wish that Moses should hear God directly, and then mediate between God and you. Second, he carefully begins his book by heralding Moses in a most attractive way: Dt 1:1-5 places him in a wondrous, remote time, surrounded by memories evoked by a series of sounding names from the past; v. 4 recalls the great victories of Moses over the fabulous Transjordanian kings Sihon and Og; and v. 5 evokes the thought that this preaching occurs on the eve of salvation. Third, the Speaker chooses to repeat this heralding after his first historical discussion, and before the exhortation begins, in 4:44-49. Fourth, the Speaker brings Moses closer to the reader by pointing out that he shares in the punishment which is the reader's lot (3:23-29). This impression was later reinforced by the addition of a Priestly account of the same story, in which Moses shares even in the sin (32:48-52). Fifth, the Speaker identifies for the reader more concretely the familiar authorities who bring Moses' words into their daily lives (thus shielding them from the fire of God, and possibly from the hot breath of the king, or from foreign conquerors). He does this by introducing the officials whom Moses appoints (1:9-18). This vignette does not belong here historically, as the tradition had it occur immediately after leaving Egypt, before arriving at Sinai-Horeb (Ex 18:13-

27); nor does it belong here logically, as the same information occurs in its proper place among the laws about Israel's authorities (Dt 16:18-20; 17:8-13). The Speaker wanted to put this here because the reader is to feel the Voice of the text as divine in origin, but spoken by the beloved Moses, and carried by familiar mediators.

Thus the Speaker has made this voice of exhortation as pleasant as possible. Finally, as indicated above, the harshness of command is subtly softened by casting the whole book as an archive, i.e., by the introduction of objectifying labels in 1:1; 4:44; 28:69; and 33:1. We are not too directly challenged, but rather we overhear this ancient speech. We feel close to Moses, but we also feel the interposed reflective presence of the Speaker.

A feeling of familiarity or intimacy is increased toward the end of our text, in respect to the mediation of the text itself: "For this commandment which I command you this day is not too hard for you, neither is it far off. It is not in heaven ... Neither is it beyond the sea ... But the word is very near you; it is in your mouth and in your heart, so that you can do it (Dt 30:11-14).

One more important aspect of mediation forms the voice of this Speaker. It has to do with the core of Deuteronomic reform, i.e., the centralization of cult in Jerusalem. Throughout the exhortation of chs. 5-11, Moses is depicted as arguing passionately for the exclusivity of divine worship: Yahweh alone. The whole force of this rhetoric climaxes in its first concrete applications in the 32 verses of ch. 12, which legislate about eliminating all cultic practices outside "the place which Yahweh will choose to make His name dwell there." There is one God, and He is to be worshiped in only one place. Nothing in ch. 12 makes this connection explicitly, but juxtaposing these materials in this order creates the inevitable rhetorical effect. The practice of restricting cult to Jerusalem is contrasted in ch. 12 with "this day", when we find "every man doing what is right in his own eyes" (12:8). This phrase, at some point at least, expressed the need of a central king. It was the phrase which was connected in Judges to the need of a central king. It was the phrase which was used systematically to express the moral chaos of the terrible tale in Judges 17-21, a state of the nation whose cause is specifically assigned to the fact that "there was no king in Israel" (Judges 17:6; 21:25; cf. also 18:1 and 19:1). In this view, the people are not to have direct access to divine revelation, not only because they are afraid of God as a burning fire, as we saw, but also because individualized religion leads to all forms of idolatry and moral chaos. The king can impose order, and assure authentic revelation. The mediatory role of a king in Jerusalem must have been very important during the time when this author wrote. In the exilic form of Deuteronomy, which is our canonical text, little or no importance is given to the king (Dt 17:14-20). Rather it is the law itself, in the place where Yahweh has set His name, which preserves Israel from individual madness and assures the valid relationship of the community with God.

Thus, the Speaker's voice in Deuteronomy is wild with the power of God, but beneficent, familiar, and orderly, because of its mediation through Moses, local authorities, and the book of Deuteronomy.

Deuteronomy 1-3

The first chapter begins with a list of sounding names of ancient places (vv. 1-2), setting an impressive scene for Moses, who is immediately portrayed as a military hero (v. 4). In v. 3, and again in v. 5, what comes first is that Moses spoke; that he spoke according to what Yahweh told him comes only second. If one contrasts Isaiah 1:1-2, or Jeremiah 1:1-4, or Ezechiel 1:1-3, the difference can be felt quite clearly. (In introductions to the Minor Prophets it is sharper still.) Isaiah, Jeremiah and Ezechiel begin with the human person, and have God second, but the human person is passive, and the speaking is done by God. In Dt the speaking itself is the speaking of Moses.

In 1:8 it is Moses who has set the land before them, and who tells them to conquer it, and in vv. 20-21 Moses sends them again. In v. 32 the people have sinned because, despite Moses' word, they have not trusted Yahweh. The people are depicted by Moses as having dealt directly with Moses, and only indirectly with God. The reader, too, feels this authoritative voice. Moses is presented in the 3rd person, but he then addresses us in the 1st person! It is Moses who appoints intermediary authorities in vv. 9-18, it is to Moses that the people respond in v. 41, and Moses who gives orders again in v. 43, orders which the people would not obey. Later Yahweh will not hearken to the people when they weep (v. 45).

The sin of the people is a lack of trust in God's power to protect them. The people want to send scouts to check God's words out in v. 20; the people don't trust the scouts whom Moses sent in v. 26; Moses condemns them for this in vv. 26-33; God does the same in vv. 34-36. In a subsequent story, the people have trust in themselves, rather than in God (vv. 41-46). These stories are drawn from Numbers 13-14, but the reader feels that it has all been rhetorically reshaped to make the Speaker's point, to carry the Speaker's tone of authority, regret, and condemnation.[5] The readers must feel the need to lower their own eyes and discover this weakness in their own lives. Moreover the smoothness and formulaic quality of the telling, and the pairing of two stories, one about cowardice and the other about brashness, give a tone closer to parable than to history. The lesson one learns is not just a feeling of guilt, but also a model for action which one can use either to direct one's future (reform similar to the reform of Josiah), or to explain one's past (reconciliation in exile). This Speaker, like the Yahwist, looks for God to intervene in history. We shall see that this Speaker, unlike the Yahwist, expects God to intervene directly in response to human virtue and vice, and to intervene by cursing and blessing within Israel rather than by cursing and blessing other nations.

Chs. 2-3 give an account of wondrous and effortless victories under the direction of God and Moses. Moses is the key actor, and he recounts the memory. These stories too are parables, and their theme is summed up in 2:7: "For the Lord your God has blessed you in all the work of your hands; He knows your going through this great wilderness; these forty years the Lord your God has been with you; you have lacked nothing." After ch. 1, the conclusion is inescapable that trust, courage, and unquestioning obedience to God through Moses bring great rewards. Finally, we learn that this state of economic blessing will continue under Yahweh, provided that this second generation obey Moses' successor Joshua in regard to the land of Israel which they are about to possess (3:21-22, 28).

The Speaker expects God to intervene by granting victory and prosperity if only the people will act aggressively in establishing themselves where God sends them, and in obeying the commands of the leader. In the stories, the commands were strategic instructions. Then, later, the same lesson will apply to the laws of Israel.

Reacting to this Speaker, a reader may tend to search his or her own psyche in order to identify some contemporary voice which urges on to victory through courageous action in obedience to some code of prescriptions. If one fails to find such a voice, if there is no King Josiah in one's world, no Charlemagne, no Richard III, no Luther, no great Pope, one might be tempted to turn to another biblical author! Time for dialectic ... Is my problem an objective lack of contemporary leadership? Or is it within myself? Do I fail to perceive any messengers of God who demand energetic and courageous action, simply because I am lazy and cowardly? Or because I too do not trust in God's help? Or do I have a theological doctrine opposed to possession of land and power? If so, is my opposition based on too narrow an interpretation of this teaching in Deuteronomy?[6]

Conversely, those who belong to the right wing of religion and politics should have a very positive feeling with regard to these three chapters. They should feel vindicated and energized. Their wealth is due to divine blessing, and their way lies clear to converting the lax doubters around them. However, they also must undertake a dialectic to be sure that their expectancy does not exclude the end of ch. 3, and that the instruction to attack has really come from God, through Moses and the ark.

Deuteronomy 7:1-24

This text is chosen because, at first reading, it seems direct and simple, and typical of deuteronomic exhortation, or "paraenesis" as the scholarly literature likes to call it; and also because it presents that facet of the Deuteronomic Speaker which repels many modern readers. This obstacle must be faced and overcome, before going any farther.

The first two verses set the problem. Many readers will instinctively take the side of the poor Hittites, Girgashites,

Amorites, Canaanites, Perizzites, Hivites, and Jebusites, who are to be shown no mercy but utterly annihilated. One will probably feel this way, even if one is aware that, at the time of writing, these nations were no longer a political reality in Israel. The modern reader may simply not want to belong to the "you" to whom this passage is addressed! Israel here is about to invade a settled country, a land which belongs to Yahweh and has been willed to Israel, but which nevertheless is settled by people who have offended no one, as far as the reader knows. We shall see that this difficulty arises now from the literal meaning of the text, but it did not arise from the "original" meaning intended by the author, whether he wrote in the 6th century, as seems most likely, or earlier during the reign of Josiah. It did not arise for the Israelites who lived at that time. However, it may be easier to come at this indirectly, by first reading vv. 17-24, and then returning.

Amid the flow of deuteronomic formulas in vv. 17-24, one feels a uniquely countrified and familiar quality of mind in the detail about hornets (v. 20), or in the argument that, if Israel has not succeeded in totally wiping out the Canaanites, it is only because God wanted some of them to remain for a while to help fight jungle animals (v. 22). This seems facile, very *ad hoc,* and transparent. One feels the special pressure toward proof and persuasion which moves the Speaker in this text.

The text is so violent, that I, at least, have a hard time concentrating on it, and registering it. Translators may sometimes tend to soften the language as best they can, but the verbs meaning "destroy" or "annihilate" pile up inexorably. Five different Hebrew verbs are used, all of which in this context signify genocide.[7]

However, the fact is that no command to extirpate the Canaanites occurs in this passage. Here the exhortation is not to do violence, but rather to be without fear. This command is repeated twice (vv. 18, 21). And the reason given is not that you have military power, but rather that God has power, and He is in your midst to help you (vv. 19-21). Moreover, He will use that power precisely against those whom you fear (v. 19b)!

The potential object of fear intended by the text are the various peoples of the Canaanites, whom Israel is expected to wipe out. During the reign of Hezekiah or Josiah, when the

Jerusalem king alone had an army in Israel, and was nego-
tiating with invading emperors at the head of their armies,
"fear" of local "nations" was simply not part of the picture.
And certainly for exiled Jews, there was no meaning at all to
the concept of fear in connection with these ancient inhabitants
of Canaan. The original readers of this chapter, whatever one's
precise theory about the date of its writing, could not have
avoided understanding this text as referring, not to settled
Canaanites, but to the powerful armies of Assyrians, or
Babylonians, or Egyptians. The reasons for fearing them were
very solid indeed. If one has ever had the occasion to see the
images of terror given to the idols of Assur, for example, one
may have a special sympathy with this text. Once this is
understood, a modern reader may no longer automatically
side with the so-called Hittites, Girgashites, and so forth!

One way of handling fear of invading armies was to capit-
ulate to the enemy, and specifically to adopt their religion,
placing their idols in the temple and in their homes. This
technique was most flagrantly adopted under Manasseh, but
we may presume that it was practised to some extent under
other kings.[8] The whole point of our passage, and of the
exhortation to fear not, and of recalling the ancient Girgashites
and so forth, is to be found in the concluding verses (25-26),
where the Israelites are instructed to burn and reject anything
connected with "their gods." *This is an exhortation, not to
violence, but to cultic purity.*

In this perspective, the earlier command to annihilate the
nations (v. 2), which is picked up in v. 17, was to be understood
rhetorically. Similarly, Dt 20 contains the laws for war, which
appear normal, or merciful, for that era. But then the special
case of the seven nations of Canaan is introduced as an
exception (vv. 15-18), and the rhetoric of the ban takes over.
The Israelites for whom Dt wrote simply could not carry that
command out in any real military activity, but only in their
own minds, or at most culturally and ritually. Current anti-
American rhetoric in parts of the Arabic world today is similar
in intent: citizens are urged to execrate the United States, in
order to stand tall, and to dare to be proud and loyal in the
face of unimaginable military power. A complex rhetorical
logic is employed by the Deuteronomist here: he has the reader

hear an ancient command to exercise limitless military power
with the help of Yahweh, not with the idea that the reader
should feel directly addressed by the command, but only to
recall the power of God in the past, as shown in Egypt (vv.
18-19), and also as shown in the land of Israel (vv. 20-24). The
reader recognizes that in fact the Hittites, Girgashites,
Amorites, Canaanites, Perizzites, Hivites, and Jebusites are no
longer political peoples, visible "nations," in Israel. That fact
itself serves as evidence of Yahweh's power, so that they might
be fearless enough to refuse cultural and religious capitulation
to the invading empires.

This handling of invaders might be termed a "sub-text" of
the literal meaning. However, the truth is that it was the prime
intent of the text for writer and original readers. The "nations"
were the Assyrians before Josiah, and the Babylonians,
Persians, and eventually Romans in successive stages of subsequent history.

We shall now return to consider briefly the first 16 verses of
Dt 7. If the Canaanites had disappeared politically, there
remained, nevertheless, a cultural presence of the seven indigenous "nations" in the form of various idolatrous practices,
which had been received when Yahwism had appeared to be
defeated by the Assyrians. These are addressed in vv. 3-5. The
command to extirpate the indigenous nations in vv. 1-2 (and
reiterated in v. 16), a command from a very remote past,
serves now only to motivate radical concern for exclusive
Yahwism. It establishes one basis for God's right to demand
exclusive worship. It has no further meaning.

The remaining verses, 6-15, are an extended plea to observe
the Law and the laws. As this plea is framed by vv. 1-5 and 16,
and as it is followed by vv. 17-26, all the laws may be intended;
but certainly the emphasis is on the first commandment.

After this relatively complex historical reconstruction of the
original meaning, it becomes possible correctly to read the
elemental meaning of the text, and to feel the stance of expectancy in the Speaker. It is the stance of one who is fighting
his/her own fear, and who feels that his/her society is losing
its way, falling apart, being assimilated, losing its soul.
Revelation/salvation is expected personally when one acknowledges Yahweh and His exclusive rights, and collectively when

one celebrates the covenant and carries out the laws. Revelation/salvation will be experienced as economic prosperity.

What are the immediate demands of this fundamental stance of expectancy? A way must be found to stand tall in the face of danger. One's central dignity, or personal worth, or collective pride, can be discovered and felt, even amid chaos or defeat, in the experience of one's unique relationship with God. Affirming this experience is the beginning of strength. In modern times one would tend to subjectify the uniqueness of the relationship. One might say something like this: "Fully conscious of my story and my being, I stand before God as a unique and special person." In Dt, on the other hand, the uniqueness of the relationship is objectified: the relationship is unique because it regards Yahweh alone, a God unique among the gods, who alone has chosen Israel and made it special. This the author affirms, and imposes with every resource of argument and rhetoric.

This fundamental stance of expectancy is familiar from Dt 1-3. God will be revealed in the prosperity of your family and of your nation, provided you cultivate radically your personal and collective basic religious commitment, and affirm this vigorously in your world. For Dt, of course, this basic commandment implies the other laws as well. Observing the laws would, in turn, normally tend to assure personal and national prosperity. The laws themselves will imply horizons of social justice which the reader can easily use to advantage in determining futher specific demands of this Speaker upon himself or herself. However, apart from a brief discussion of the laws in ch. 15, it will not be possible here to enter that complex field.[9]

Historically, this text must have recalled for the exiles the great "deuteronomic reform" under Josiah, in which the uniqueness of Yahweh was militarily imposed throughout Judah and even up into Benjamin, and institutionalized in the uniqueness of Jerusalem as the sole place for worship. At that time, fearlessness had been the order of the day, as the weakness of Assyria permitted Josiah to reassert military, political, and religious control.

The reader may cast about in his or her mind to identify some enemy of whom one is afraid, to whom one has capitulated. This text tells the reader that Yahweh is far more terrible and ruthless than any enemy, and Yahweh is on your side. The Deuteronomic Speaker writes from that stance, and demands the same energetic affirmation of Yahweh and of self on the part of the reader.

Deuteronomy 15:1-18

As half of the book Deuteronomy consists of laws, it would be unthinkable to overlook those texts completely when discussing the author's basic stance of expectancy, and the resulting demands upon the reader. The collection of ch. 15:1-18 has been selected because of its peculiar focus on the community of Israel.

In reading this text, one is struck by the contradiction between v. 4 which says "there will be no poor among you," and v. 11 which affirms that "the poor will never cease out of the land." Between the two verses one can feel the efforts of the legislator to make v. 4 true, turning the year of release into radical social concern. One perceives a delicate psychological sense in vv. 8-10 which oblige prosperous Israelites to "lend" to poor Israelites, even on the eve of the time for releasing debts. Moreover, the obligation extends even to the inner attitude of the prosperous, since they must feel no resentment of the poor (v. 10). Motives for this generosity are provided: Yahweh commands a year of release (v. 2); it is Yahweh who owns and gives the land to you in the first place (v. 4); Yahweh wants no one poor, and, therefore, those who are poor must be helped by a generous social order (vv. 4, 11); Moses commands this (v. 11); Yahweh will bless you with further prosperity if you are generous (vv. 4, 6, 10). The legislator notes a difference from the law of release, which is directly from Yahweh, and the law of generous social order, which is based on the experience of poverty in the promised land, deduced from Yahweh's intent in the light of this experience, and presented as a command from Moses (v. 11).

It is important to note that this generosity is not to be viewed as merely a virtue. It is a legal reform. It is part of a new economic law, integrating cult and community feeling, which begins in Dt 14:22 and extends to 16:17.[10] A new economic structure is envisaged, and imposed. It proposes a legal and religious foundation for what in our day has been termed a welfare state.

In vv. 12-18 the same social doctrine is evident in the command to provide generously for the slaves you release (vv. 13-14), and again the demand that there be no resentment connected with the release (v. 18). According to this law, the slave is not only to be freed, but also he must be given all he will need to provide for himself and his family in the future (15:14). This very concrete and personal responsibility can be felt more sharply if one notes how the laws here have been evolved from the earlier forms of this legislation, which we find in Ex 23:10-11 and Ex 21:2-11.

Motives for generosity are also provided in this section: since Yahweh has given you prosperity in Israel, so you should give your brother and sister prosperity (v. 14); since you were once a slave and Yahweh freed you, so you should do likewise (v. 15); Yahweh will bless you if you are generous in your heart (v. 18b); economic sense demands that you be not resentful (v. 18a).

Generosity is directed to fellow Israelites only (vv. 3, 12). This economic law is based on a religious grasp of society: the basic motive for generosity is Yahweh, and Yahweh has chosen the Israelites. It is up to other gods to take care of their own in their own manner.

What is the foundational stance of expectancy in the author of this legislation? Once again revelation/salvation is expected to occur in the ongoing personal and collective prosperity of Israel. This expectancy demands that the Israelites join Yahweh in bringing it about, acting generously as Yahweh acted generously, and providing social well-being as Yahweh has provided the land of Israel. The demand is not presented as an exhortation. It is a law. A reader who accepts the stance of the Speaker will feel obliged to share his or her own prosperity, a gift from God, with others whom God loves. Only in this way can one be sure that one's own blessings will continue. The reader will also feel obliged to be prosperous and concerned for general prosperity, in order to be like Yahweh! This basic stance can have many expressions. No doubt the most familiar of these is the so-called "Protestant ethic."

Deuteronomy 26:17-19

Before beginning the discussion of this text, we must first introduce one aspect of the rhetorical style of this author which has been recovered by historical research in this century.[11] It has been observed that the book of Deuteronomy as a whole is organized with the following logic:

1. Introduction (1:1-6)
2. History of relations between Yahweh and Israel (1:9-3:29)
3. History and fundamental obligation arising from it (5-11)
4. Specific stipulations arising from this obligation (12—26:16)
5. Blessings for observance and curses for failure to do so (28)
6. Ritual celebration (26:1-15; 27; parts of 29-33)

This logic, or literary form, has not only shaped the book as a whole, but also, within the book, it has repeatedly shaped the organization of materials in smaller unities, even in texts inserted in a post-exilic editing, such as ch. 4.[12] Such a literary form has a rhetorical force, and its power is felt, even if not easily identified, by readers today. Research has discovered that the form is derived from international treaties, legally binding documents between kings, which were made in the Ancient Near East.[13] The book of Deuteronomy, therefore, although it is not a treaty document of contract in itself, is entirely impregnated with the language, logic, and feel of contractual obligation. It is presented by Moses as an authoritative expression of God's rights to exclusive worship and to obedience to the laws, and also of Israel's (i.e., "your") reciprocal obligation to obey the laws, and to worship exclusively. At the same time, it is an expression of "your" corresponding rights to expect God's blessing, prosperity and long life in the land.

The weight of emphasis is overwhelmingly upon God's right and Israel's obligation, whereas the corresponding rights of Israel and obligation on God, which are expressed in terms of blessing and of promises, are more indirectly present. It is difficult to feel one's way into the exact tone of the legal and binding character of this language. However, we may note that ritual acts are imposed upon Israel (e.g., 26:1-15, or 31:24-29), but there is no ritual imposed upon God. There is no counterpart to Gen 15 in Deuteronomy. The fact is that the treaty form outlined above served precisely for treaties between great kings and their vassals, not for treaties between equals.

In this respect, 26:17-19 is a key text. It clearly refers to a ritual act, possibly a covenant cutting, in which, first, God affirms His rights and your obligations (v. 17), and then "you" answer by affirming your rights and God's obligations (vv. 18-19). The text should be translated somewhat as follows:

> 17) You have this day accepted (under oath) what Yahweh declared to you, namely that He would act as God for you, and that you should walk in His ways, observe His laws, precepts and commandments, and obey His voice.

> 18) And Yahweh has this day accepted (under oath) what you declared to Him, namely that you would act as His very own people as He had promised you, that you would observe all His precepts, 19) but that He must elevate you in praise, and in fame, and in honour, above all the peoples whom He has made, and that you would be a people apart with Yahweh, your God, as He had said.[14]

One must imagine a spokesperson for God on the one hand, and a representative of Israel on the other, addressing formal declarations to each other. The mutuality, almost equality, which one finds in this liturgy may be unique.[15] Certainly it is not easy to find a parallel. It gives to the contractual feel of the whole book of Deuteronomy an expectation that God will act as God on one hand, but that "you," on the other, must act within the same framework of obligation and responsibility as God does! Or, conversely, that "you" must keep the Law and the laws because you have freely bound yourself to do so, but in full consciousness that God has freely bound Himself in the self-same legal act to give you prosperity in the land.

Theologically, this asserts no more than the familiar doctrine that God is love, and can desire only what is good for us. But the communication of this doctrine in such a framework reveals a very special stance of expectation. It is not the stance of one who is helpless and in need, expecting salvation from the merciful and all-powerful God. Rather it is the stance of one who is a full citizen in a divine kingdom; one who is free and competent; one who expects prosperity, not as a gift, but as a right; one who stands tall in the world, and before God; one who takes responsibility with full confidence in the future. This is not pride in a negative sense. The stance is not based on one's virtue, or ability, as we saw earlier, but rather it is based on God's free choice to love Israel, to save Israel, to take this oath, to give "you" this feeling of power and confidence.

It is true that readers of Dt through the centuries were unaware of the treaty forms which underlie this text. And the text itself has been badly translated in many instances, because of the confusion which arises if the translator does not clearly advert to the reciprocal intent of the text. However the challenge of the Speaker here to meet God seriously, face to face, must be felt by any reader. Historical research has sharpened, not created, that challenge.

Dt 28

This chapter, important as it is in revealing the stance of the Speaker in Deuteronomy, does not invite much comment. It speaks eloquently for itself. The Speaker has not stretched himself to create imaginative blessings and curses, but rather has taken most of them from literary materials commonly found in the Ancient Near East.[16] In this text, it is clear that an exilic Deuteronomic author has rewritten parts of the curse section in order to make of it, not a threat of future punishment, but rather an explanation of the devastation which the exiles were then experiencing. For example, v. 47 shifts from the logic of saying "if" you do not keep the laws then a curse will come upon you, to the logic of saying that "because" you have already acted badly therefore you are in servitude. Moreover, some of the curses are so concretely related to the experience of the Babylonian exile, that one feels they are a description, rather than a threat.

We have here a different feel resulting from the same basic expectation that God will intervene, or be revealed, in the realm of personal, family, or national economic well-being. For this editor, God is not about to be revealed in blessings and curses, but rather is already revealed in curses. The suffering reveals the religious dimensions of past transgressions, the seriousness of sin, the reality of divine concern. Suffering is seen as divine punishment, and as an invitation to an examination of conscience, and eventually to conversion (30:1ff). The demands which result now from the Speaker's fundamental stance are different from what we have mentioned so far: the Speaker demands that we stand tall as before, but now we must stand tall enough to face our sinfulness, to contemplate our failure, our poverty, or sickness, or alienation, and take it as revelation: suffering reveals the power of our sinfulness before God who is all powerful and who has loved us. It is a reverse way of believing again in the goodness of God and the dignity of people. We shall meet this posture again when we read Dt 32.

If we read ch. 28 without the exilic overwriting, or without adverting to an exilic context, taking it all as straight blessings and curses, then the chapter fits perfectly into the treaty form outlined above. It is the clincher in motivating future observance of the Law and the laws. We must note that the form of reciprocal treaty is not fully applicable here, as one cannot imagine a fully reciprocal blessing/curse section directed at Yahweh, even though the treaty is reciprocal in other respects.

It is hard to take this chapter seriously today, and yet it is evident that the ancients, like primitives today, took blessings and curses very seriously indeed. For the Speaker, this is where divine revelation or salvation will occur. His expectancy is that God intervenes in human affairs in the realm of economic well-being. God intervened in the past to set up this kingdom of God, and the book of Deuteronomy is an instrument for celebrating what was done. In the future, God will intervene to bless the good (and that comes first), or to curse the sinners. It is a very simple universe!

Viewed theologically, this stance of expectancy immediately evokes the problem of evil and the discussion one finds in the book of Job. Deuteronomy explains evil as a curse visited on those who do not observe the obligations of this treaty. Such evil is from God! It is a positive thing in that it shows forth

God's truth or trustworthiness. It also shows by implication the importance He attaches to a human oath, and, by implication, His respect for humans.

In order to take this chapter seriously, it might help if one attempted to express the religious belief in more philosophical terms. A person, or a people, that retains its sense of worth and of being irrevocably related to Infinite Value, and that establishes a society of order and justice as an expression of this belief, will prosper and endure. But a person or a people that reduces itself to superficiality by understanding itself only in terms of meaningless drives and reactions and satisfactions, losing its sense of unique personal or collective worth and of irrevocable relatedness to Infinite Value, is certainly headed for disaster. The disaster will demonstrate in its own way the significance and power of what was lost. For example, if an individual loses love by choosing sex alone, or justice by choosing money alone, or self-esteem by choosing success alone, or if a people loses prestige by demanding victory alone, or prosperity by demanding legality alone, or security by demanding military power alone, then the inevitable result will show, in reverse, how deep and full human life was supposed to be. The disaster will reveal the real (i.e., spiritual) wellsprings of human prosperity.

Now this does not answer Job. Job focusses on evil in a case where one has loved God and kept the law. Deuteronomy simply does not address that question. One should not on that account reject Deuteronomy. Its truth is valid as far as it goes. To answer Job, insofar as this is possible, one would have to begin by laying a philosophic groundwork which is remote from the horizon of Deuteronomy. We shall not attempt that here. What is important for us is the realization that the Speaker we hear in Deuteronomy stands tall in expecting God's blessing in the future, and demands of the reader that we too stand tall, by relating to Yahweh alone with all our heart and mind, and by obeying His voice, with full confidence that only blessing lies ahead. Revelation and salvation will be experienced in the fulness of our life. This may be simplistic, but surely as a basic stance in life it is the only way to begin. A positive starting point allows of any number of sophisticated developments and distinctions and explanations. Conversely, a person who is unable to share this initial stance with the Speaker will have a hard time loving God, or being joyful in life, or hopeful about the future.

Dt 32:1-43

This final song of Moses, which focuses throughout on the supremacy and uniqueness of Yahweh, is so coherent with the teaching of the book of Deuteronomy, that one suspects it may have played some originating role in this tradition. Verses 1-25 recall God's care for Israel, Israel's sin of idolatry, and God's threat of curses; vv. 26-35 treat of the foolishness of the nations who underestimate Yahweh; 36-42 celebrate the exclusive worship of Yahweh. A Dt editor, who fashioned the unit 28:69—32:52, wrote an introduction to the song in 31:16-22.[17] He must have viewed this song as the concluding text in his material, a hymnic climax, since chs. 33-34 appear to be external to Dt thought, and placed there in order to link Dt back to the other Pentateuchal sources.

The date of the poem is hard to fix. Scholars have placed it in the fifth, seventh, eighth, ninth, and eleventh centuries, with consensus possibly heading toward the eleventh.[18] Source critics have held that its first insertion was into the Elohist source, before landing in the Dt context.

Also the structure is hard to determine. There are astoundingly few structural clues apart from the regularity of couplets. Patrick Skehan has argued on the basis of numbers to a scheme of three strophes consisting of 33 couplets each: vv. 1-14; 15-29; 30-43.[19] There may be some truth to that view, but it obscures what appears to be the most important division from the perspective of content, i.e., the entirely new direction of thought in v. 26. In its present context, this division is given added emphasis by the fact that the Dt editor who introduced this poem in 31:16-22 commented on it only up to v. 25.[20]

To discuss the structure of the poem in Dt we must begin then by recognizing a division after v. 25. One might further remark that the poem begins with an announcement of praise and a hymnic imperative plural in v. 3, and it ends with a hymn of praise introduced by an second hymnic imperative plural (v. 43). Surprisingly, it begins with praise of Yahweh,

but ends with praise of Israel.[21] Thirdly, vv. 3-5 seem to state
the problem to which the song is an answer: how should a just
God act in the face of ungrateful and perfidious creatures?
Fourthly, there are two speeches of Yahweh, one beginning in
v. 20, and a second in v. 37. Finally, it may be remarked that
although the language of the poem is not typically deuteronomic, still its themes fit the logic of covenant-treaty. On these
five bases, and on the basis of content, one may suggest the
following structure:

vv. 1-2	Prelude: Song addressed to the universe
vv. 3-6	Overture: Praise Yahweh, a Rock outraged
vv. 7-18	First Strophe: The Sacred History
	vv. 7-14 - God's choosing and care
	vv. 15-16 - Israel spoiled, careless
vv. 19-35	Second Strophe: Yahweh's speech
	vv. 19-25 - I will shatter the cosmos in punishing Israel
	vv. 26-35 - A limit: The Nations are foolish, vicious: I will avenge
vv. 36-42	Third Strophe: Yahweh's Taunt Song
	v. 36 - Intro: Israel restored
	vv. 37-38 - Idolatry mocked
	vv. 39-42 - Yahweh's boast
v. 43	Hymn of Praise

The song recognizes the reality of other gods, but celebrates
the power of Yahweh and His care for Israel, as a reason for
exclusive worship. It is addressed to the heavens and the earth,
and it invited the whole universe to praise Yahweh (v. 3), and
at the end it invites "the nations" to praise Israel (v. 43).

The probably exilic Dt editor who inserted this ancient song
into his work remained consistent with the Speaker of the
earlier Deuteronomy, since the song centered on the same
themes. In ch. 28, as we saw, this editor's additions introduced
a new slant from a later point in time, emphasizing the expe-

rience of exile and the mystery of sinfulness. This aspect is partially present in the poem in ch. 32, where the sins of Israel are not enumerated as future conditions of curse, but as already committed and recognized (vv. 15-18). Also partially present is the aspect of conversion, which the exilic editor introduced in ch. 30. At least in v. 36 it is indicated that Israel has hit bottom, and has been restored. What is totally new to the pre-exilic Dt text in ch. 32 is precisely the material in vv. 26-35, and the commands to praise in vv. 3 and 43. Thus the earlier schema (Yahweh's care and resulting rights, chs. 1-3; Yahweh's care and resulting demands, chs. 5-26; Yahweh's blessings/ curses, ch. 28) has been completed by this later editing as follows: the experience of evil (ch. 28: additions, and ch. 32:15-18); conversion (ch. 30, and ch. 32:36); Yahweh's vengeance on your enemies/ praise God and praise Israel (ch. 32:26—35: 3-4, 43). The Speaker has come full circle. He began by challenging the reader to *trust God* who is all powerful, and who has chosen "you" in preference to others; and now, after the experience of sin and punishment, he challenges the reader to *praise God* who punishes your enemies.

This Speaker has a single fundamental stance of expectancy, but now his horizon is broader, as he stands outside Israel somehow, and tells the universe or the nations to praise. On its own, the song promises nothing about a future economic restoration of family and nation, but within the continuity of the book all of that remains within the expectancy of the Speaker. Within the song itself, the Speaker thinks only of an end to punishment, and a vindication of Yahweh. It demands that the reader stand taller than ever, in the face of adversity.

It is Israel that is to be praised when Yahweh restores it (v. 43). This will take place only after Israel has become reduced to nothing (v. 36). A similar conviction appears to have played an important role in shaping the book of Ezechiel, who refused all prophecy until news of Jerusalem's final destruction is brought to him (Ez 33:21-22). The collections of prophecy in Ezechiel are arranged in a dated sequence, but appear to be grouped around this turning point. In Dt 32:36, the idea of a foregoing complete annihilation serves to enhance the role of God: nothing comes of oneself, but everything will certainly come from Yahweh, after one's own efforts have come to a final end. This is the nub of apocalyptic thinking.

The intervening experience of evil determines the tone of everything. The Speaker is not addressing a warning to a victorious empire. Rather it is addressing encouragement to a diaspora. In this, the Speaker's, but especially the reader's, stance has been altered. Where before the demand was that one should stand tall, and remain observant of the law, now the message is that one should regain lost courage, and have confidence that in the end it may be possible to reestablish the holy community. The feelings evoked in the reader are no longer the fierce idealism of early adolescence, but rather the realistic determination of an adult. The reader begins, not as an innocent person choosing between good and evil, but rather as a sinner required to reestablish his or her self-esteem, culture, and civilization, with the help of God who remains all-powerful, and who cares passionately about His reputation.

Conclusion

The Deuteronomic Speaker possesses a unique Voice. We overhear God and Moses challenging us directly, demanding action, addressing us as free covenanters with God, who must stand tall and act courageously, establishing justice and prosperity for our families and nations.

This Speaker expects God to be revealed in economic welfare (blessing). Such a stance might imply a materialistic philosophy, since revelation and salvation are to consist of material well-being. However, the Speaker also expects God to be revealed in suffering (curse). In this contradiction we are forced to redefine our understanding of the expectancy. The realm of revelation is the welfare or suffering of a people who stands facing Yahweh in a unique contractual relationship.[22] The demand for exclusive worship of Yahweh does not result from the fundamental stance of expectancy, but rather constitutes it.

Because this Speaker allows us to overhear precisely a law-giving, it is not easy to distinguish between the fundamental expectancy and the demands (laws) which would result from it. Certainly the Speaker demands of the reader that we be free: free of constraints from other gods, and standing tall before other nations (Dt 7), and dealing with Yahweh face to face (Dt 26:17-19). It demands that we be ready for energetic and aggressive action in following God's will, confident in God's help (Dt 1-3). It demands that we be prosperous, and judge of our spiritual health by its results in the economic sphere (Dt 28). It demands that we practice the laws of the land in order to assure social order, and thus assure this prosperity (Dt 12-26). It demands that we institute a generous social welfare within our community (Dt 15).

The Dt Speaker fills a gap left by the Yahwist Speaker. The Yahwist expects God, an absent landlord, to bring blessing and curses to other nations, in order to give political protection to Israel. For the Yahwist, God is revealed only at the international political level, leaving the people free to run their ethical, social, and economic lives as they please, and responsible for their own prosperity (i.e., blessing). The Dt Speaker on the other hand expects God to bring blessing and curses on Israel itself. In this view, God is revealed specifically at the ethical, social, and economic level.

This voice is heard, and this stance felt, in every part of the book. A reader of Deuteronomy will be very uncomfortable indeed with this Speaker, unless he or she has assumed a responsible and active role in building society. The book of Deuteronomy is pivotal in biblical thought, since it serves both as the conclusion to the Pentateuch, and as the introduction to the Deuteronomistic History. The Voice of this Speaker must be thought to have prevailed at times in the painful growth toward social consciousness in Western Society. If I may borrow a sentence from a lesser context: "The writer printed the person he is on every page of his books, and we can read him into our own lives, if we want, in the privacy of libraries."[23]

7

Original Meaning and Contemporary Theology

Summary and Restatement of the Problem

This book has been an exercise in reinventing the wheel. Throughout the past two millennia and more, believing Jews and Christians have found no difficulty in nourishing their spiritual vitality by reading the Bible. Recently, among religious Jews and Christians who try to unite their faith with contemporary culture, the Bible appears to be increasingly less useful for this purpose. And this is true, despite the fact that two centuries of outstanding biblical scholarship have come to fruition in filling our library shelves with excellent critical commentaries. Ironically, the trouble seems to lie in the precise historical objectification of biblical meaning made possible by that scholarship, and made available in those commentaries. The wheel needs to be reinvented. A method of reading needs to be described which is intelligible and respectable within the terms of contemporary culture, and yet which makes available once again the vitality we know the Bible contains.

The proposal of chapters 1 and 2 of this book is that we recognize formally and effectively that the Bible is literary in nature, and must not be read as though it were philosophy, or science, or history in a modern sense. It must be read for literary truth. A contemporary reading of ancient literature requires, however, the use of historical-critical methodology, as that is the only means we have of getting beyond our own ideas to really read the intent of a text from another era.[1]

The argument is made that the truth of literature, i.e., the form of affirmation about reality found in literature, the lasting normative force of literature, is not the truth of doctrines. Rather it is a subjective sort of truth. It is the author's self-affirmation, the implicit affirmation of a foundational stance. This essential affirmation is not any situation-specific "message" or "kerygma" of the historical author, even though many literary texts do contain such meanings; but rather it is an implied teaching which is affirmed in the style, in the choice of themes, in the omissions, and in the horizons of the Speaker. Literary truth is expressed as elemental meaning in the text.

How does this relate to religion? The foundational stance of biblical authors includes expectancy about God, revelation, salvation. The reader is directly challenged by the implied foundational stance of the author: challenged to share its religious implications more actively, or challenged to convert and learn them. The reader may be all the more powerfully moved by this elemental meaning the less he or she directly adverts to it.

How does one set about adverting to and describing this elemental meaning of texts? We have proposed a dialectical method, beginning with feelings, on the grounds that our intellectual habits may lead us too narrowly and easily to the articulated meanings of text, whereas our feelings lead us to the challenge of the author whose authorial stance is elementally expressed in the text. We ask the question: in what realm of human meaning or activity does this text expect meaning, revelation, salvation to occur? In war? In family life? In obeying the law? In prayer? and so forth. This line of questioning proved to be a useful tool. There may well be other even more useful lines of question.

Chapters 3 to 6 applied this approach to major texts in the Pentateuch, and found that the realms addressed by elemental meaning in these texts were diverse. In the Yahwist text, God is shown revealing Himself by specific interventions in the past, and His trace is to be sought in the larger political and cultural realities which determine our lives. For the Elohist Speaker, God is revealed precisely where the heart is torn in our deepest inter-personal relationships, particularly in family relationships. The elemental meaning of the Deuteronomist's texts would have God revealed as blessing in the socio-economic prosperity of our lives, or as curse in the decline of our fortunes. For the Priestly Writer, God is in complete command of all that happens, and all of life is sacred, but God's glory appears only in the sacred land, and in the aesthetic experience of great liturgy.

As Torah, the Pentateuch has challenged readers through millennia to respond to God through their actions in each of these realms. Reading the Yahwist, we have been drawn to recover our authentic selves by accepting the constraints constituted by our historical origins, and by energetically fighting evil in the pursuit of prosperity. Reading the Elohist, we have learned to trust in God's direct care during storms of personal grief, provided we do not back away from family strife when the heart is torn. From the Deuteronomist, we have learned that we should be courageous and enterprising in socially responsible action, and civil obedience. From the Priestly Writer, we know that we should be munificent and aesthetically exigent in providing for the worship of God.

The task for biblical scholars, then, is clear. First we must continue the work of recovering original meanings, using contemporary critical methods. This constitutes real knowledge of the text, and is the necessary condition for any honest interpretation. Second, however, we must specifically address the question of original elemental meanings, and attempt to describe the foundational expectancies of biblical Speakers. The results of such study will be helpful both to theologians and to homilists. It will lead these beyond discussion of ancient history, and beyond the consideration of ancient ideas or teachings which usually were intended only for specific past situations. In other words, it will go beyond what is after all merely the scholarly preparation for understanding ancient text. It will allow theologians and homilists to focus their attention upon the passionate faith of biblical authors, and invite them to deal directly with normative elemental expressions of Jewish and Christian spirituality.

Scripture and Theology

What is the precise relation between the original meanings of Scripture and the truths of Theology as a formal discipline? In a discussion of this subject, the point of departure is crucial. The term "Scripture," on the one hand, designates a complex reality surrounded by a vast sea of theoretical discussion, and the term "Theology" on the other designates an even wider ocean of ideas and realities. As a result, discussing the relation of one to the other is like discussing the relation between plants and humans. Where does one begin?

If one begins with a traditional doctrine, such as that of divine inspiration or the inerrancy of Scripture, (doctrines which labour under inadequately analysed theories of knowledge), then one finds oneself in a never ending and sterile posture of defence. One tends to explain Scripture away, rather than focus on its value. There are too many statements in the Bible which are not true, in the simplistic sense of that word. Generally one ends up with somewhat strained positions about the "real" meaning of Scripture, positions which seem to answer objections, but which leave one inclined to just quietly do something better than read the actual Bible.

The most massive attempt to bridge from inerrant Scripture to true Theology was the patristic and medieval technique of formulating allegorical meanings. This technique may elicit aesthetic admiration, but it seems strained and fanciful to the modern reader. Certainly it requires a posture of defence!

A similar technique is often used today, not so much to save inerrancy as to make up for the apparent doctrinal poverty of Old Testament texts. I am referring to attempts to find a "spiritual sense" in biblical texts, according to which the divine author has put meanings in the text beyond what the human author could have intended, meanings which emerge in a subsequent era, as for example making "the Servant Songs" of Second Isaiah refer directly to Jesus Christ. This not only demands some suspension of disbelief, but also tends to overlook the real meaning of the text in favour of something very weak indeed. (For knowledge of Jesus Christ, it would ask Second Isaiah to compete with the Gospels!). More importantly, such approaches forget that Scripture is literature.

A more sophisticated technique for covering over biblical deficiency with regard to doctrines is to bury the meaning of individual sentences in the overall meaning of whole books, or in the meaning of the Bible as a whole. This can be creative and valuable, but it frequently overlooks the real power we feel in those offending texts.[2] Such discussions wrongfully imply that biblical (divine) teaching must be defended within a conceptual polarity between propositional error and propositional truth. Often they head toward a solution in which another kind of truth, never defined, is vaguely envisaged.[3]

Our own approach will employ an empirical strategy. For the first term of the relation between Scripture and Theology, namely "Scripture," we shall draw upon the original meanings of scriptural texts as experienced by the reader and defined in preceding chapters, i.e., the foundational stances of expectancy concerning revelation and salvation affirmed as elemental meaning by biblical Speakers. For the second term, namely "Theology," we shall draw on the work of Bernard Lonergan who, in his first book, enables the reader to experience and understand his or her own thought processes, and who then, in a second book, applies this empirical self-awareness to a formal definition of the tasks of theology.[4]

For Lonergan, Theology must mediate between a given "cultural matrix and the significance and role of religion in that matrix."[5] The contemporary cultural matrix he deals with is Western culture, which has learned through its history and literature to approach reality, not only with common sense, but also with theoretically precise language, and by the progressively improved understanding of data (both subjective and objective) made possible by scientific methods employed variously by a large number of communicating inquirers.

Theology itself comprises a number of diverse operations, all of them essential. First there is the task of recovering the truth contained in our tradition. This is done through four operations: *research,* which establishes the texts and facts; *interpretation,* which goes back to original meanings in the texts; *history,* which imagines what was going on behind those texts; and *dialectic,* which separates authentic from inauthentic knowledge provided by the research, interpretation, and history surrounding a given question. Second, there is the task of formulating new theological knowledge as required by contemporary culture. This is achieved through a second group of four operations: *foundations,* which define the method of study, the categories of truth, the canons of relevance, and the horizon of inquiry, which govern the first four operations enumerated above, as well as the final three operations we shall now enumerate; *doctrines,* which select and accurately formulate those truths which are theologically relevant; *systematics,* which create a theoretical framework within which doctrines can be accurately conceived and related one to another; and finally *communications* in which the sophisticated product of the previous seven operations is now translated into stories, essays, institutions, actions, images, music, and so forth, within the artistic and common sense realms of various cultures and societies. All of this is Theology. All of these are operations of the human subject. All of these are carried on with self-correcting critical awareness, not by any one individual, but by a community of communicating specialists.

This description of Theology does not mention Scripture, because Scripture is a source for Theology, not an operation of the theologian. Hence the enumeration of operations will not include it. Where does Scripture fit?

First, it is clear that Scripture will fit in the first group of four operations dealing with the task of recovering the truths of our tradition. In fact if we recall applications of *research, interpretation,* and *history,* the first instances which leap to mind are their extensive uses in scriptural studies. In these three operations contemporary foundational norms have governed Scripture rather than the reverse, because contemporary culture has been more demanding than Scripture was about establishing original texts and meanings, and more sophisticated in reconstructing history. When we come to the fourth operation, *dialectic,* however, the authority of Scripture governs the theologian, even though contemporary critical categories control the theologian's use of Scripture. We shall return to dialectic in a moment.

With regard to the second group of operations, Scripture seems at first to have no place, since these deal with contemporary formulation. Still many verbal *communications* about Theology will tend to formulate propositions as far as possible in biblical language, and will cite the Bible as an authority for its positions. We have seen that this use of the Bible frequently seems abusive to scholars, in that the original meaning is often overlooked in such citation. Biblical phrases are used (or abused), not for what they really mean in themselves, but only because they will sound familiar to readers who go to church, and because they smack of ancient truth and authority. *Communications* are not involved in teaching biblical truth, however. They are involved in teaching theological truth, i.e., a product of research, interpretation, history, foundations, doctrines, and systematics, in which the Bible has played a key but limited role. Using biblical words in *communications* is no more, and no less, abusive than using wooden beams to decorate a modern ceiling. The beams appear to, but do not in fact, support the structure. The beams are there to suggest the nature of structure in general, and to impart a familiar atmosphere and warmth, a warmth hard to define but felt archetypically in images drawn anywhere from King Arthur's great hall to Santa's workshop.

Similarly those who write *systematics* and *doctrines,* and who do not take care to distinguish the operations of historical inquiry, for example, from those of systematic thinking, may well cite Scripture in their footnotes in ways which annoy Scripture scholars, exhaust and bore other theologians, and discredit Theology as a critical enterprise.[6] As clarity in theological method grows, it is to be hoped that these confusions will diminish.

But it is in the first operation within this group, i.e., *foundations,* that Scripture plays its chief role, and it is as foundation that Scripture rules Theology. It is true that foundations will decide about contemporary categories and legitimate processes of proof, independently of Scripture. However, Theology begins as "faith in search of understanding," and faith is primarily a stance of openness to the transcendent, implying trust and love. Faith, in this sense, is a gift of God, and is habitual, and foundational. The faith of a believer may not operate foundationally in all aspects of thinking and deciding. We may well prescind from faith, for example, while shopping for bargains, or while working on crossword puzzles. However, for theologians, faith must be actively foundational in their Theology. Jewish and Christian theologians learn this faith from their parents and teachers, no doubt; but eventually it must come to them through Scripture. Not just any faith is normative. The faith of the biblical Speakers is the normative faith of Jewish and Christian Theology. And it cannot be the faith of selected biblical Speakers, a canon chosen within the canon, but rather the faith of all biblical Speakers. This will be a minimal foundation for Jewish Theology, or for Christian Theology. We are not speaking here of a set of doctrines of the faith, but rather of the original meaning of Speakers, their foundational expectancy, their horizons for meaning and their realms of salvation, their Voices to which we all react instinctively, and which make such demands on us, demands which human growth alone, often painful and life-long growth, will enable us to meet. Not everyone is called to write authentic new theological knowledge, because it is not given to everyone to share the totality of this biblical faith.[7]

This may sound pretty oppressive, particularly when one thinks about certain biblical texts which one does not like at all. It is here that we must return to the final operation of the first group, i.e., *dialectic*. It will be best to treat this in a concrete example.

The glossator's treatment of the divine name in Ex 3:14 offers the advantage that we have already discussed this text at some length in the opening sections of this book. To focus on *dialectic* with this text, we shall first have to circle the subject, showing how the operations of *interpretation*, and *history* have functioned in our earlier study of the text, and then discuss the move to *doctrines*.

We concluded that Ex 3:14 taught that Yahweh was radically free in bringing Israel out of Egypt. In saying this, we reduced the text from a foundational expectancy to a proposition. There was also the more obvious proposition, namely that the etymology of "Yahweh" was to be explained on the basis of the Hebrew root *HYH*, corresponding partially to the English verb "to be." However, our reduction did not entirely block out the Voice of the Speaker, because in pursuing our *interpretation* we were able to point out the author's concern: namely, not just to *name* God, but rather to *describe the divine nature* as acting freely, independently of Israel's virtue, or liturgy, or suffering. Moreover, adding *history* to interpretation, we pointed out that the author's concern may have arisen when Samaria fell, i.e., in a context where God did *not* intervene to save Israel; and we pointed out that this concern belongs in a stream of discussions which would eventually terminate in the doctrine of "grace." All of this was by no means a paraphrase of Ex 3:14. Rather it was a series of hypotheses and observations and probabilities about the *history* of what was going forward behind the text, to be placed in the service of interpreting the original elemental meaning of the text.

What then are the *doctrines* of the text? One is a philological doctrine about the etymology of "Yahweh." This doctrine would not be accepted by any expert in comparative philology, who might point out that the glossator's account overlooks the vowels, and specifically the "hiphilic" form of the name as it is written in Hebrew. Moreover, he does not support his statement through reference to other Semitic languages. Nor does he provide footnotes about the form of the name as it occurs in "halleluya," for example: is the "ya" a familiar shortening of the name, or is it the original form of the name? Now the author, in a sense, knew more about classical Hebrew than does any modern philologist. But his foundations about philological method were entirely different. The modern philologist would enter into dialectic with the glossator, and reject him, judging him to be serious about religion but not serious about philology as a modern understands it. That would be legitimate. And the philologist would not have to reject the Judeo-Christian tradition of religious belief, because the foundations rejected here are foundations concerning categories and methods, not concerning revelation and salvation.

How about the "*doctrine*" of divine freedom in choosing Israel? We must first note that the affirmation of Ex 3:14 is *not* formulated as a doctrine about freedom. It might serve as a basis for diverse doctrinal complexes. It might be communicated in a philosophical mode as a formal doctrine about the essence of God, i.e., about the manner of all divine choosing. In that case, apophatic theology would protest that we know nothing of God's interior; and scholastic philosophy would protest that since God is totally in act, doctrines which suggest deliberation in divine choosing (any before and after in God) are anthropomorphic distortions. A quite different doctrinal complex would be invoked if one were to argue that the affirmation of Ex 3:14 should be understood as an historically limited, theologico-political directive concerning the method of decision appropriate only to Moses and to the kings of Israel: you kings of Israel must exercise power without hesitation, since your power is a free gift from Yahweh, who is whenever He is, and needs no justification. Such a doctrine would imply corollaries about the power of Yahweh over the gods of other nations. Certainly theologians in the royal court of Egypt, and other surrounding kingdoms, would have disagreed. A third manner of communicating the same affirmation could be a psychological and a historical doctrine such as the following: all personal power is the gift of God, and can be withdrawn in an instant; therefore be humble (recognizing the source of all greatness), and attentive to changes in the divine will. This doctrine would imply a complex system of corollaries concerning the definitions of grace, of humility, of the existence and knowability of a changing divine will. One may or may not be prepared to accept every part of that system. Or again the glossator's teaching might be communicated in a more sociological type of doctrine such as this: when groups of people acquire a realization of corporate power, they may project a myth of unquestioned divine election by a God who favours whomsoever He favours. The effect of this myth might be both to counter feelings of guilt about the exercise of power, and also to maintain and enhance the feeling of power. Such a sociologically formulated doctrine also implies a system of definitions and beliefs about group communication, about the role of myths in society and the manner of their origin, about the instinctive aims of groups, and so forth. Now all of these possible doctrines and their corollaries pertain to belief, and arise on the basis of various types of faith. They all shed light on Ex 3:14, at least by providing various models for possible implications of the text. It is not at all clear that the glossator would agree to any one of them. Certainly his text does not express any one of them! It follows that a contemporary theologian is not bound by any doctrines of Scripture either to accept or reject any one of them. If a contemporary reader is repelled by the Speaker in Ex 3:14, it might just be because he or she wrongly attributed to the Speaker one or other of these doctrines.

However, a contemporary reader may have worked hard enough at interpretaion to realize that all such doctrines are pseudo-problems, and yet still be unable to accept this Speaker. He or she is repelled specifically by the foundational expectancy of the Speaker. It is here that *dialectic* must enter the picture. What precise aspect of foundational expectancy of the glossator is offensive to me? That is a hard question. There is a still harder one: what aspect of my own foundational expectancy is offended?

One might imagine a dialectic proceeding as follows: the Speaker offends me by seeking for an explanation, a kind of formulation or law, expressive of divine favour. And does not find it! Am I offended by the seeking, or by the not finding? Am I afraid that God is not there at all, so that I find intolerable the Speaker's uncertainty while inquiring into limits of divine presence and care? It can't be that, because the Speaker's inquiry has in fact a reassuring feel: the glossator is assured of God's presence and care, and his concern is only to explain God's non-intervention in a specific case, for, otherwise, he would not have written a gloss to Ex 3; rather he would have deleted that chapter. Well then, maybe I am offended at the Speaker's avoiding a real divine name, a descriptive formulation or explanation or law of grace? If so, what precisely in my foundational expectancy is offended? Am I convinced that the name Jesus, "Saviour," which does imply a law of Grace, contradicts and condemns this glossator's nonsense? Or, conversely, am I distrustful of God's radical goodness so that I can't endure the refusal of formulas which would force God to take care of me? Do I want to control God through guilt? Such *dialectic* with the Speaker in Ex 3:14 could, obviously, take many other directions and forms, and evolve to a great subtlety. The point is to understand how the foundations of the Speaker challenge my foundations, demanding some form of conversion or growth on my part.

In dealing with dialectic, Lonergan treats of intellectual,

moral, and religious conversions, and presents the dialectician as accepting some positions and rejecting others on the basis of evidence of these conversions in the authors who propose the positions. The biblical authors have been included in the canon precisely because the Jewish and Christian communities recognized in them that form of conversion which springs from the presence of the Holy Spirit in their souls on the one hand, and the effective operation of that divine foundation in their knowing and writing on the other. Contemporary dialectic may feel free to reject their doctrines, or, better, free to reject communication of their thought in the form of doctrines, on the grounds that these doctrines were based on incomplete data, or inadequate theory. But it is not free to reject their "conversion," their foundational expectancy as expressed as elemental meaning within the original meaning of the text, unless it is prepared to reject the Judeo-Christian tradition. Contemporary dialectic is an occasion for discovering the positions and stances in oneself which cannot agree with those of the biblical Speakers, and for opening oneself to grace through prayer.

Conclusion

This chapter has presented, not a simple, but rather a complex set of relations between the elemental meanings of Scripture on the one hand, and the eight operations of Theology on the other. However, it concluded with a lengthy discussion of dialectic, as applied to Ex 4:14, because the most common misunderstandings about the relation between Scripture and Theology occur precisely in confusing the operation of dialectic with that of doctrines.

A theologian must first come to the end of a dialectic process with the glossator in Ex 3:14, possibly experiencing a conversion in his foundational expectancy about revelation and salvation, before formulating doctrines about grace. The theologian, on the basis of a converted foundation, is prepared to argue about the doctrines which might be communicated on the basis of Ex 3:14. The theologian's arguments will be drawn from philosophy, psychology, sociology, and so forth, as indicated in the foregoing discussion, but they will conclude to authentic positions within the Jewish and Christian traditions only insofar as they are, not only scientifically valid within the canons of a given culture, but also authentically founded on conversion.

To present it schematically, the elemental meanings of Scripture lead to conversions. Conversions have implications for one's style of life, and for one's beliefs. A style of life may lead a community to ethical practices which must be questioned in the light of ethical clarification from other sources. Similarly, beliefs can be formulated as truths, and these occasion questions in the light of other truths, theoretical and empirical. These are the areas of inquiry which theologians, as opposed to scripture scholars or historians of religion, are chiefly engaged in.

Thus Scripture creates a community of living and thinking out of which the questions for Theology arise. Theologians, in undertaking these questions, must personally begin by that normative conversion which is demanded by Scripture.

The approach presented here supposes that God has created us in the world as we know it, in order to care for and understand ourselves and that world in communion with the love He has poured out in our hearts and revealed to us in Scripture. The alternative would seem to suppose that God revealed a normative culture in the Bible to which we should conform by denying the world as we know it, and by caring for and understanding ourselves and others in a radical counter-culture. The approach presented here supposes that Western culture has advanced beyond that of Ancient Israel, and it may be open to the charge of softness or compliance. The alternative would have us return to an earlier purity, and may be open to the charge of ignorance or arrogance. Each of these approaches has something to learn from the other.

Appendix A

The Elohist Source: A Synopsis
(Drawn from J.A. Grindel:
Cf opening paragraph of ch. 4)

	NOTH	*JENKS*	*GRINDEL*
Genesis	15:1b,3a,5, 13-16	15:1-6,13-16	(15:1-6, 13-16)
	20:1b-18	20:1-17	20:1-18
	21:6,8-21	21:8-21	21:8-21
	21:22-34	21:22-34	21:22-34
	22:1-14, (15-18),19	22:1-14,19	22:1-14, (15-18),19
	28:11-12, 17-18, 20-22	28:11-12, 17-18, 20-22	28:10-12, 17-22
	30:1-3,6, 17-19, 22-23	————	————
	31:2,4-16	31:4-16	31:4-16
	31:19b,24- 25a,26, 28-29,30b 32-35, 36b- 37,41-45, 50,53b-55	31:17-24,25- 42,45, 49,50, 53-54	31:17-24, 25-42
	32:1-2,13b-21	————	————

	NOTH	JENKS	GRINDEL
	33:4-5,8-11	33:5-11	33:5-11
	33:19-20	———	———
	35:1-5, 7-8, 14	35:1-8	35:1-8
	35:16-20	———	———
	37:3b,22-24, 29-36	37:21-24,28a 29-30,36	———
	40:2-23	40	———
	41:1-33,34b, 35a,36-40, 47-48, 50-54	41	———
	42:1a,2-3, 6-7,11b, 13-26, 28b-37	42:1a,2-3, 6-7,11b, 13-26, 28b-38	———
	45:2-3,5b-15	45:2-3,5-15	———
	46:1-5a	46:1-4	46:1-5a
	47:5b, 6a, 7-12	———	———
	48:1-2,7-22	48:1-2,7-14 17-22	48:1-2,8-14, 17-22
	50:10b-11, 15-26	50:15-26	50:15-26
Exodus	1:15-21	1:15-21	———
	3:1, 4b, 6, 9-15	3:1, 4b, 6, 9-13 15	3:1,4b,6,9-13, 15
	4:17, 18, 20b	4:17, 18, 20b	———
	———	7-12: Fragments	———
	13:17-19	13:17-19	13:17-19
	14:5a, 7, 11-12 19a,25a	14:5a,19a	———
	———	15:20-21	———
	17:3	17:4-7	———
	———	17:8-16	(17:8-16)
	18:1-27	18:1-27	(18)
	19:3a,16-17, 19	19:2b-3a,4-6 16-17,19	(19:2b-3a, 4-6, 16-17,19)
	20:(1-17), 18-21	20:18-21	(20:18-21)

	NOTH	*JENKS*	*GRINDEL*
	24:1-2,9-11	24:1-2,9-11	(24:1,9-11)
	_____	24:12-15a, 18b	(24:12-15a, 18b)
	32:1b-4a, 21-24	32:1-6,15-20	(32:1-6, 15-20)
	_____	33:3b-6,7-11	(33:7-11)
Numbers	_____	11:1-3,16-17, 24-30;12	(11-12)
	20:14-18,21	_____	_____
	21:21-35	_____	_____
	22:2-3a, 9-12, 20,38	22:2-21, 36-40	
	22:41-23:27	22:41-23:26	_____
	23:29-30	_____	_____
Deuteronomy	_____	31:14-15,23	_____
	_____	34:10-12	_____

() - Uncertain

Appendix B
Some Probably Elohist Texts

It is generally agreed among source critics that most of the legal traditions in Exodus, whatever their earlier origins and history, were absorbed through the Elohist framework. Moreover, the "conditional covenant" tradition is generally taken to be Elohist in origin. This implies a specific asceticism of the Elohist, enjoining one to keep both ethical laws and civil laws, as all of these are laws of God (cf., for example, B. Childs, *The Book of Exodus,* Westminster Press, 1974, pp. 351-360 and 452).

Within this context, the role of Moses as law-mediator is very important. Moses (and whatever replaces Moses as the community goes through historical developments) becomes the locus of divine revelation. In terms of spirituality, one expects God to be revealed and to intervene where law is promulgated and applied. This topic, in fact, is central in many of the texts which Grindel lists as probably Elohist in origin.

Ex 17:8-16 dealing with enmity between Israel and Amalek, is very much focussed on the mediatory role of Moses. There are introduced other elements, with roles to play which evoke rather a later liturgical situation than an historical narrative: the rod in v. 11, which is not given a place in the rest of the account; the sudden introduction of Joshua at the head of the army, without narrative preparation; the stone to sit upon, and the support of Aaron and Hur; the gesture of Moses which determines how the battle goes; the hand upon a banner of Yahweh in v. 16. Whatever the history behind this story, or the point of the narrative itself, the Moses function in Israel is presented as determinative of Israel's success in war.

Ex 18 is quite different: a domestic scene, a family reunion, an encounter with preparation in advance (vv. 6-7), expressions of mutual feeling: the divine milieu for the Elohist! The rejoicing over God's care for Israel is repeated three times (vv. 8, 9,10-11), in an encounter in which the reader participates. In this story, Moses is presented as a judge, who "makes known the statutes of God and his decisions" (v. 16) in Israel. The kindly father-in-law intervenes (v. 14), and Moses obeys him (v. 24). The point of the story seems to be to validate the divine authority of lower levels of administration of justice in Israel. An extended judiciary is created of men chosen because they are able and "fear" God (v. 21), but Moses remains the sole mediator, or place of revelation for Israel (v. 19-20). Typically, the Elohist has been unable to do this without narrating the event within family relations. Typically Elohist again is the fact that a foreigner, the Midianite priest Jethro, is the one who was empowered by God to tell Moses about this proper disposition of powers. Finally, local courts were considered so important by the Elohist that he ascribed their creation to divine command, and dated it back to the time of Moses. This indicates once again the religious relevance of justice in Elohist foundations. Both 17:8-16 and ch. 18 prepare for the theophany by establishing authoritative mediation: God will be known through Israel's leaders and judges.

The theophany on the mountain is related by the Elohist in *Ex 19:2b,3a,4-6,16-17,19; 20:18-21.* This account stresses the idea that, even though the people have a role of priesthood vis-à-vis the other nations, their stance before God is one of "fear," and one which requires the mediatorship of Moses. The priesthood of Israel can express Israel's special election, while leaving God free to reveal Himself to God-fearing foreigners. Finally, once again, the place of revelation is the place of mediation of law and justice.

In *Ex 24:1, 9-11, 12-15a, 18b* we read of further encounters with God on the mountain.

In *Ex 32:1-6,15-20* we have the retelling of a Yahwist story contained in the other verses of this chapter. The retelling has the effect of placing the blame on Aaron. One may suspect some special pleading about the priesthood at Bethel as opposed to that in Jerusalem. In terms of foundational stance we learn nothing new, although the significance of Bethel is affirmed once again. There is also an added specific prohibition against statues and religious dancing.

In *Ex 33:7-11* the mediator role of Moses is again stressed. Once again Joshua is introduced, as he has been in all these texts, though his exact role is usually not clear.

Num 11 again deals with the role of Moses. It is a tale of emotional confrontation which one can easily believe to be Elohist. Moreover it deals with trusting God in the affairs of everyday life, i.e., food to eat. Moses is unable to bear the burden of mediating all alone between the numerous people of Israel and God, as he was not in Ex 18. And once again the solution is found by spreading the burden around among other chosen men. The story troubles to recall, and to answer, an objection to this arrangement (vv. 26-29), and to make the point that it would be nice if all the people were prophets, but that this is not the case (v. 29). Eventually, although God is angry with the people because of their constant dissatisfaction, and although he punishes the complainers through a plague, still he sends quail in great numbers to provide food. This story presents God as providing food on the one hand, but on the other it focusses on dissatisfaction with manna and with the divine mediation of Moses. It is important to us, because it is the first sin commented upon by the Elohist. It is a sin against the foundational stance so powerfully expressed in Gen 20-22, i.e., the expectancy that God has taken care from the beginning that no harm should come to those who fear Him. It is also a sin against the authority of Moses' mediatorship. This story reinforces Elohist teaching by showing the evils of going against it.

Num 12 is the same as Num 11, dealing with Moses' mediatorship, and recounting a sin of desrespect on the part of Aaron and Miriam.

Conclusion

To understand exactly the Elohist kergyma in these chapters, in his correcting of Yahwist tradition or in presenting his own meaning, one would have to know more than we do about the institutions of authority in the Northern Kingdom. However, our aim was not to recover the Elohist's kerygma. Rather it was to define the foundational stance implicitly expressed in the text, and subliminally received by readers throughout history.

The "probably Elohistic" texts examined in this appendix emphasize the legal dimension of the Elohist stance as summarized at the end of chapter IV. The Elohist Speaker expects to meet God in reciprocal obligations and covenant, in following the laws and decisions of divinely authorized authority. Every reader will feel the demands of this Speaker in different ways: divinely authorized authority may be thought to reside in the king, the Pope, the elected government, the communist party, exclusively in one's own conscience, and so forth.

This aspect of the Elohist's foundational stance was already expressed in the Genesis texts, but Exodus and Numbers provide much more clarity about it, and gives it much greater emphasis. The divine milieu remains familial, and brotherly, but God, revelation, salvation, and meaning come to the family through authorities, laws, courts and priests. All of this was needed to complete and correct the Yahwist's exclusive concern for international relations.

Appendix C

The Priestly Narrative
(cf. ch. 5, footnote 2)

Genesis

1:1-31
2:1-4a
5:1-28,30-32
6:9-22
7:6,11,13-16a,
  17a,18-21,
  24
8:1,2a,3b-5,
  13a,14-19
9:1-17,28f
10:1-4a,5a*-7,
  20,22f,31f
11:10-27,31f
12:4b,5
13:6,11b,
  12ab**
16:1,3,15f
17:1-27
19:29 (follows
  13:12)
21:1b-5
23:1-20
25:7-11a,12-
  17,19f

26:26b,34f
27:46
28:1-9
31:18a***b
33:18a
35:6a,9-13,15,
  22b-29
36:1-14
37:1f
41:46a
46:6f
47:27b,28
48:3-6
49:1a,28b-33
50:12f

Exodus

1:1-5,7,13f
2:23a*b,24f
6:2-12
7:1-13,19,20a*
  21b,22
8:1-3...11b,

12-15
9:8-12,35b
11:9-10
12:1,3-14,28,
  40-41
14:1-4,8a,
  10ab*,15-
  18
  20a*b,22f,
  26,27a*,28f
15:27
16:1-3,6f,9-
  13a...14b*
  16ab*-20,
  22-26,31a,
  35b
17:1ab*
19:1,2a
  (reverse)
24:15b-18a
25:all

26:all
27:1-19
28:1-41
29:1-37...

42b-46
31:18
35:1a,4b-10,
  20-29,
  (30-33)
36:2,(8-38
  after
  37:24)
37:(1-24)
38:(1-7,9-20)
39:(1-31),32,
  43
40:17,33b,34,
  (35)

Leviticus

8:(1-10a*,
  12-36)
9:1-24

Numbers

1:(1-47)

2:(1-34)
3:(14-15)
8:(5-10,12-15a,20)
9:(15-18)
10:11f
13:1-3a,17a*,21,25,26a*,32
14:1a,2,5-7,10,26-29a*,35-38
20:1a*,2,3b,4,6f,8a**b*,10,11b,12,22,23a*,25-29
21:4a*(to *hhr*)
22:1b
27:12-14a,15-23

p^g *possibly*

1:1-3,19b-43,45-47
3:14-16,39

Deuteronomy

1:3
32:48-52
34:1a...7-9

Joshua

4:19*
5:10-12
14:1,2*
18:1
19:51

Endnotes

Notes, Chapter 1

[1]Cf. Jonathan Culler, *The Pursuit of Signs, Semiotics, Literature, Deconstruction*, Cornell University Press, Ithaca, 1981, p. 6.

[2]Cf. Michel Foucault, *The Order of Things, An Archaeology of the Human Sciences*, Vintage Books, New York, 1973, p. 306.

[3]This source division is classical, and it enjoys consensus. For the sources of Ex 3-4, cf. Brevard S. Childs, *The Book of Exodus, A Critical, Theological Commentary*, Westminster Press, Philadelphia, 1974, pp. 51-64. For 3:13-15, cf. the bibliography and analysis of Magne Saebo, "Offenbarung oder Verhüllung? Bemerkungen zum Character des Gottesnamens in Ex 3, 13-15," in J. Jeremias and L. Perlitt (eds.), *Die Botchaft und die Boten, Festschrift Wolff*, Neukirchener Verlag, 1981, pp. 43-55. Wellhausen and Eissfeldt attributed v. 14 to the Elohist, but more recent scholarship has correctly seen that it is in discontinuity with vv. 13 and 15. Classical source theory is very much disputed at the present time. For useful overviews, cf. for example, E. Zenger, "Wo steht die Pentateuchforschung heute?", *Biblische Zeitschrift*, NF 24, 1980, pp. 101-116; Hans-Christoph Schmitt, "Die Hintergründe der 'neuesten Pentateuchkritik' und der literarische Befund der Josefsgeschichte Gen 37-50," *Zeitschrift für die alltestamentlische Wissenschaft* 97, 1985, pp. 161-179. Source criticism is its own specialization, requiring meticulous research and proof. This book cannot enter that field without losing its own objectives. It will accept the results of source critics where possible, or take a reasoned position where necessary. Where no solid probability can be identified, it will avoid drawing conclusions.

[4]One can reject the search for original meanings of texts on theological, philosophical, or practical grounds. This will be the subject of a detailed discussion in the second section of this chapter.

[5]Of course the same meanings might emerge out of ahistorical questions, such as "What can I derive for my own living from this text?" The inadequacy of this direct approach, without historical research, is discussed below in a second section of this chapter, under the heading of practical grounds for rejecting historical methodology.

[6]Cf. Wolfgang Richter, *Die sogenannten vorprophetischen Berufungsberichte*, Vandenhoeck & Ruprecht, Göttingen, 1970, p. 176. Richter concludes to two separate origins for oral call forms, i.e., the leader in Holy War and the prophet, which have been fused in literature by the time of the Yahwist. His refined analysis of Ex 3-4 differs from the presentation above only in ways which do not affect our discussion.

[7]For a useful survey and analysis of positions, the reader is referred to Frank Lentricchia, *After the New Criticism*, University of Chicago Press, 1980. Cf. further Jonathan Culler, *The Pursuit of Signs: Semiotics, Literature, Deconstruction*, Cornell University Press, Ithaca, N.Y., 1981; Terry Eagleton, *Literary Theory: An Introduction*, Basil Blackwell, Oxford, 1983; Edgar V. McKnight, *The Bible and the Reader, An Introduction to Literary Criticism*, Fortress Press, Philadelphia, 1985.

[8]F.R. Leavis held many chairs in English universities, and his approach to Literature dominated the Empire and Commonwealth through the first half of this century. The central doctrine of the "New Criticism" dictated the style of "Oxford Editions" of

literary texts and anthologies: no biographical or historical notes are provided; the text alone speaks. The text is its own complete world, and its meaning must be derived, not from external clues, but from the relations of elements within it. R. Wellek and A. Warren, *Theory of Literature*, Harcourt Brace, New York, 1949, prescribed this approach in textbook form in the United States. Hans-Georg Gadamer is a philosopher of culture, who taught at the University of Heidelberg, and has often been a guest in North America. His influential work, *Wahrheit und Methode*, Mohr (Siebeck), Tübingen, 1965, was translated as *Truth and Method*, Seabury Press, N.Y., 1976.

[9]Not to mention the "consciousness criticism" of what was known as the "Geneva School" of literary criticism. Cf. Sarah Lawall, *Critics of Consciousness, The Existential Structures of Literature*, Harvard University Press, Cambridge, 1968.

[10]Cf H.-G. Gadamer, *Wahrheit und Methode*, pp. 97-127, and 462-465.

[11]Cf H.-G. Gadamer, "On the Problem of Self-Understanding," in *Philosophical Hermeneutics*, (translated and edited by David E. Linge), University of California Press, Berkeley, Los Angeles, London, 1976, p. 58.

[12]Cf. H.-G. Gadamer, *Wahrheit und Methode*, p. 119.

[13]Cf. *Ibid.*, p. 369.

[14]Cf. Northrop Frye, *Anatomy of Criticism, Four Essays*, Princeton University Press, 1957, paperback ed. 1971, pp. 120-121.

[15]Cf. Jacques Derrida, *L'écriture et la différence*, Editions du Seuil, 1967, p. 23.

[16]Cf. T.S. Eliot, "The Perfect Critic," in *The Sacred Word*, Methuen and Co., London, 1920, paperback ed. 1960, pp. 1-16. Also the "Polemical Introduction" to Northrop Frye's *Anatomy of Criticism*, pp. 3-29 offers a similarly caustic argument against the theory that "critics are intellectuals who have a taste for art but lack both the power to produce it and the money to patronize it" (p. 3).

[17]Cf. H.-G. Gadamer, *Philosophical Hermeneutics*, p. 57.

[18]Cf. for example H.-G. Gadamer, *Wahrbeit und Methode*, pp. 106-122.

[19]Similarly Northrop Frye takes scholarship for granted, but when he comes to writing at a theoretical level he appears, not only to overlook it, but also to deny its validity. His recurring affirmation of the primacy of "centripetal meaning" over "centrifugal meaning" of literary texts in his recent *The Great Code, The Bible and Literature*, Academic Press, Toronto, 1982, v.g. pp. 60-61, is helpful when attacking fundamentalist approaches, but in itself it is a misleading simplification. Most literary texts, including biblical texts, contain many words, sentences, and whole passages whose primary referent is not internal to the text, unless primacy of reference is established by the force of grammar alone. When the Bible tells us in 1 Kgs 11:43 that "Solomon slept with his fathers, and was buried in the city of David his father; and Rehoboam his son reigned in his stead," one can treat "Solomon" as referring to the verb "slept" as its subject, or treat the whole sentence as referring to the foregoing chapters as their "conclusion," and the coming chapter as a "transition." And these references are "primary" in the sense that grammar and literary form hold them in connections for us as we listen. However in an equally true sense their primary reference, i.e., dominant reference in the reader's mind, is to two men who are familiar and judged to be real on the basis of this and other texts, and to a grave which might conceivably be uncovered one day by an archeologist. Of course other sentences are more mythical in meaning, more centripetal. But poems like "Kubla Khan" are the exception, not the rule, in literature.

[20]Cf. H.-G. Gadamer, *Wahrheit und Methode*, pp. 369-373.

²¹This convoluted text was approved on April 8, 1546. Cf. Denzinger-Rahner (eds.), *Enchiridion Symbolorum*, Herder, 1960, no. 783. It may be translated as follows: "The most holy Synod ... constantly mindful of its purpose that the very purity of the Gospel should be preserved in the Church freed from error, as something which was promised by the Prophets in holy Scriptures, which Jesus Christ the Son of God with his own lips was the first to promulgate, and which He then commanded through the Apostles that it be preached to every creature as the source of all salvific truth and moral discipline (Mt 20:19-20; Mk 16:15): and perceiving that this truth is contained in written books and in unwritten traditions, which were received by the Apostles from the lips of Christ himself or else have come down to us handed on as it were from hand to hand by the same Apostles at the dictation of the Holy Spirit, having followed the examples of the orthodox Fathers, receives and venerates with equal feelings of piety and reverence all the books both of the Old and of the New Testament since one God is author of both, and also those same traditions pertaining to faith and morals insofar as they were dictated either orally by Christ or by the Holy Spirit and were conserved through continuous succession in the Catholic Church."

²²Cf. Frederick E. Crowe, *Theology of the Christian Word, A Study in History*, Paulist Press, New York, Ramsey, N.J., Toronto, 1978; Geza Vermes, *Scripture and Tradition in Judaism*, E.J. Brill, Leiden, 2nd ed. 1973. For an illuminating analysis of the *sola scriptura* ideal in Protestant thought, cf. Charles Clifford Hefling, *Lonergan on Development: "The Way of Nicea" in Light of his More Recent Methodology*, University Microfilm International, Ann Arbor, 1982, pp. 302-354.

²³Cited from Abbot and Gallagher (eds.), *The Documents of Vatican II*, Guild Press, New York, 1966. The document was signed by Pope Paul VI and the Fathers of the Council on Nov. 21, 1964.

²⁴Cf. Robert P. Carroll, *From Chaos to Covenant, Uses of Prophecy in the Book of Jeremiah*, SCM Press, London, 1981, pp. 216 and 219.

²⁵It is interesting to note one way in which early Judaism accommodated Jeremiah's exclusion of teachers. The Torah was intended as a teaching for everyone, and made available to everyone each Sabbath. Jews "do not resort to persons learned in the law with questions as to what they should do or not do, nor yet by keeping independent transgress in ignorance of the law, but any one of them whom you attack with inquiries about their ancestral institutions can answer you readily and easily. The husband seems competent to transmit knowledge of the laws to his wife, the father to his children, the master to his slaves." Philo, *Hypothetica*, 7.12, cited by A.I. Baumgarten, "The Torah as a Public Document in Judaism," *Studies in Religion* 14, 1985, pp. 17-24, cf. pp. 17-18.

²⁶Cf. Brevard Childs, *The Book of Exodus, A Critical Theological Commentary*, Westminster Press, Philadelphia, 1974, pp. 80-89.

²⁷Cf. *Ibid.*, p. 81. This appears to be a return to a medieval definition of the spiritual sense as a meaning, not of the words but of the things spoken of in the text. Cf. for example: "whereas in all sciences words have meaning, what is peculiar to this science is that the very things meant by words also have their meaning" (cum in omnibus scientiis voces significent, hoc habet proprium ista scientia, quod ipsae res significatae per voces etiam significant aliquid." Thomas Aquinas, *Summa Theologica*, Pars Ia, art. 10. This clarification is in fact a confusion: things do not of themselves signify anything; rather the things spoken of can be thought about and given meaning by the reader. All of this shows that Jesus (and Matthew) were not intending to deceive by their interpretation. It also shows that they would have been less confusing had they first interpreted the text in its original meaning, and then added their additional

178   *Endnotes*

thoughts about resurrection, not as immediate conclusions from Ex 3:6, but as the result of a sophisticated logical process.

²⁸Cf. pp. 81-82. For further study of New Testament interpretation of the Old in a similar style, and for extensive bibliography, cf. Anthony Tyrrell Hanson, *The New Testament Interpretation of Scripture*, SPCK, London, 1980. This point is directly explored in S. McEvenue, "The Spiritual Authority of the Bible," in T.P. Fallon, S.J., and P.B. Riley (eds.), *Religion and Culture, Essays in Honor of Bernard Lonergan, S.J.*, State University of New York Press, Albany, 1987, pp. 205-219.

²⁹Cf. p. 89.

³⁰Cf. Umberto Cassuto, *Commentary on the Book of Exodus*, Magnes Press, Jerusalem, 1967, pp. 30-44. For a discussion of classical Jewish exegetical methods, cf. Brevard Childs, "The Sensus Literalis of Scripture: An Ancient and Modern Problem," in H. Donner, R. Hanhart and R. Smend (eds.), *Beiträge zur alttestamentischen Theologie, Festschrift Walter Zimmerli*, Vandenhoeck & Ruprecht, Göttingen, 1977, and the literature he cites, particularly W. Becher, *Die exegetische Terminologie der jüdischen Traditionsliteratur*, Leipzig, 1899-90, and Darmstadt, 1965; also R. Loewe, "The 'Plain' Meaning of Scripture in Early Jewish Exegesis," *Papers of the Institute of Jewish Studies London I*, Jerusalem, 1964, pp. 140-185. For an extreme position, cf. Morton Smith, *Palestinian Parties and Politics that Shaped the Old Testament*, New York and London, 1971; and for a nuanced discussion cf. Joseph Blenkinsopp, "Interpretation and the Tendency to Sectarianism: An Aspect of Second Temple History," in E. Sanders, A. Baumgarten, and A. Mendelson (eds.), *Jewish and Christian Self-Definition*, vol. 2: *Aspects of Judaism in the Greco-Roman Period*, Fortress Press, Philadelphia, 1981, pp. 1-26.

³¹A most striking Old Testament study of this doctrine is to be found in the Ark Narrative. Cf. Antony Campbell, *The Ark Narrative (1 Sam 4-6; 2 Sam 6), A Form-Critical and Traditio-Historical Study*, Scholar's Press, Missoula, 1975.

³²Cf. *Sententiae*, 24; M. Martin (ed.), *Oeuvres de Robert de Melun*, iii, Louvain, 1947; cited by Beryl Smalley, *The Study of the Bible in the Middle Ages*, Basil Blackwell, Oxford, 1952, p. 229.

³³Cf. *De Scripturis*, vv. 13-15; cited by Beryl Smalley, *op. cit.*, pp. 93-94.

³⁴For a compelling demonstration of the impossibility of paraphrasing poetry, cf. Cleanth Brooks, *The Well Wrought Urn, Studies in the Structure of Poetry*, Harcourt Brace Jovanovitch, New York and London, 1947, especially ch. 11, "The Heresy of Paraphrase," pp. 192-214. The specific application of this thesis to the Old Testament is argued in S. McEvenue, "Theological Doctrines and the Old Testament," in S. McEvenue and B. Meyer (eds.), *Lonergan's Hermeneutics, Its Development and Application*, Catholic University Press, Washington, 1989.

³⁵It will be helpful to read Bernard Lonergan's description of "common-sense" knowledge as compared to "specialized" knowledge, in *Understanding and Being, An Introduction and Companion to "Insight"*, (ed. by Morelli and Morelli), Edwin Mellen Press, New York and Toronto, 1980, ch. 4, pp. 101-125. For the general theory of knowledge and of interpretation which bases this discussion, I am totally indebted to Bernard Lonergan, S.J., *Insight, A Study of Human Understanding*, Philosophical Library, New York, 1957; and *Method in Theology*, Darton, Longman and Todd, London, 1972, especially ch. 7, "Interpretation," pp. 153-173.

³⁶Cf. Bernard Lonergan, *Method*, pp. 355-368.

³⁷For scholarly studies concerning these texts the reader can be referred to the critical commentaries of Gunkel, Von Rad, Cassuto, Speiser, Vawter and others.

³⁸Cf. our treatment of this story in ch. 4 below.

³⁹For further precisions concerning the Yahwist's meaning, cf. our treatment of the text in ch. 3 below.

⁴⁰This may seem at first to be an idiosyncratic approach to interpretation. It is in fact common. Cf., for example, Cleanth Brooks, *The Well Wrought Urn* (cited above in note 34), who develops a whole theory of meaning in poetry based on contradictions within the poem, which he calls "paradox" or "irony." Wolfgang Iser has analysed successful communication through reading in terms of the reader's activity: filling in the gaps introduced into the flow of language by the author—cf. Edgar V. McKnight, *The Bible and the Reader, An Introduction to Literary Criticism*, Fortress Press, Philadelphia, 1985, pp. 78-82, and Bibliography. Cf. further Meier Sternberg, *The Poetics of Biblical Narrative, Ideological Literature and the Drama of Reading*, Indiana University Press, Bloomington, 1987, ch. 6 "Gaps, Ambiguity and the Reading Process," pp. 186-229. The valuable contribution of Jacques Derrida, Hillis Miller, and other "deconstructionist" literary critics has been to focus on the significance of edges and logic-breaks in texts, to show that meaning is not fully accounted for by the interrelation of textual elements. Certainly the meaning of humour is the gap between what the words lead one to expect and the punch line; and the meaning in history writing is often to be found in the gap between what the author imperceptibly implies about possible or ideal outcomes and the actual outcomes as he/she describes them. It seems that reading between the lines is precisely the way reading is done! In any case, the reader must decide about the validity of the small, but central, point we have adduced toward the interpretation of Gen 12:9-13:2, and about our account of the method implied. This will be further explored in the next chapter.

Notes, Chapter 2

¹The main ideas in this chapter were first worked out and presented in a different conceptual framework in a paper entitled "The Spiritual Authority of the Bible," published now in T.P. Fallon, S.J. and P.B. Riley, *Religion and Culture, Essays in Honor of Bernard Lonergan S.J.*, State University of New York Press, Albany, 1987, pp. 205-219.

²For a caustic exposition of this position, cf. Northrop Frye, *Anatomy of Criticism, Four Essays.* Princeton University Press, 1957, pp. 20-24.

³It might be argued that an analogous, or even very similar, process was involved in the formation of the Hebrew, and eventually the Christian, canon of Scripture. This topic pertains to the sociology of knowledge, and the social history of that period. The present study restricts itself to the contemporary reading of Scripture.

⁴The present discussion aims specifically at the relation of biblical literature to theology. It cannot usefully be carried out at a sufficiently abstract level of reflection to serve simultaneously as a complete general theory about the relation of literature to common-sense reality, or the relation of literature to literary criticism.

⁵The terms "foundation" and "stance" are drawn from Bernard Lonergan, *Method in Theology,* Darton, Longman and Todd, London, 1971, pp. 267-293. Lonergan distinguishes between foundational reality and its expression. He describes foundational reality as intellectual, moral, and religious conversion. He further distinguishes simple foundations (e.g., the initial syllogism in a linked series of syllogisms) from complex foundations, which is method itself as outlined in his book. In this, Lonergan is prescribing the foundations appropriate to contemporary theology. Our discussion

is about the foundations of authors in general. As a result our use of the category cannot be nearly as precise.

We have termed foundational stance "subliminal" or "implicit" in the text, because these are familiar categories which are close to the right idea. It is however expressed in the text as "elemental meaning." Foundational stance forms, and elemental meaning informs, a text just as attitude forms and voice tone or smile or body language informs spoken communication.

[6]Jacques Derrida provides precise descriptions of this experience. Cf. for example, *L'écriture et la différence,* éditions du Seuil, Paris, 1967, pp. 15-27, where he argues that the text you write is not an expression of what you know, but rather a creation of something new.

[7]It is important to note that one's foundational reality is normally subliminal, but not unconscious. It can be adverted to when needed. It is "collective," in the sense that most of it is usually shared by contemporary participants in one's culture, and much of it shared by all humankind in varying degrees. However it is not at all a collective unconscious in the sense of a form of life diverse from that of conscious psychic activity.

[8]I add the word "fulfillment" to "meaning" in order to be sure that meaning is not reduced to a merely rational content.

[9]An example of this may be found in the work of Harvard professor Daniel Aaron, who edited the diaries of Arthur Inman after his death in 1963. As a true scholar Dr. Aaron succeeded in entering Inman's unique world-view: "Nobody can tell me anything I don't know about him. I just know him. I can predict his response to anything. Anything . . . I certainly know him better than any member of my family." Dr. Aaron spent seven years editing the diaries, and recently described his experience: ". . . I became stuck, absorbed, caught up in it. . . . And while I disliked him intensely—I couldn't be further away from his political, economic, nearly all his attitudes—I became fascinated by his unique opportunity to indulge himself in a way no one else could. . . . You have to read the whole diary through. You begin by despising him and end up sympathizing, even admiring him—while not embracing his attitudes." Cf. TIME magazine, Dec. 2, 1985, pp. 8-9.

[10]"Compact Consciousness" is a term invented by Ernst Voegelin to describe undifferentiated consciousness in which methods of thought and realms of meaning are not distinguished.

[11]As in the book of Judges.

[12]As in "The Succession Narrative," 2 Samuel 9-20; 1 Kings 1-2.

[13]As in accounts of the appearances of Our Lady at Lourdes, or at Fatima, or at Medugorje.

[14]As in Muslim belief.

[15]As in the programme to build the temples of Solomon and Herod, the medieval cathedrals, the Roman and High Church liturgies.

Notes, Chapter 3

[1]David J.A. Clines, *The Theme of the Pentateuch,* JSOTSS 10, Sheffield, 1978, reduces this teaching to a single luminous paragraph on p. 29. A symptom of the inadequacy of this approach may be seen in the fact that to gain this clarity he simply overlooks the whole legal tradition in the Pentateuch. I provide a detailed critique of Clines' study in "Theological Doctrines and the Old Testament,

Lonergan's Contribution," in S. McEvenue and B. Meyer (eds.), *Lonergan's Hermeneutics, Its Development and Application,* Catholic University Press, Washington, 1989.

²For a convenient summary of the situation, cf. the first 13 pages of Hans-Christoph Schmitt, "Die Hintergründe der 'neuesten Pentateuchkritik' und der literarische Befund der Josefsgeschichte Gen 37-50," *ZAW* 97, 1985, pp. 161-179; Erich Zenger, "Wo steht die Pentateuchforschung heute?", *BZ NF* 24, 1940, pp. 101-116; Erich Zenger, "Auf der Suche nach einem Weg aus der Pentateuchkrise," *Theo Rev* 78, 1982, pp. 353-362. Further literature on this topic is cited in footnote 3, in chapter 1.

³A whole series of recent articles and books delight in celebrating the inconclusive character of specific source-critical conclusions, or in establishing minor source-critical hypotheses on the basis of specific texts. Regarding the Yahwist specifically, cf. Frank Crüsemann, "Die Eigenständigkeit der Urgeschichte, Ein Beitrag zur Diskussion des 'Jahwisten'," in J. Jeremias and L. Perlitt (eds.), *Die Botschaft und die Boten, Festschrift Hans Walter Wolff,* Neukirchen, 1981, pp. 11-29, who shows some discontinuity between Gen 12:1-3 and the Jahwist sections of Gen 2-11. He argues to the possibility of a post-Priestly origin for these 3 verses, and to the independence of the Proto-history. After establishing some plausibility for his position (very weak in my opinion), he concludes that this uncertainty leads on to endless further uncertainty, i.e., to "far-reaching questions about a redaction history of the Pentateuch which cannot here be followed through." His article leaves us with a hypothetical Proto-history without literary form or historical context on the one hand, and with an undescribed remnant of the Yahwist text (almost unintelligible now without Gen 12:1-3) on the other. This will be useless until a new Wellhausen devotes a new lifetime to following through all the questions toward a new synthesis. In the meantime a careful strategy based on selected probabilities must be used. In some measure, our attention to foundational stance of authors implies a new criterion for source-criticism, one which classical source-critics may have used inadvertently. Cf. further R. Rendtorff, "The Yahwist as Theologian," *Journal for the Study of the Old Testament* 3, 1977, pp. 2-10; R.B. Coote and D.R. Ord, *The Bible's First History,* Fortress Press, Philadelphia, 1988.

⁴"Knowing good and evil" must be read as "polarity," i.e., a figure of speech in which two extremes are named in order to denote the whole range of things between them. For a biblical example, in Gen 1 "heaven and earth" really means simply everything. Familiar examples in modern English are "from soup to nuts" or "from a to z." "Good and evil" seem to encompass, not only a narrowly defined area of ethics, but the whole sphere of human appetite and aspiration. A similar anxiety about the limitlessness of human inquiry is found in Qohelet 3:11 which reads literally: "He has made everything beautiful in its time; also He has put eternity at the heart of everything, yet so that man cannot find out what God has done from the beginning to the end." It is, in fact, man's capacity for the beautiful, the true (infinite and eternal), and the good, which makes us both perennially dissatisfied with life, and desirous of God.

⁵The answer to this question may have to wait until more is understood about Egypt's cult of the serpent. Carl Jung's discussion of the serpent as earth energy, and as feminine, may provide some initial indications about why the Yahwist gave such prominence to this figure.

⁶Cf. for example columns 4-6 in the Atrahasis Epic, analysed in Claus Westermann, *Genesis 1-11, A Commentary,* SPCK in London, and Augsburg Publishers in Minneapolis, 1984, pp. 68-69.

[7]This apparently unfulfilled threat has always been a problem for commentators. It occurs in contexts which involve very serious punishment for crimes: cf. I Sam 14:44; 22:16; I Kings 2:37, 42; 2 Kings 1:4, 6, 16; Jer 26:8; Ez 3:18; 33:8, 14. Cf. Westermann's commentary, pp. 222-225, for an excellent survey of opinions, where he points out that none has solved the problem. His own solution is based on the interweaving of two traditions which were originally separate, and on the explanation that this is a warning, not a sentence. In Westermann's analysis the Yahwist turns out to be an editor who preserves sources, and does profound theological connecting, but is careless of story. In fact some raggedness in the text (i.e., the inadequate preparation for the 4 rivers and 2 trees) shows perhaps that he was not concerned for perfect smoothness. However, too many generations have praised his talent for story-writing to allow easy credence to Westermann's reconstruction of the Yahwist's process. Moreover, it is hard to imagine that the Yahwist was totally unconcerned about the overall impression Yahweh makes in his text. I conclude that the character of the warning is hard to explain except in terms of the lightness of this narrative style, and the limits on God's power and knowledge presented in this text.

[8]This theme is taken up again in the New Testament, with the addition of an eschatological tradition: cf. Mt 13:24-30, 36-43.

[9]For an excellent survey and source-critical study cf. Brevard Childs, *The Book of the Exodus, a Critical, Theological Commentary,* Westminster Press, Philadelphia, 1974, pp. 604-609. For the actual law collection, cf. J. Halbe, *Das Privilegrecht Jahwes, Ex 34:10-16.* (FRLANT 114), Vandenhoeck & Ruprecht, Göttingen, 1975.

[10]Even if sources cannot be successfully separated out, it is clear that J narrated these events. Cf. the source-critical sections of Childs' commentary.

[11]The enlightening essay of Hans Walter Wolff, "The Kerygma of the Yahwist," *Interpretation* 20, 1966, pp. 131-158, has dominated study of the Yahwist since it was first published in *EvTH* 24, 1964, pp. 73-98. Cf. the critique of Wolff's study in my article cited above in note 1.

[12]Norbert Lohfink convincingly demonstrates that v. 3 is a clarification of the obscure v. 2, added by a later writer, that vv. 13-16 are an editorial addition, and that the rest of the text is an original Yahwist creation, whose form he describes as "imitation narrative." Cf. *Die Landverheissung als Eid, Eine Studie zu Gn 15,* (Stuttgarter Bibelstudien 28), Verlag Katholisches Bibelwerk Stuttgart, 1967, esp. pp. 35-44.

[13]The usual translations of *magen* here have "shield" instead of "patron" or "benefactor," because they mistakenly understand the opening "Fear not" in a literal sense. Actually "Fear not" is a stereotypical phrase for introducing a favourable oracle in the temple (cf. Lohfink, *Op. cit.,* p. 49). The meaning of *magen* is not to be determined by the concept of "fear," but rather by the following clause about the great benefaction or reward Abraham is to have. The root *mgn* has the meaning of "bestow" or "gift" in Ugaritic, and this meaning can be found in biblical Hebrew in Prov 4:9, as well as here.

[14]This is a paraphrase, but close to the intended meaning. I use the word "trust" rather than "faith," because the latter is too freighted with theological theories. Similarly, to translate *tsedaqah* as "righteousness" is traditional but misleading. Cf. G. Von Rad, *Old Testament Theology,* vol. 1, Harper and Row, New York, 1962, pp. 370-418. The term refers to the correct concrete relationship, in this case between Abram and God. Abram's trust was acknowledged by God as real, and as the proper relationship.

¹⁵For example, much of Shakespeare's vocabulary and imagery are drawn from falconry. It is dominant in *The Taming of the Shrew,* where Petruchio tames Katherine by starving her and keeping her from sleeping, as a falconer tames a falcon. The metaphor is made explicit in Act 4, Scene 1; but the play is replete with bird imagery and vocabulary.

¹⁶This gift is termed "religious conversion" by Bernard Lonergan, and very clearly analysed in *Method in Theology,* Darton, Longman & Todd, London, 1972, esp. pp. 107, 241-243, 282-283.

¹⁷Detailed source criticism here becomes very complicated. Cf. for example, G.B. Gray, *A Critical and Exegetical Commentary on Numbers,* (The International Critical Commentary), Edinburgh, 1903. However the predominance of J is generally agreed upon. Here I am following the source as isolated by Martin Noth, *Das vierte Buch Mose, Numeri,* Vandenhoeck & Ruprecht, Göttingen, 1966. There is no female presence or initiative in this pericope, but Noth points out that the mention of Kadesh in 20:1 is connected with the burial of Miriam, in whom the Yahwist shows a special interest in Ex 15:20-21 and Num 12:1ff (Noth, p. 128).

¹⁸The "sons of Anak" in vv. 22 and 28 must be translated "sons of the giant" in a context of giant grapes and terrified spies.

Notes, Chapter 4

¹Cf. Alan W. Jenks, *The Elohist and North Israelite Traditions.* (SBLMS 22), Scholars Press, Missoula, 1977.

²Every source critic who admits the existence of an Elohist recognizes his distinctive marks here. Elsewhere I have argued to a trilogy structure for these chapters, and to the unity of authorship: cf. S. McEvenue, "The Elohist at Work," *ZAW* 96, 1984, pp. 315-332. Some of the data considered in that study will be presented in the ensuing pages, but our discussion will assume, rather than prove, its more general conclusions. Cf. Jean Louis Ska, "Gn 22:2-19. Essai sur les niveux de lecture," *Biblica* 69, 1988, pp. 324-339, whose final conclusion tends toward a moralizing reading only because he includes vv. 14-18 in the text he studies, i.e., not the original Elohist.

³I translate "The God" because the Elohist chooses not to give God a final name until Ex 3, and not to describe Him until Gen 35:1-8. In this regard, though he leaves the Yahwist intact, he is clearly "correcting" the tradition.

⁴For a useful survey of these traditions, and for bibliography, cf. James Swetnam, *Jesus and Isaac, A Study of the Epistle to the Hebrews in the Light of the Aqeda,* (Analecta Biblica 94), Rome, 1983.

⁵Julius Wellhausen, *Die Composition des Hexateuchs und der historischen Bücher des Alten Testaments,* 4th edit., Walter de Gruyter & Co., Berlin, 1963, p. 34, points out this peculiar trick of style, and states that it is found nowhere in the Yahwist text. He indicates its presence in the following E Texts: Gen 22:2, 7, 11; 27:1; 31:11. To this list we can add Gen 46:2-3a; Ex 3:4b, 6a. It is not found in the Priestly Writer.

⁶For details the reader is again referred to S. McEvenue, "The Elohist at Work," *ZAW* 96, 1984, pp. 315-332. It was puzzling over Gen 20 which led to the research laid out in that article.

⁷Brevard Childs makes such correction one of the basic principles of canonical criticism: since the biblical text corrected itself as it was edited and added to over the centuries, only the final whole Bible is authoritative. Cf., for example, a most explicit

statement in "The Exegetical Significance of Canon," *VTS* 29, 1978, pp. 66-80, especially p. 69.

[8]These two texts were pointed out to me in this connection by John Grindel. My own treatment of these texts is given at the appropriate places in the present chapter.

[9]The name "Yahweh" supports their position: i.e., that the verse is a gloss. Cf. J. Wellhausen, *Die Composition,* p. 29; H. Gunkel, *Genesis,* pp. 224-25; O. Eissfeldt, *Synopse,* p. 33. However B. Vawter, *On Genesis,* p. 244, considers the verse Elohist, and points out that some Septuagint manuscripts and the Samaritan text show *'elohim* here. The MT error has occurred by attraction to 21:1.

[10]In v. 9 we can safely follow MT; whereas in v. 10 the Septuagint, Vulgate, and Samaritan tradition must prevail. The argument in both cases is *lectio difficilior,* and the fact that reasons for editorially adding the name are evident. In v. 9, the translations had lost the pun, and had to restore sense by adding the name. In v. 10, those MT editors who removed "great" in v. 13a to avoid glorifying the Ishmaelites (cf. Vawter, *On Genesis,* p. 249) added Isaac's name here to give him more prominence. The Elohist had in fact written a story concerned only with the Ishmaelites.

[11]This observation will be slightly modified in our reading of 35:1-8 immediately below. Of course the Dt tradition will develop the *maqom* theme, and eventually the meaning will be shifted to Jerusalem, an ironic reversal of intent.

[12]Subsequently the classical prophets will not approve of the religious practises developed specifically at Bethel: Hos 10:5; Amos 3:24; 4:4; 5:5; Jer 48:13. However, support for a temple, and tithing, has a long and honourable history in biblical and later Judaism.

[13]Undoubtedly 27:1, 2a is Elohist in origin: cf. note 5 above. The Elohist narrative consistently depends on the Yahwist for its intelligibility. Gen 27 is a Yahwist text, but the Elohist had no need of correcting it, since it was a family story in itself, and basically sympathetic to the foreigner, i.e., Esau. The Elohist added vv. 1, 2a in order to heighten the inter-personal character of the legendary event.

[14]Gen 33:5-11, discussed below, provides a sharp contrast with the Yahwist text in 32:2—33:17.

[15]The verb has "heart" as its object in vv. 20 and 26. In v. 27, the object is simply "me," but the unique meaning is retained. This argues in favour of an Elohist origin for this verse. Elsewhere in the Bible this verb occurs with the object "heart" only in 2 Sam 15:6, where Absalom "steals" the hearts from David, i.e., in a sense closer to the normal stealing.

[16]Cf. the discussion of *pahad* as thigh, symbolizing the family god, in M. Malul, "More on *pahad yishaq* (Gen xxxl 42, 53) and the oath by the thigh," *VT* 35, 1985, pp. 192-200.

[17]Cf. George W. Coats, *From Canaan to Egypt: Structural and Theological context for the Joseph Story* (CBQMS 4), Washington, 1976, pp. 67-68.

[18]The Elohist's involvement with covenant is generally acknowledged by source critics, as will be indicated in dealing with Exodus texts in Appendix B. This reciprocal covenant experience of God may have been appropriated by the Jews from the "Baal-berith" cult at Shechem (cf. Judges 9 and Joshua 24), and, according to the Elohist tradition, brought from Shechem to Bethel as now no longer a foreign liturgical practise (Gen 35:1-8).

[19]Cf. also Appendix A. The texts in brackets are viewed by Grindel as probably Elohist.

Notes, Chapter 5

[1]The history of this research may be found in the classical Introductions to the Old Testament. A useful discussion of these texts may be found in Martin Noth, *A History of Pentateuchal Traditions,* Scholars Press, Chico, California, 1981, pp. 8-19. Bibliography and further particular studies may be found, for example, in commentaries to Leviticus and Numbers, particularly those by Karl Elliger and Martin Noth, and in monographs such as Rolf Rendtorff, *Die Gesetze in der Pristerschrift, eine gattungsgeschichtliche Untersuchung,* Vandenhoeck & Ruprecht, Göttingen, 2nd edit. 1962; Henning Graf Reventlow, *Das Heiligkeitsgesetz formgeschichtlich untersucht,* (WMANT 6), Neukirchener Verlag, Neukirchen, 1961; Norbert Lohfink. "Die Abänderung der Theologie des Priesterlichen Geschichtswerks im Segen des Heiligkeitsgezetzes," in H. Gese and H.P. Ruger, *Wort und Geschichte, Festschrift Elliger,* Neukirchen-Vluyn, Neukirchen, 1973, pp. 129-136; Diether Kellermann, *Die Priesterschrift von Numeri 1, 1 bis 10, 10* (BZAW 120), Walther de Gruyer, Berlin, 1970.

[2]Cf. Karl Elliger, "Sinn und Ursprung der priesterlichen Geschichtserzälung," *ZThK* 49, 1952, pp. 121-143, and reprinted in his *Kleine Schriften zum Alten Testament,* (Thb 32), 1966; Brevard Childs, *The Book of Exodus, A Critical Theological Commentary,* Westminster Press, Philadelphia, 1974, especially pp. 131-151; Norbert Lohfink, "Die Priesterschrift und die Geschichte," *VTS* 29, Brill, Leiden, 1978, pp. 189-225, esp. p. 198. The footnotes in Lohfink's article provide an excellent survey of research touching Pg over the past 20 years.

[3]Cf. Karl Elliger cited in note 2 above.

[4]For a history of research cf. S. McEvenue, *The Narrative Style of the Priestly Writer,* Biblical Institute Press, Rome, 1971, especially pp. 1-9.

[5]The bracketed verses may be either Pg or Ps. One may simply skip them. However it is interesting to see in these examples how the supplemental material has the effect of carrying futher the intention of Pg.

[6]For understanding Ezekiel the reader is referred to Walther Zimmerli, *A Commentary on the book of the Prophet Ezekiel,* 2 vols, Fortress Press, Philadelphia, 1983. The German version was published by Neukirchen-Vluyn, Neukirchen, 1969.

[7]The symbols, their origins and significance, are thoroughly analysed in Jon Douglas Levenson, *Theology of the Program of Restoration of Ezekiel 40-48,* (Harvard Semitic Monographs 10), Scholars Press, Missoula, Montana, 1976.

[8]For a study of the temple imagery in the New Testament, cf. Ben F. Meyer, *The Aims of Jesus,* SCM Press, London, 1979, especially pp. 181-185, 200-202, 220-222.

[9]This has been worked out in some detail in S. McEvenue, "The Style of a Building Instruction," *Semitics,* 1974, pp. 1-9.

[10]Cf. Walther Zimmerli, "Sinaibund und Abrahambund, Ein Beitrag zum Verständnis der Priesterschrift," in *Festgabe für Walter Eichrodt,* (ZTBas 16), 1969, pp. 268-280, and reprinted in his *Gesammelte Aufsätze,* (TB 19), Munich, 1963. For an extensive demonstration of how the Priestly Writer remains faithful to his sources, while changing the perspective, cf. my book cited in note 4 above, especially pp. 24-36, 92-96, 117-127, 149-155.

[11]These literary techniques in Pg are studied extensively in McEvenue, *Op. cit.,* note 4 above, pp. 29 and 157-158, and are there illustrated in many Pg texts: cf. the Index, under "palistrophe," on p. 217. All observations in this chapter about Pg's style may be found demonstrated in detail in that book.

[12]Cf. Norbert Lohfink, "Die Ursünden in der Priesterlichen Geschichtserzählung,"

186   *Endnotes*

in G. Bornkamm and K. Rahner, *Die Zeit Jesu, Festschrift H. Schlier,* Freiburg, 1970, pp. 38-57.

¹³This static aspect of Priestly style is fully studied by Norbert Lohfink, *Op. Cit.,* in note 2 above, under the title "Die Rückverwandlung der Geschichte in Mythos," and he characterizes the Priestly stories as paradigms artificially linked by genealogies and calendar, rather than history: pp. 202-215.

¹⁴For the meaning of *mabbul* and its use in Pg, cf. J. Begrich, "Mabbul, Eine exegetisch-lexikalische Studie," *ZS* 6, 1928, pp. 135-142, and McEvenue, *Op. Cit.,* in note 4 above, pp. 26-27.

¹⁵Cf. Brevard Childs, *loc. cit.,* note 2 above.

¹⁶Cf. Louis J. Puhl, *The Spiritual Exercises of St. Ignatius,* Loyola University Press, Chicago, 1951, p. 12.

¹⁷The style, structure, and relation to a glossed Yahwist/Elohist source is thoroughly analysed in McEvenue, *Op. Cit.,* in note 4 above, pp. 90-144. For the translation of *twr*, cf. pp. 120-121.

¹⁸Cf. Rudolf Kilian, "Die Priesterschrift—Hoffnung auf Heimkehr," in Josef Schreiner (ed.), *Wort und Botschaft, Eine theologische und kritische Einführung in die Probleme des Alten Testaments,* Echter Verlag, Wurtzburg, 1976, pp. 226-243.

Notes, Chapter 6

¹For points of source criticism, and historical criticism, I shall try to follow the position developed by Norbert Lohfink, because it results from the most minute and extensive study of the text, the most careful analysis of other positions, and the most convincing critical arguments. This position has developed in numerous publications from 1960 to the present, and will eventually be drawn together in the commentary on Deuteronomy to appear in the "Hermeneia" series, Fortress Press. In the meantime, the reader can be referred to his book, *Das Hauptgebot, Eine Untersuchung literarischer Einleitungsfragen zu Dtn 5-11,* Rome, 1963; and the dictionary articles "Deuteronomium" in a forthcoming new edition of *Bibellexikon,* and "Deuteronomy," *International Dictionary of the Bible, Sup.,* pp. 229-232. Cf. also "Kerygmata des Deuteronomistischen Geschichtswerks," in J. Jeremias and L. Perlitt (eds.), *Die Botschaft und die Boten, Festschrift H.W. Wolff,* Neukirchen, 1981, pp. 87-100; "Zur Neueren Diskussion über 2 Kon 22-23," in N. Lohfink (ed.), *Das Deuteronomium, Entstehung, Gestalt und Botschaft,* (BETHL 68), Louvain University Press, 1985, pp. 24-48; "Glauben Lernen in Israel," *Katechetische Blätter,* 1983, pp. 84-99.

For an excellent review of recent scholarship in Deuteronomic and Deuteronomistic source criticism, cf. Anthony F. Campbell, *Of Prophets and Kings, A Late Ninth-Century Document (1 Samuel 1—2 Kings 10),* CBQMS 17, Washington, 1986, pp. 1-16.

The text of Deuteronomy has the form of a collection of four addresses given by Moses on a single day, identified in turn by four notices or labels: 1:1; 4:44; 28:69; 33:1. Chs. 33-34 do not belong to the original core of Dt, but rather serve to link this book externally back to the Pentateuch. Ch. 4 is a post-exilic addition, and moreover much of legislation in chs. 19-25 did not belong to the original core, but rather were added after the exile. The core of the book is to be thought of as a composition inspired by a national-religious revival in Judah under Hezekiah, or possibly Josiah. It is substantially the book whose introduction as law is narrated in 1 Kings 22.

²Only in Ezechiel does the reader feel directly in contact with a divine Speaker. There the text is composed of words addressed to Ezechiel, with only very rare objectifying narrative in which Ezechiel might answer, or report, or fulfill commands.

So the reader may feel the divine word as directed immediately at himself or herself. But that feeling is not really justified: the massive vocation narrative in chs. 1-3, and the discussion of Ezechiel's responsibility as prophet in chs. 14 and 33:1-9, serve to establish the realization that the "you" in this book is not the reader but only Ezechiel himself.

³Cf. George Minette de Tillesse, "Sections 'tu' et sections 'vous' dans le Deutéronome," *VT* 12, 1962, pp. 29-87, and Henri Cazelles, "Passages in the Singular within Discourse in the Plural of Dt 1-4, *CBQ* 29, 1967, pp. 207-219. For more recent discussion, cf. C.J. Labuschagne, "Divine Speech in Deuteronomy," in Norbert Lohfink, *Das Deuteronomium*, 1985, cited in note 1 above, pp. 111-126, esp. pp. 113-115, and J. Vermeylen, "Les sections narratives de Deut 5-11 et leur relation à Ex 19-34," *Ibid.* pp. 174-207. The singular and plural forms appear to be traces of levels in the text in some places. However Norbert Lohfink demonstrated in 1963 that the text of Dt was so meticulously unified through vocabulary, formulas, and structural techniques that the retention of singular and plural forms has to be read as intentional, as part of the meaning. This position has shaped subsequent discussion. Cf. Norbert Lohfink, *Das Hauptgebot*, 1963, cited in note 1 above.

⁴For the political and contractual sense of "love" cf. William Moran, "The Ancient Near Eastern Background of the Love of God in Deuteronomy," *CBQ* 25, 1963, pp. 77-87. For the theological import of "remember," cf. Brevard Childs, *Memory and Tradition*, (Studies in Biblical Theology 37), Allenson, Napierville, 1962. For the meaning of *yrš* (hiph) cf. Norbert Lohfink, "die Bedeutungen von hebr. *yrs qal* und *hif*," *BZ* 27, 1983, pp. 14-33. This word occurs in Dt 7:17, for example, and is translated "disposses" in the RSV. In other places it is translated as "drive out." Lohfink shows that in Deuteronomic tradition the real meaning is "to annihilate some one so that his property can be taken over."

⁵For a careful analysis of Dt's reshaping of the tradition, cf. Norbert Lohfink, "Darstellungskunst und Theologie in Dtn 1, 6—3, 29," *Biblica* 41, 1960, pp. 105-134.

⁶Lohfink has shown that, after the fall of Jerusalem, an exilic Deuteronomist set forth an interpretation of this tradition which repudiated the supremacy of political power, subordinating human authorities to the divine will expressed in the Law. This is to be found principally in the reediting of 1 Sam 8-12, and in the expansion of Dt 16:18—18:22 into a full-blown political thoery. Cf. "Die Sicherung der Wirksamkeit des Gotteswortes durch das prinzip der Schriftlichkeit der Tora und durch das Prinzip der Gewaltenteilung nach den Ämtergesetzen des Buches Deuteronomium (Dt 16, 18—18: 22)," in H. Wolter (ed.), *Testimonium Veritati, Festschrift W. Kempf*, 1971, pp. 143-155. Cf. further N. Lohfink, *Great Themes from the Old Testament*, Clark, Chicago and Edinburgh, 1982.

⁷The following roots occur: *yrš* hiph. (v. 17), *'bd* (vv. 20,24); *nšl* (v. 22), *klh* (v. 22), *šmd* hiph. (vv. 23, 24).

⁸Cf. H. Spieckermann, *Juda unter Assur in der Sargonidenzeit*, FRLANT 129, Göttingen, 1982.

⁹For a discussion of nomistic thinking in the Dtr tradition, cf. recent research from the Göttingen school reviewed by Anthony F. Campbell, *Op. Cit.*, in note 1 above, pp. 9-14.

¹⁰Cf. Georg Braulik, "Die Abfolge der Gesetze in Dt 12-26," in Norbert Lohfink, *Das Deuteronomium*, 1985, cited in note 1 above, pp. 252-272, esp. p. 259.

¹¹The work was set in motion in articles by George Mendenhall, published in *Biblical Archeology* in 1954, and collected in a book: *Covenant Forms in Israelite Tradition*, Pittsburgh, 1955. It was further extended by Kurt Baltzer, *Das*

Bundesformular, Neukirchen, 1960, now available in translation: *The Covenant Formulary in Old Testament, Jewish, and Early Christian Writings,* Fortress Press, Philadelphia, 1971. A survey of this research is to be found in D.J. McCarthy, *Der Gottesbund im Alten Israel, Ein Bericht über die Forschung der letzten Jahre.,* Verlag Katholisches Bibelwerk, Stuttgart, 1966, updated in D.J. McCarthy, *Old Testament Covenant, A Survey of Current Opinions,* John Knox Press, Atlanta, 1972. For a more recent bibliography, cf. Horst D. Preuss, *Deuteronomium,* (Erträge der Forschung 164), Wissenschaftliche Buchgesellschaft, Darmstadt, 1982, pp. 217-219.

[12]Cf. Dennis McCarthy, *Treaty and Covenant, A Study in Form in the Ancient Oriental Documents and in the Old Testament,* 2nd edit., Pontifical Biblical Institute, Rome, 1978.

[13]Treaty texts in translation are readily available in J.B. Pritchard (ed.), *Ancient Near Eastern Texts Relating to the Old Testament,* Princeton University Press, 3rd edition 1969.

[14]For this translation cf. Th.C. Vriezen, "Das Hiphil von 'amar in Dt 26:17-18," *Jaarbericht van het Vooraziatish-Egyptisch Genootschap, Ex Oriente Lux* 17, 1964, pp. 207-210, and Norbert Lohfink, "Dt 26, 17-19 und die 'Bundesformel,'" *Zeitschrift für Katholische Theologie* 91, 1969, pp. 517-553, especially pp. 529-535. In v. 18, the phrase "you would act as His very own people" is differently translated by Lohfink, making it an obligation, not on Israel, but on God. This introduces an unnecessary complication, since the word *sequlah,* "possession" may not be as sharply defined as Lohfink supposes. There is no reason to suppose it cannot connote both a favourable status and its obligations: clearly it is connected with obligation on Israel in Ex 19:5-6, and Dt 7:6. Like being "holy," being a "possession" of Yahweh was a status which was desirable but onerous. In Dt 28:9 being holy is more a blessing, but in 14:21 it is more an obligation.

[15]Lohfink points out that in Hittite treaty texts, there is no reciprocal text when the Hittite king covenants with a vassal. There is one when he covenants with an equal ally. The reciprocal nature of Dt 26:17-19 seems to mirror this equality. Cf. Lohfink, *Op. Cit.* in note 11 above, pp. 535-540. He refers, for example, to treaties between Hattusil III and Pharaoh Ramses II, which can be found in *ANET,* pp. 199-203.

[16]Cf. D.R. Hillers, *Treaty Curses and the Old Testament Prophets,* Pontifical Biblical Institute, Rome, 1964; R. Frankena, "The Vassal Treaties of Esarhaddon and the Dating of Deuteronomy," *OTS* 14, Leiden 1965, p. 122-154; M. Weinfeld, "Traces of Assyrian treaty Formulae in Deuteronomy," *Biblica* 46, 1965, pp. 417-427.

[17]Cf. Norbert Lohfink, "Der Bundesschluss im Land Moab," *Biblische Zeitschrift* 6, 1962, pp. 45-56.

[18]Cf. G. Ernest Wright, "The Lawsuit of God: A Form-Critical Study of Deuteronomy 32," in B.W. Anderson and W. Harrelson, *Israel's Prophetic Heritage, Festschrift James Muilenberg,* Harper and Brothers, New York, pp. 26-67, esp. pp. 36-37; also Georg Fohrer, in Sellin-Fohrer, *Introduction to the Old Testament,* Abingdon Press, Nashville and New York, 1965, p. 190. The consensus affects both the German and American schools: cf., for example, Georg Fohrer, *Loc. Cit.;* Otto Eissfeldt, *Das Lied Moses Dt 32:1-43 und das Lehrgedicht Asaphs Psalm 78 samt einer Analyse der Umgebung des Mose-Leides,* Leipzig, 1958; George Mendenhall, "Samuel's 'Broken Rib': Dt 32," in J.W. Flanagan and A.W. Robinson, *No Famine in the Land, Festschrift John L. McKenzie,* Scholars Press, Missoula, 1975, pp. 63-74, especially pp. 64-68. Most recently J. Luyten, "Primeval and Eschatological Overtones in the Song of Moses (Dt 32, 1-43)," in Norbert Lohfink (ed.), *Das Deuteronomium,* 1985, cited in note 1 above, pp. 341-347, recognizes remnants of an ancient form of the song, but argues from its fitting ill into the Dt framework (Dt 31 and 32, esp. 31:19

and 21), and also from its piling up of motifs, parallels of which are found in such a variety of Old Testament texts, that the present text appears to represent a post-Deuteronomic synthesis. The argument has weight. Against it is the evidence that, elsewhere, such late editing is characterized first, by making things fit their frames quite well, and, second, by introducing strong structural elements, such as palistrophes, or at least chiasm. One is left, then, with a primitive, but uniquely rich, poem, whose motifs have been drawn upon by a great number of later biblical writers.

[19]Cf. Patrick W. Skehan, "The Structure of the Song of Moses in Deuteronomy," *CBQ* 13, 1951, pp. 153-163.

[20]Cf. Norbert Lohfink, *Op. Cit.,* note 14 above.

[21]There is considerable doubt about the text of v. 43. P.-M. Bogaert, "Les trois rédactions conservées et la forme originale de l'envoi du cantique de Moise (Dt 32, 43)," in N. Lohfink, *Das Deuteronomium,* 1985, cited in note 1 above, pp. 329-340, attempts to construct an original text which would explain MT and other variants, especially on the basis of a Qum Rhan fragment and of the Septuagint translation. He argues that the original text read: "Rejoice you gods with Him (i.e., Yahweh). Because He will take vengeance etc." MT, which RSV renders "Praise His people, O you nations," has thus shifted the meaning because of a repugnance to having gods and Yahweh so involved with each other. I shall remain with MT here, because, if Bogaert is right, still we cannot say whether it occurred at the time of the first Deuteronomist, before him, or after him.

[22]I was delighed to discover that the first Puritans, who founded American political culture, derived the same elemental meaning as I had. A study of John Winthrop (1588-1649) first governor of the Massachuchusetts Bay Colony, cites his sermon before landing, which described "a city set upon a hill," which they would found: "We must delight in each other, make others conditions our own, rejoyce together, mourn together, labour and suffer together, always having before our eyes our community as members of the same body." The author goes on to describe this ideal: "The Puritans were not uninterested in material posperity and were prone when it came, unfortunately, to take it as a sign of God's approval. Yet their fundamental criterion of success was not material wealth but the creation of a community in which a genuinely ethical and spiritual life could be lived. During his twelve terms as governor, Winthrop, a relatively rich man for those days, devoted his life to the welfare of the colony, frequently using his own funds for public purposes." Cf. R.N. Bellah, R. Madsen, W.M. Sullivan, A. Swidler, S.M. Tipton, *Habits of the Heart, Individualism and Commitment in American Life,* Harper and Row, New York etc., 1985, pp. 28-29.

[23] This sentence, originally applied to Nevil Shute, is taken from the beginning of ch. 5 in Richard Bach's recent novel *The Bridge Across Forever, a Love Story,* New York, 1984.

Notes, Chapter 7

[1]For a recent, spirited, and very compelling demonstration of the need to maintain the discipline of historical-critical method, in the face of Narratologists and others, cf. L. Perlitt, "Deuteronomium 1-3 im Streit der exegetischen Methoden," in Nortbert Lohfink (ed.), *Das Deuteronomium, Entstehung, Gestalt und Botschaft,* Leuven University Press, 1985, pp. 149-163.

[2]A collection of leading Roman Catholic articles in this direction is to be found in *Giornale di teologia,* 21, "La 'verità' della Bibbia nel dibattito attuale," editrice Quiriniana, Brescia, 1968. On the Protestant side, a programme of "canonical criticism" was created by Brevard Childs, *Biblical Theology in Crisis,* Westminster Press,

Philadelphia, 1970, and given a solid skeleton in his *Introduction to the Old Testament as Scripture,* Fortress Press, Philadelphia, 1979. Its aim was to solve the general problem outlined in the first chapter of this book by focussing on the final meaning of the Bible as a whole. Cf. my critique of the proposal in "The Old Testament, Scripture or Theology," *Interpretation,* 1981, pp. 229-242, and my critical bookreview of the skeleton in *CBQ,* 1980, pp. 535-537.

[3]A prestigious example of this vagueness may be found in the "Dogmatic Constitution on Divine Revelation," promulgated on Nov. 18, 1965, by the Second Vatican Council. In handling inerrancy at the beginning of chapter III, the Council rejected the formula "salvific truth" as a descriptor of the inerrant content, because that seemed to weaken truth too much, but chose instead the phrase "that truth which God wanted put into the sacred writings for the sake of our salvation." However this did not represent a careless or crude affirmation of doctrinal inerrancy, for the official footnote takes a careful step back toward the rejected formula by citing a text from Thomas Aquinas: "Any knowledge which is profitable to salvation may be the object of prophetic inspiration. But things which cannot affect our salvation do not belong to inspiration." Cf. Abbott and Gallagher (eds.), *The Documents of Vatican II,* Guild Press, New York, 1966, p. 119. The whole dogmatic constitution is an admirably sophisticated statement, remaining evasive throughout in regard to "inspired" knowledge content. There was no alternative, unless the Council was prepared to adopt a specific theory of knowledge.

[4]Cf. Bernard Lonergan, *Insight, A Study of Human Understanding,* Philosophical Library, New York, 1957; and *Method in Theology,* Darton, Longeran and Todd, London, 1971. *Method in Theology* is a short book, relatively easy to read. In offering the following résumé of its contents, I hope that those who have read the book will find it helpful; but those who have not will undoubtedly find it obscure and unsatisfactory.

James Barr, in *Old and New in Interpretation,* SCM Press, London, 1966, and in *The Bible in the Modern World,* SCM Press, London, 1973, provides a lucid and balanced exploration of the terms and positions and possibilities surrounding the relation between Scripture and Theology. I would agree with virtually every detail of his presentation. However, he does not begin with an adequate theory of knowledge. Specifically he does not formulate the nature and value of common sense thought, or the relation between common sense thought and scientific thought; he provides no general description of Theology as a distinct discipline; he does not articulate his view of culture in general. Without such a framework, one can come to understand the problem very well without ever outlining a convincing solution. It is at this point that Lonergan's self-discoveries and philosophical clarifications are valuable and even indispensible to biblical scholars.

[5]Cf. *Method,* p. xi.

[6]One might contrast the work of James D.G. Dunn, for example in *Christology in the Making, A New Testament Inquiry into the Origins of the Doctrine of the Incarnation,* Westminster Press, Philadelphia, 1980, with that of Edward Schillebeeckx, *Jesus, An Experiment in Christology,* (transl. H. Hoskins), Crossroad, New York, 1981. They cover roughly the same ground with equally exact and painstaking scholarship. The former is methodically writing *history,* whereas the latter intermingles *history* with *doctrine,* and *communications.* The former book is 443 pages in length, easy of access, and therefore very useful as a reference tool. The latter is 767 pages in length, and for its intelligibility must be read from beginning to end, because "to pick and choose among the chapters or change the order in which they are read will only rob the book of its inner dynamic," as the author warns us in his

"Foreword." The virtuosity of Schillebeeckx, and his theological depth, have won him much recognition. Still his book, which is always referred to in general, is not always referred to in detail. Cf. also David Kelsey, *The Uses of Scripture in Recent Theology*, Fortress Press, Philadelphia, 1975. Kelsey analyzes very precisely recent abuses in methodology, although it is not clear that he sees it in that light. And finally, religious leaders, whether they be fundamentalist or hierarchical, frequently blame biblical scholars for undermining the faith of the flock. There is much truth to that charge, but usually it is not the scholars who are at fault. The fault lies in those preachers, or in those theologians, who force Scripture to play a doctrinal role for which it is not intended.

[7]As Jewish and Christian and Muslim traditions diverged and split into diverse religious communities, further criteria for creating authentic contemporary theological knowledge for a specific group have been added. Further Speakers were added. But also diverse doctrinal systems became diverse criteria for orthodoxy; and ever multiplying religious authorities took responsibility for truth. If one could reestablish biblical orthodoxy, as outlined in this chapter, as a common realm for religious thought, one real value of the Bible to the modern world would be reestablished. Of course, it too could be subverted, if used to unite Jews, Christians, and Muslims against the rest of humanity!

Author Index

Aaron, Daniel, 180
Abbot, 177, 191
Alter, Robert, 1
Anderson, R.W., 190
Anselm, 41
Aquinas, Thomas, 177, 191
Augustine, 34
Austen, Jane 39
Avila, Theresa of, 72

Bach, Richard, 191
Baltzer, Kurt, 189
Barr, James, 1, 192
Baumgarten, A.I., 177, 178
Becher, W., 178,
Beckett, Samuel, 45
Begrich, J., 187
Bellah, R.N., 191
Blenkinsopp, Joseph, 178
Bornkamm, G., 187
Bogaert, P.M., 190
Braulik, Georg, 189
Brescia, Quiriniana, 180 191
Brooks, Cleanth, 178, 179

Campbell, Antony, 178, 188, 189
Carroll, Robert P., 177
Cassuto, Umberto, 34, 178
Cazelles, Henri, 188
Chaucer, 22, 23
Childs, Brevard, 1, 116, 125, 169, 175,
    177, 178, 183, 185-88, 191
Clines, David J.A., 182
Coates, G.W., 110, 186
Coote, R.B., 183
Crowe, Frederick, 1, 177
Crüsemann, Frank, 182
Culler, Jonathon, 175

Dante, 39
Denzinger, 177

Derrida, Jacques, 17, 21, 57, 175, 179,
    180
Donner, H., 178
Dryden, John, 23
Dunn, James D.G., 192

Eagleton, Terry, 175
Eissfeldt, Otto, 107, 185, 190
Eliot, T.S., 22, 49, 175
Elliger, Karl, 116, 186
Elliot, George, 51
Ezekiel,

Fallon, T.P., 178, 179
Flanagan, J.W., 190
Foucault, Michel, 175
Fohrer, Georg, 190
Frankena, R., 190
Frye, Northrop, 1, 21, 175, 179

Gadamer, Hans-Georg, 17, 19-24, 29,
    30, 175
Gallagher, 177, 191
Gese, H., 186
Glazier, Michael, 2
Gray, G.B., 184
Gray, John, 45, 47
Grindel, John A., 88, 107, 115, 166-68,
    186
Gunkel, Hermann, 52, 107, 178, 185

Halbe, J., 183
Hanhart, R., 178
Hanson, Anthony Tyrrell, 178
Harrelson, W., 190
Hefling, Charles Clifford, 177
Herodotus, 59
Hillers, D.R., 190
Homer, 18, 39, 69
Hopkins, Gerald Manley, 21, 22, 60

Inman, Arthur, 180
Iser, Wolfgang, 179

Jeremias, J., 175, 182, 188
Jenks, Alan, 88, 166-68, 184
Joyce, James, 21
Jung, Karl, 53, 183

Keats, John, 39
Kellermann, Diether, 186
Kelsey, David P., 192
Kierans, Hugh, 1
Killian, Rudolf, 187
Knowles, John, 70

Lawall, Sarah, 176
LeCarré, John, 49
Leavis, F.R., 17, 175
Lentricchia, Frank, 175
Levenson, Jon Douglas, 187
Loewe, R., 178
Lohfink, Norbert, 116, 184, 186-90
Lonergan, Bernard, 1, 4, 156, 178, 179, 184, 192
Loyola, Ignatius, 54, 72
Luyten, J., 190

Madsen, R., 191
Malul, M., 186
Martin, M., 178
McCarthy, D.J., 189
McEvenue, S., 178, 185, 187
McKnight, Edgar V., 175, 179
McShane, Philip, 1
Melun, Robert of, 35
Mendelson, A., 178
Mendenhall, George, 189, 190
Meyer, Ben, 1, 178, 187
Miller, Hillis, 179
Mills, John Steward, 47
Moran, William, 188

Neth, 166-68, 184, 186

Ord, D.R., 183
Origen, 25

Perlitt, L., 175, 182, 188, 191
Preuss, Horst D., 189
Pritchard, J.B., 189
Puhl, Louis J., 187

Rahner, K., 187, 177
Rendtorff, R., 183, 186
Reventlow, Henning, Graf, 186
Richter, Wolfgang, 175
Riley, P.B., 178
Ruger, H.P., 186

St. Victor, Hugh of, 35
Salinger, J.D., 19
Sanders, E., 178
Schmitt, Hans-Christoph, 175, 182
Schillebeeckx, Edward, 192
Schreiner, Josef, 187
Shakespeare, William, 18, 184
Shute, Nevil, 191
Ska, Jean Louis, 185
Skehan, Patrick W., 190
Smalley, Beryl, 178
Smend, R., 178
Smith, Morton, 178
Speiser, E.A., 178
Spieckermann, H., 189
Sternberg, Meier, 1, 179
Sullivan, W.M., 191
Swetnam, James, 185
Swindler, A., 191

Thomas, Dylan, 45
Thompson, William, 1
de Tillesse, George Minette, 188
Tipton, M. 191

Vawter, Bruce, 107, 178, 185
Vermes, Geza, 177
Vermeylen, J., 188
Voegelin, Eric, 180
VonRad, C., 178, 184
Vriezen, C., 189

Warren, A., 176
Welleck, R., 176
Weinfelf, M., 190
Wellhausen, J., 63, 107, 116, 182, 185
Westerman, Claus, 183
Wilde, Oscar, 69
Wolter, H., 189
Wordsworth, William, 46-48, 60
Winthrop, John, 191
Wright, G. Ernest, 88, 190

Zenger, Hans-Erich, 175, 182
Zimmerli, Walther, 187

Biblical Index